Capability Building and Global Innovation Networks

This book explores the dynamics of global innovation networks and their implications for development. Knowledge is often seen as the main determinant of economic growth, competitiveness and employment. There is a strong causal interaction between capability building and the growth in demand for, and supply of, technical and organizational innovation. This complex of skills, knowledge and innovation holds great potential benefit for development, particularly in the context of developing countries. However, despite evidence of the increasing importance of knowledge and innovation, there has been relatively little research to understand the distribution and coordination of innovation and knowledge-intensive economic activities on a global scale – and what this might mean for economic development.

Each chapter – though sharing an underlying conception of innovation systems, innovation networks and their relation to capability building and development – takes a different theoretical stance. The authors explore the emerging relationship between competence building and the structure of global innovation networks, thus providing a valuable new perspective from which to critically assess their development potential.

This book was originally published as a special issue of *Innovation and Development*.

Michael Gastrow is a Senior Research Specialist in the Education and Skills Development programme at the Human Sciences Research Council, South Africa. His research focuses on innovation systems, skills development, and the public understanding of science.

Glenda Kruss is a Director in the Education and Skills Development programme at the Human Sciences Research Council, South Africa. Her research focuses on higher education, innovation and development, exploring responsiveness to economic and social needs, and skills development.

Capability Building and Global Innovation Networks

Edited by

Michael Gastrow and Glenda Kruss

Routledge
Taylor & Francis Group

LONDON AND NEW YORK

First published 2016 by Routledge

2 Park Square, Milton Park, Abingdon, Oxfordshire OX14 4RN
711 Third Avenue, New York, NY 10017

Routledge is an imprint of the Taylor & Francis Group, an informa business

First issued in paperback 2017

British Library Cataloguing in Publication Data
A catalogue record for this book is available from the British Library

ISBN 13: 978-1-138-93773-4 (hbk)
ISBN 13: 978-1-138-29986-3 (pbk)

Typeset in Times
by RefineCatch Limited, Bungay, Suffolk

Publisher's Note
The publisher accepts responsibility for any inconsistencies that may have
arisen during the conversion of this book from journal articles to book chapters,
namely the possible inclusion of journal terminology.

Disclaimer
Every effort has been made to contact copyright holders for their permission to
reprint material in this book. The publishers would be grateful to hear from any
copyright holder who is not here acknowledged and will undertake to rectify
any errors or omissions in future editions of this book.

Contents

Citation Information

The chapters in this book were originally published in *Innovation and Development*, volume 2, issue 2 (October 2012). When citing this material, please use the original page numbering for each article, as follows:

Chapter 6

New trends in an old sector: exploring global knowledge and HR management in MNCs and the North–South divide in human capital formation
Eike W. Schamp and Andreas Stamm
Innovation and Development, volume 2, issue 2 (October 2012) pp. 285–302

Chapter 7

Skills and the formation of global innovation networks: a balancing act
Michael Gastrow and Glenda Kruss
Innovation and Development, volume 2, issue 2 (October 2012) pp. 303–323

For any permission-related enquiries please visit:
http://www.tandfonline.com/page/help/permissions

Notes on Contributors

Gustavo Britto is based in the Centro de Desenvolvimento e Planejamento Regional – Cedeplar, Belo Horizonte, Brazil.

Cristina Chaminade is Full Professor in Innovation Studies at Lund University, Sweden, and Coordinator of the research area on Globalization of Innovation at CIRCLE.

Claudia De Fuentes is based in the Sobey School of Business at Saint Mary's University, Halifax, Canada.

Ana Valéria Carneiro Dias is a Professor in the Department of Production Engineering at the Universidade Federal de Minas Gerais, Belo Horizonte, Brazil.

Michael Gastrow is a Senior Research Specialist in the Education and Skills Development programme at the Human Sciences Research Council (HSRC), South Africa.

Stine Jessen Haakonsson is an Associate Professor in the Department of Business and Politics in the Copenhagen Business School, Denmark.

Glenda Kruss is a Director in the Education and Skills Development programme at the Human Sciences Research Council (HSRC), South Africa.

Jo Lorentzen was a Chief Research Specialist in the Education and Skills Development research programme at the Human Sciences Research Council (HSRC), South Africa.

Maria Cecília Pereira is a Professor in the Department of Production Engineering at the Universidade Federal de Minas Gerais, Belo Horizonte, Brazil.

Eike W. Schamp is a Professor in the Institute for Human Geography at Goethe University, Frankfurt, Germany.

Andreas Stamm is a Senior Researcher in the German Development Institute, Bonn, Germany.

Dedication

The book is dedicated to Jo Lorentzen, to honour the passion with which he built the international INGINEUS research team, to guide the conceptualisation and empirical investigation of global innovation networks in the North and South.

Preface

The chapters of this book are articles that originally appeared in one of the special issues of *Innovation and Development*, an inter-disciplinary international journal from Globelics network, published by Taylor & Francis. http://www.tandf.co.uk/journals/RIAD

Innovation and Development is a relatively young journal born at a particular juncture in the discourse on development. The closing decades of the last century witnessed unprecedented changes in different spheres of economies and societies. This was induced by, among others, technological innovations led mainly by information communication technology and institutional innovations, resulting in increased integration between countries under globalization. In the emerging context of heightened competition, international competitiveness became the only means of survival. With the expanding global production networks and global innovation networks, different sectors across countries got themselves located appropriately in the global value chains. Instances of high rates growth sustained even for decades tended to suggest that achieving faster economic growth is within the reach of the developing world. Unfortunately, however, the episodes of high growth turned out to be not inclusive and sustainable. The challenge, therefore, is to accomplish development that is sustainable and inclusive.

The mandate of *Innovation and Development* has its roots in this new millennium development challenge. Since the role of innovation in development is increasingly being recognized in both the developed and the developing world, an enhancement of our understanding on the interface between innovation and development might help to find ways of addressing many of the developmental issues and making growth process inclusive and sustainable. Hence, understanding the link between innovation, capacity building and development has emerged as a critical issue of concern for academia, practitioners and policy-makers, including international organizations such as the World Bank or United Nations.

But our understanding of the links between innovation and development remains at best rudimentary, notwithstanding an unprecedented increase in studies on development and innovation on the one hand and a heightened interest in development practice on the other. While the two disciplines (development studies and innovation studies) have been growing in parallel, as they are traditionally separated with limited linkages, in recent years there has been an upsurge of interest in innovation issues in development studies. At the same time, with an increasing engagement of civil society organizations in developmental issues, innovative development practices are becoming more visible and their impact felt more than ever before.

By adopting a broader approach to innovation (to include technological, institutional, organizational and others) the journal and this book series aims to provide a forum for discussion of various issues pertaining to innovation, development and their interaction, both in the developed and developing world, for achieving sustainable and inclusive growth.

PREFACE

It is matter of great satisfaction that *Innovation and Development* has been able to lay the strong foundations for integrating innovation studies and development studies through the high quality articles contributed by scholars across the world. These articles dealt with issues pertaining to diverse contexts ranging from primary agriculture to high-end services, and from low technology sectors to high technology sectors operating in both the developing and developed world. In tune with the Globelics research agenda, *Innovation and Development* has also been promoting research and discourse on innovation at the national, regional, sectoral and societal level to facilitate building up systems for learning, innovation and competence building. A unique feature of *Innovation and Development* is its supplementary sections that publish PhD abstracts, web resources for research and innovations in practice.

The editorial board of *Innovation and Development* also takes pride in highlighting the significant contribution of this journal during the last five years of its existence through its special issues that focused on subjects of much relevance for theory and policy. The special issues brought out by the journal dealt with issues that include:

a) Sustainability–oriented innovation systems in China and India, guest editor Tilman Altenburg;
b) Capability building and global innovation networks, guest editors Glenda Kruss and Michael Gastrow;
c) Innovation and global competitiveness: case of India's manufacturing sector, guest editors N. S. Siddharthan and K. Narayanan;
d) Innovation for inclusive development, guest editor Fernando Santiago;
e) New models of inclusive innovation for development, guest editors Richard Heeks, Christopher Foster and Yanuar Nugroho.

We place on record our appreciation for all our guest editors for joining hands with us in our endeavor to take forward the agenda of *Innovation and Development*. We also take this occasion to acknowledge the liberal support that we received from the Editorial Advisory Board and the Scientific Committee. Our special appreciation goes to Taylor & Francis for bringing out this book series from the special issues of *Innovation and Development* and Emily Ross for taking this project to its local conclusion.

It is our hope that this book series will be useful to the academia at large, innovation scholars in particular and the policy-makers concerned.

K. J. Joseph (Editor in Chief),
Cristina Chaminade, Susan Cozzens, Gabriela Dutrénit,
Mammo Muchie, Judith Sutz and Tim Turpin
Editors, *Innovation and Development*

INTRODUCTION

Global innovation networks, human capital, and development

Michael Gastrow and Glenda Kruss

In this Special Issue, we explore the dynamics of global innovation networks (GINs), and their implications for development. In the neo-Shumpeterian and 'new trade theory' context, knowledge is seen as the main determinant of economic growth, competitiveness and employment (Lundvall and Borras, 1998; Archibugi and Lundvall, 2001). The relationship between skills and innovation has been widely investigated (Lall, 2001; teVelde, 2005; Fagerberg and Verspagen, 2007; Martin, 2008; Toner, 2011), and has generated theoretical frameworks such as that of 'absorptive capacity' (Cohen and Levinthal, 1990). The evidence in this body of literature suggests that there is a strong causal interaction between capability-building and the growth in demand for, and supply of, technical and organizational innovation. Taken together, this complex of skills, knowledge and innovation holds great potential benefit for development, particularly in the context of developing countries (Grossman and Helpman, 1991; teVelde, 2005; Lorentzen, 2009).

Globalization has influenced the international distribution of economic activity, and production chains are increasingly co-ordinated through global production networks (GPNs). These trends are well researched in the economic literature (Henderson et al., 2002; Gereffi, 2005). Despite the evidence of the increasing importance of knowledge and innovation, there has been relatively little research to understand the distribution and coordination of innovation and knowledge-intensive economic activities on a global scale – and what this might mean for economic development.

The original research articles in this volume contribute to address this gap. They draw on a research programme on the *impact of networks, globalization and their interaction with EU strategies*, a first large-scale international attempt to understand the emergence and evolution of GINs. Chaminade (2009) defines GINs as 'globally organized networks of interconnected and integrated functions and operations by firms and non-firm organizations engaged in the development or diffusion of innovations'. These innovation networks are 'global' when developing countries are also involved in knowledge-intensive innovation activities. The research considered the roles of countries, regions, sectors, firms and institutional frameworks in driving the emergence and structure of GINs. Cutting across, and central to such analysis, is the role of competence building. The global distribution of human capital is a major determinant of the global distribution of

---

This Special Issue is dedicated to the memory of Jo Lorentzen. Jo was a well known and loved member of the innovation studies community. He was central to the conception of the INGINEUS project, and led the way in understanding the relationship between capability-building and GINs. Jo tragically passed away in 2011, shortly before the conclusion of the project. He was passionate about the power of innovation to drive human development, and we hope that this publication represents one small step towards achieving this.

innovation activity. However, this relationship has never been comprehensively studied before – hence, the focus of this Special Issue.

Taken together, the articles have a broad coverage – sectorally, geographically and theoretically. They include cases from the ICT sector, the agro-food sector and the automotive manufacturing sector, thus covering a range a high, medium and low-tech enterprises. Comparative analysis reveals the important role played by sector-specific factors in shaping GINs, such as value chain dynamics, tacit knowledge and market requirements.

Three of the articles in the Special Issue are written from the perspective of developed countries, including Denmark, Sweden and Germany. Two are written from the perspective of developing countries – South Africa and Brazil. The final article presents an overview of cases from both the developed and developing world. This range of geographical coverage reveals two sides of a global story. The developed country perspective emphasizes the offshoring of innovation activity, and the manner in which firms search the globe for strategically suitable capabilities – in the context of other factors such as costs, markets and regulation. The developing country perspective is focused on the means of attracting innovation activity into local subsidiaries, capability upgrading to support increased innovation activity and co-evolutionary learning through insertion into the internal knowledge networks of multinational firms. At the same time, there is an emerging trend of firms from developing countries outsourcing innovation activities to developed economies and purchasing strategic knowledge assets in the 'North'. Overall, this body of research shows how these perspectives are part of an integrated story, in which innovation and capability-building are truly globalized and multi-polar.

Each of the articles, while sharing an underlying conception of innovation systems, innovation networks and their relation to capability-building and development, approach the question from a somewhat different theoretical stance. This renders a diverse set of findings that shed light on distinct aspects of the relationship between the globalization of innovation and evolving capabilities in developing countries.

An analytical distinction between innovation for the purposes of 'exploitation' and 'exploration' is utilized by Haakonsen. This model provides an evolutionary understanding of the development of innovation networks from the point of view of MNCs engaged in the internationalization of innovation. In this view, international exploitation refers to the marketing of nationally produced innovations beyond the company's home market. Exploration entails corporations re-organizing their activities beyond the home economy and (re)locating innovative activities in host countries. In this context, Haakonsen examines the internationalization of innovation in agro-processing firms in Denmark as an emergent phenomenon, associated with exploration strategies, that engages with capabilities in the host economy.

Within the framework of 'knowledge exploiting' and 'knowledge exploring' strategies of firms, Chaminade and De Fuentes employ a primary analytical distinction between the roles of competences as 'drivers' and as 'enablers'. Their examination of case study and survey findings indicates that, for Swedish ICT firms, firm-level competences are an enabler for the globalization of innovation, particularly for offshoring. Competences at the regional level are important drivers for globalization of innovation, particularly for offshoring and collaboration. This suggests that the breadth and depth of competences available in host countries determine the type of innovation activities that the subsidiary performs, as well as the role that it plays in the global innovation strategy of the firm.

The role of knowledge management in the setting of transnational R&D and engineering functions of multinational firms is explored by Schamp and Stamm. Case studies of three German automotive manufacturers with subsidiaries in India provide an exploratory analysis of knowledge and human resources management tools and how they are related to the globalization of innovation – including the relation between knowledge management within multinational firms and the national education and training policies in the host country.

Writing from the developing country perspective, Lorentzen and Gastrow retain an analytical focus on the relationship between firm strategies and human capital in the host country, and what this implies for the management and structure of technological change and innovation. They examine five case studies of the globalization of innovation within automotive firms, including three German firms with subsidiaries in South Africa, and two South African firms with subsidiaries in Europe. The cases show that the offshoring of innovation is taking place in the automotive sector, which traditionally has concentrated knowledge-intensive activities in the home country. This offshoring is bi-directional, with firms based in developed economies taking advantage of growing local capabilities in developing countries, and firms based in developing countries acquiring strategic knowledge assets in developed countries.

Dias et al. also examine case studies from the automotive sector, in this instance from Brazil, including a large European automotive assembler and four automotive systems suppliers. They demonstrate how the establishment and deepening of GINs in this context has been driven by both technological and market incentives and, how, over time, participation in such GINs can increase technological and innovation capabilities at the local level.

An overview paper by Gastrow and Kruss develops an analytical framework that incorporates concepts of dynamic upgrading with the distinction between centripetal and centrifugal forces that act to expand or contract GINs. Their analysis of 14 case studies of 11 multinational firms suggests that skills act as a centrifugal force distributing innovation around the globe. However, this general pattern overlays many other influential factors at the macro, meso and micro levels, including factors related to market characteristics, sectoral characteristics, policy contexts, geographical location, cultural contexts and micro-level determinants. Within each individual network, they identify a unique and complex interaction between these sets of forces, which together shape the emergence and structure of GINs. This model is particularly useful for understanding innovation in a multipolar world where the 'North–South' polarity may not always be descriptively or analytically accurate.

Together, these papers create a new picture of the emerging relationship between competence building and the structure of GINs. This, in turn, provides a valuable new perspective from which to critically assess their development potential. Firms from developing countries can play active roles as primary agents within GINs. As such, developing countries are empowered to search the globe for skills and markets that motivate for the expansion of the networks that drive knowledge production and innovation and, hence potential for economic and social development.

References

Archibugi, D., and Lundvall, B. (eds) (2001) *The Globalizing Learning Economy* (Oxford: Oxford University Press).

Chaminade, C. (2009) On the concept of global innovation networks. *CIRCLE Working Paper 2009/05*.

Cohen, W.M., and Levinthal, D.A. (1990) Absorptive capacity: A new perspective on learning and innovation. *Administrative Science Quarterly*, 35, pp. 128--152.

Fagerberg, J., and Verspagen, B. (2007) Innovation studies – the emerging structure of a new scientific field. *TIK Working Papers on Innovation Studies No. 20090104*.

Gereffi, G. (2005) The global economy: Organisation, governance and development, in: S. Smelser and R. Swedberg (eds) *Handbook of Economic Sociology*, Princeton University Press and Russel Sage Foundation: Princeton, NJ, pp. 160–182.

Grossman, G.M., and Helpman, E. (1991) *Innovation and Growth in the Global Economy* (Cambidge, MA: MIT Press).

Henderson, J., Dicken, P., Hess, M., Coe, N., and Yeung, H. (2002) Global production networks and the analysis of economic development. *Review of International Political Economy*, 9(3), pp. 436--464.

Lall, S. (2001) *Competitiveness, Technology and Skills* (Cheltenham: Edward Elgar).

Lorentzen, J. (2009) Learning and innovation: What's different in the (sub)tropics and how do we explain it? A review essay. *Science, Technology & Society*, 14, pp. 177--205.

Lundvall, B., and Borrás, S. (1998) *The Globalising Learning Economy: Implications for Innovation Policy* (Brussels: Commission of the EU).

Martin, B.R. (2008) The evolution of science policy and innovation studies. *TIK Working Paper on Innovation Studies No. 20080828*.

teVelde, D.W. (2005) Globalisation and education: What do the trade, investment and migration literatures tell us? *Working Paper 254* (London: Overseas Development Institute).

Toner, P. (2011) Workforce skills and innovation: An overview of major themes in the literature, *OECD Education Working Papers, No. 55* (Paris: OECD).

Competences as drivers and enablers of globalization of innovation: the Swedish ICT industry and emerging economies

Cristina Chaminade[a] and Claudia De Fuentes[b]

[a]CIRCLE, Lund University, Lund, Sweden; [b]Sobey School of Business, Saint Mary's University, Halifax, Canada

This paper explores the relationship between competences and global innovation networks in the Swedish ICT industry. More specifically this paper combines econometric techniques and case study analysis to capture the interplay between firm level competences (competences as *enablers*), the availability of competences in the host country (competences as *drivers*), and the specific strategy of the firm for engaging in global innovation networks. Our results show that for Swedish ICT firms, firm-level competences are an important *enabler* for globalization of innovation, particularly for offshoring. Home regional competences also play an important role for the mode of globalization of innovation that firms engage in. Host regional competences are important *drivers* for globalization of innovation, particularly for offshoring and collaboration. The results suggest that the breadth and depth of competences available in host countries actually determine the type of innovation activities that the subsidiary performs, as well as the role that it plays in the global innovation strategy of the company.

1. Introduction

The objective of this article is to discuss the relationship between competences and global innovation networks (GINs) in the Swedish ICT industry using both survey data and information from a case company. This article portrays the interplay between firm-level competences, the availability of competences in the host country and the specific strategy of the firm for engaging in GINs. GINs are defined in this article as 'a globally organized network of interconnected and integrated functions and operations by firms and non-firm organizations engaged in the development or diffusion of innovations' (Chaminade, 2009). Firms can globalize their innovation activities by engaging in the global exploitation of innovations (exports), global sourcing of technology, global research collaboration and offshoring of innovation (Archibugi and Michie, 1995; Audretsch and Feldman, 1996). This article is concerned with the last two forms of GINs.

This article starts by discussing the interplay between competences and GINs, distinguishing between regional and firm-level competences. Competences may influence GINs in at least two ways: as drivers of globalization and as enablers of globalization. Scholars in international business and innovation studies (Arora et al., 2001; Arora and Gambardella, 2004, 2005) argue that offshoring MNCs pursuing an asset seeking strategy (Howells, 1990) may be attracted to a certain region to tap into the specific competences available there (Narula and Zanfei, 2004; Cantwell and Piscitello, 2005, 2007; Lewin et al., 2009). Therefore, competences may play a role as a *driver* for the establishment of GINs, notably, for global research collaboration and offshoring for innovation, as the evidence of knowledge hubs like Bangalore shows (Arora et al., 2001; Saxenian, 2001b; Parthasarathy and Aoyama, 2006; Chaminade and Vang, 2008). That is, firms may be driven to certain locations to access competences available there. In this sense, competences as drivers refer to the role of regional competences attracting innovation activities to a particular region. On the other hand, firm-level competences may also be *enablers* for the establishment of GINs (Nooteboom, 2000, 2004; Nooteboom et al., 2007), that is, firms may need a certain level of in-house competences to engage in global research collaboration or offshoring in faraway locations. Competences define the absorptive capacity of a firm (Cohen and Levinthal, 1990) which in turn, influences the ability of an organization to benefit from engaging in collaboration with other organizations. It also affects the ability of the firm to operate in international environments. Thus, competences are also an enabler for the engagement in GINs.

Through regression analysis using survey data and in-depth interviews with TELEQUIP in different world locations (Sweden, South Africa (SA), India and China), the article explores the interplay between globalization of innovation and competence building, from two perspectives:

(1) Which competences companies need to engage in GINs, particularly in global research collaboration and offshoring? – competences as an enabler
(2) To what extent the access to competences may be the driver for the location of R&D labs abroad? – competences as a driver

This article is structured as follows. First, it introduces the conceptual framework exploring the relationship between firm and regional competences and globalization. The following section presents the method used for this article. Section 4 is centred on the empirical evidence of the relationship between globalization of innovation and competences in the ICT industry in Sweden in general and in multinational firms in particular. The final section of the article concludes with some reflections on the role of competences in GINs, based on the Swedish experience.

2. Conceptual framework

2.1 *Global innovation networks*

It is widely accepted that innovation is the result of the interaction and exchange of knowledge between different individuals and organizations (Freeman, 1987; Lundvall, 1988, 1992). Scholars in the innovation literature have contributed to our understanding of networks of innovators (De Bresson and Amesse, 1991; Freeman, 1991; Powell and Grodal, 2004) particularly with regards to the structure of the network (Burt, 1992; Dickens, 2007), the governance of the networks (Humphrey and Schmitz, 2002; Nooteboom, 2003; Coe et al., 2004; Gereffi et al., 2005) and its impact on knowledge distribution among the actors of the network (Giuliani and Bell, 2005a, 2005b; Giuliani, 2007) but substantially less on its geographical spread.

On the other hand, the geography of innovation networks has been the focus of economic geographers for almost two decades (Cooke, 1992; Asheim and Isaksen, 1997; Mothe and Paquet, 1998). Traditionally, economic geographers have argued that due to its tacit nature, knowledge is sticky and tends to be embedded in certain regions or territories. Local or regional networks of innovators are then considered to be crucial for innovation and competitiveness. Bathelt and Glûckler (2003) argued that the most competitive clusters were those that showed a high degree of local interactions but also strong linkages with international sources of knowledge.

With few exceptions (Fifarek and Veloso, 2010) almost all the scholarly work that has followed on local/global knowledge interactions or the geography of knowledge sourcing (Moodysson, 2008; Moodysson et al., 2008; Martin and Moodysson, 2011) has been mainly treating the international level as a black box, not analyzing whether those international linkages were with countries in close proximity or whether they were globally spread and constituted truly GINs.

As indicated in the introduction section, GINs are defined in this article as a 'globally organized network of interconnected and integrated functions and operations by firms and non-firm organizations engaged in the development or diffusion of innovations' (Chaminade, 2009). This definition highlights the main characteristics of a GIN: its global dispersion, its focus on innovation (and not production) and the combination of both internal and external networks. Following Archibugi and Michie (1995), it is possible to distinguish different forms of GINs (Plechero and Chaminade, 2010): the global exploitation of innovations, global sourcing of technology, global research collaboration and offshoring of innovation. Firms may globally exploit their innovations simply by selling their products abroad; they may innovate by acquiring technology from abroad or by engaging in research collaboration with firm and non-firm organizations located in a different country and, finally, they may also develop innovation through offshoring R&D labs abroad (global generation of innovation). This article is concerned with the last two forms of GINs. The interplay between these two forms of GINs and competences will be discussed in the following sections.

2.2 *Technological competences as an enabler for globalizing innovation activities*[1]

The resource-based view of the firm (Teece, 1980; Wernefelt, 1984) has long argued that the strategy that firms may pursue is contingent to the competences and the capabilities that the firms have (Wernefelt, 1984; Grant, 1991; Barney, 1996; Eisenhardt and Martin, 2000; Barney et al., 2001). The international business literature claims that the success of the internationalization process is also dependent on some firms' competences like the previous experience of the firm in international markets (Sousa et al., 2008) as well as the capability of the firm to organize internally the connections between the headquarters (HQs) and the subsidiaries (Dunning and Narula, 1995; Dunning et al., 1996). Finally, innovation scholars have long maintained that the capability to innovate and engage in interactive learning with other organizations and individuals is highly contingent to the technological competences that the firm has like the qualification of the human resources or the previous investment in R&D (Cohen and Levinthal, 1990; Lall, 1992; Bell and Pavitt, 1995).

Firm-level technological competences in this article are defined not only in terms of human resources but also in terms of technological effort as in Lall (1992) and Cohen and Levinthal (1990). Human resources refer to the skills of the individuals working for the firm and include the formal training as well as experience-based competences acquired on the job (Dantas et al., 2007). Technological effort refers to the investment of the firm in R&D and knowledge creation (Giuliani and Bell, 2005a, 2005b). Technological capabilities are related to the ability of the firm to connect to external sources of knowledge (domestic and international) (Bell and Albu, 1999).

Skills in general and technological skills in particular are the base on which technological capabilities are built (Lall and Pietrobelli, 2005). Qualified human capital is considered to be central for building the absorptive capacity of the firm (Cohen and Levinthal, 1990) and thus is determinant of the ability of the firm to locate, acquire and use information and knowledge from other organizations, such as other firms, users or knowledge providers (i.e. research institutions). Human capital is considered to be crucial for engaging in interactive learning which, in turn, is conducive to innovation. We might therefore expect that the qualification of the human capital is an important enabler of global research collaboration and offshoring of innovation.

Technological efforts or, more explicitly, intramural investments in R&D are expected to serve not only the generation of innovation but also to facilitate the acquisition of knowledge from external sources (Cohen and Levinthal, 1990) and the establishment of partnerships with external suppliers (outsourcing) (Mol, 2005). The more the firm knows, the more it is able to learn and therefore, the more that it will benefit from the interaction with other sources of knowledge. R&D may therefore to be considered directly an enabler of global research collaboration but also of offshoring of innovation. Firms with higher technology intensity are more likely to establish R&D subsidiaries abroad independently of production (Mariani, 2002; Audretsch and Feldman, 2004).

Both the coordination of R&D and innovation activities globally as well as the engagement in research networks requires the introduction of organizational innovations at the firm level (Dunning and Narula, 1995; Knight and Cavusgil, 2004; Sabiola and Zanfei, 2009). As acknowledged by recent international business literature, the advantages of multinationals not only emerge from the technological assets that the firms have in the HQs but also from the ability of the firm to manage international networks, including those with the subsidiaries (Kogut and Zander, 1992; Cantwell, 1995). The coordination of R&D activities between R&D subsidiaries and the HQs is very complex, as it involves the integration of both internal and external networks and requires advanced managerial and organizational competences. Those competences can be considered as enablers or facilitators for the engagement in offshoring and global research collaboration. Firms with higher organizational competences are expected to be related to global research collaboration and offshoring of innovation.

We may therefore expect that firm's level technological competences – such as the educational level, the R&D investment or the organizational innovations – may act as enablers for the engagement in GINs, particularly for global research collaboration as well as offshoring of innovations.

The region in which the firm is located has also an influence of the ability of the firm to engage in GINs. The institutional thickness of a certain region may facilitate or hamper the exchange of knowledge (Cooke et al., 1997; Asheim and Isaksen, 2002; Morgan, 2007; Gertler, 2010; Asheim et al., 2011), shape the geography of the knowledge flows of a particular region (Amin and Thrift, 1994, 1995; Tödtling et al., 2011) and be the main engine of change within the regional innovation system (RIS) (Boschma and Frenken, 2006, 2009).

We may therefore expect that the competences available in the region in which the firm is located may also act as enablers.

2.3 *Competences as a driver for the globalization of innovation activities: offshoring and global research collaboration*

One of the traditional arguments in international business literature explaining the internationalization of production and innovation activities has been the exploitation of existing advantages. The OLI (ownership, location, internalization advantage) framework developed by (Dunning, 1993, 2001) in the early nineties argued that multinational companies expanded their activities abroad to exploit their competitive advantage in terms of ownership, location and internalization. Dunning (1993) refers to four different strategies for internationalization: market seeking, resource seeking, efficiency seeking and asset seeking, being the first three more related to asset exploiting strategies (Knight and Cavusgil, 2004).

In line with March (1991), Penrose (1959) and later Wernefelt (1984) argue that the strategy of the firm is based on both the exploitation of existing resources and the exploration of new ones. The distinction between asset exploiting and asset seeking strategies is particularly relevant for offshoring and global research collaboration and has important implications for the role of competences as a driver for the engagement in GINs. While it is true that some companies may locate

R&D labs abroad to adapt existing products to the specific market needs (asset exploiting) (Verspagen and Schoenmakers, 2004), there is growing evidence of the increasing importance of asset seeking strategies in the localization of R&D abroad (Howells, 1990; Zander, 1999; Zanfei, 2000). Firms are attracted to certain regions or engage in research networks to tap into specific competences and knowledge available in that particular region or network (Lewin et al., 2009) and, in doing so, they increase the geographical concentration of innovation activities in certain knowledge hubs around the world (Fifarek and Veloso, 2010). Competences in the host region are therefore considered as drivers for offshoring of innovation.

Country or regional technological competences are defined here as the skills, knowledge and institutions that make a country or region's capacity to generate and manage change (Bell and Pavitt, 1995). Traditionally technological competences have been concentrated in a handful of developed countries and regions (Archibugi and Coco, 2004, 2005; Li et al., 2010). But the technology clubs of the world are slowly changing (Castellacci and Archibugi, 2008). In 2006, the UNCTAD published a report on R&D Foreign Direct Investment which pointed, almost for the first time, to the changing role of developing countries in the global flows of innovation-related investments (UNCTAD, 2006). It showed how R&D investments to and from developing countries had increased dramatically in a few years. Innovation had become truly global, involving organizations and regions outside the high-income countries.

One of the most often cited arguments explaining this global shift is the accumulation of competences in certain regions around the world, like Bangalore in India (Arora et al., 2001; Saxenian, 2001; Arora and Bagde, 2006; Parthasarathy and Aoyama, 2006) or Beijing in China (Altenburg et al., 2008; Athreye and Prevezer, 2008). Thus, some regions in developing countries have become knowledge hubs in global value chains (Castellacci and Archibugi, 2008), particularly in ICT industries (Chaminade and Vang, 2008).

We may therefore expect that the knowledge or technological competences available in a certain host region is an important *driver* at least for the offshoring of innovation activities.

3. Method

This article combines the analysis of survey-based data with a case study to illustrate with more detail the complex relationship between competences and GINs from a managerial perspective.

3.1 *Survey*

The survey was conducted in 2010 and was directed to the entire ICT population in Sweden. Firms were contacted by email and asked to conduct the survey online. The dataset used for the survey contains all the Swedish companies that according to Statistic Sweden operate in ICT in the following NACE 2 codes: (26.30 manufacture of communication equipment; 62.01 computer programming activities; 62.02 computer consultancy activities; 62.03 computer facilities management activities; 62.09 other information technology and computer service activities). The size of companies in the database is small, medium-size and large organizations. We excluded in the survey the firms with less than five employees.

The final number of companies contacted by mail was 1662. The final number of responses (complete questionnaires) was 171. The response rate was therefore 10.28%. The distribution of responses by firm size and sub-industry is representative of the total population of the industry (using statistics from statistics Sweden).[2]

The survey captures information about the different dimensions of the globalization of innovation for each firm, such as global technological collaboration (R&D strategy, sources of technology, establishment of networks for sourcing/developing technologies or innovations), and offshoring of production and innovation. The survey also captures information about structural characteristics of the firm, such as size, industry, specific activities and the main functions performed by the firm. Finally, it also captures information on technological competences at firm level such as qualification of the human resources, investments in R&D and organizational management techniques, etc.

3.1.1 Dependent variables

Global research collaboration. In the survey firms were asked who they actively collaborated with for the development of their most important innovation in the last 3 years. The firms were also asked to indicate the geographical location of the partner – the region, the country and a list of regions around the world (Western Europe, Eastern and Central Europe, North America, South America, Africa, Japan and Australasia and rest of Asia). The options available included clients, suppliers, competitors, consultancy companies, government and universities. We created two variables that capture collaboration within Europe, and truly global collaboration (grouping North America, South America, Japan and Australasia, Africa and rest of Asia). These two numerical variables are based on the number of partners that the firm collaborates with.

Global offshoring of production and innovation. In the survey, the firms were asked if they had offshored production and R&D activities. The firm could only answer yes/no. Although the survey did not explicitly ask the geography of offshoring, we checked their websites to investigate where the firm was offshoring. For the analysis we consider two cases, offshoring within Europe and those firms that have global offshoring (i.e. outside Europe) to destinations like India, China, Malaysia, Hong-Kong, Dubai or Bangladesh. Therefore, the two variables of offshoring of innovation are dummy variables that take the value 1 when the firm has offshored production or R&D activities and 0 otherwise.

3.1.2 Independent variables

3.1.2.1 *Competences as enablers. Firm's technological competences – skills.* We use two variables to capture the qualification of the human capital in the firm. In the survey, we asked the firms to indicate the estimated proportion of the employees by level of education. The three options were technical education/training, university degree and postgraduate degree. We created two dummy variables 'employees with university degree' and 'employees with postgraduate degree' that takes value 1 if the firm responded affirmatively to each of the categories, respectively.

Firm's technological competences – technological effort. We use three variables to capture the R&D activities of the firm. The first one is a dummy 'R&D activities' that takes the value 1 if the firm had answered Yes to the question 'do you have any significant R&D activity?'. The second one is a numerical variable with the number of full time equivalents employed in R&D. The third one captures whether the firm had engaged in intramural R&D and is derived from the question 'did your company engage in any of the following innovation activities in 2008' – being the options intramural R&D, extramural R&D, design, training and acquisition of machinery and equipment.

Firm's technological competences – organizational competences. The variable 'service innovation' captures whether the firm has introduced any service innovation in the last 3 years; the variable 'support innovation' captures whether the firm has answered positively to the question 'has the firm introduced new or significantly improved supporting activities for your processes (e.g. purchasing, accounting, maintenance systems, etc.) in the past 3 years (2006–2008)'? or to the question 'has the firm introduced new or significantly improved logistics, distribution or delivery methods for your inputs, goods and services in the past 3 years?'. These two variables are categorical variables that indicate the degree of novelty of the innovations (new to the firm, new to the country and new to the world). The variable 'advanced production systems' is a numerical variable that captures the number of systems of production organization that the firm employs. The available options were quality control systems, just in time production, continuous improvement, quality circles, internal manual and others. We use this variable also as a proxy for firm technological competences, related to organizational competences. We also asked the firms to estimate the percentage due to products 'manufactured by your unit according to design specifications provided by external buyers' (original equipment manufacturing – *OEM*), 'developed and designed by your unit according to performance requirements of buyers' (original design manufacturing – *ODM*) and 'developed and designed by your unit and sold under your own brand' (original brand manufacturing – *OBM*). We created three dummy variables that take the value 1 if the firm has performed any of those activities, respectively.

To capture the level of competences in the home region, we created the variable 'Home region Tier'. Home Region Tier is an original categorical variable that represents the dynamics and importance of the ICT in different regions in Sweden. We assigned the Tier level based on information about employment, economic dynamism and industrial activities for the ICT sector in Sweden. We have categorized regions where the firms are located in Tier 1, Tier 2 and Tier 3. Tier 1 regions are the most dynamic in the particular industry. Firms located there can have higher level of technological capabilities, also networks among agents and knowledge flows are more mature than in Tiers 2 or 3. Tier 2 regions present a medium level of interaction among the members of the network, and firms located in Tier 2 have a medium level of technological capabilities. Tier 3 regions are the least dynamic and interactions among the members of the network are weak (see Table 1).

3.1.2.2 *Competences as drivers (for offshoring of innovation only). Regional competences.* If the firm offshored production and innovation, they were asked to indicate 'what were the important regional factors in the decision to offshore production and innovation into a host region'. The different options available captured market, costs and knowledge drivers *separately* for production and innovation. For the variable 'Host-region competences' we use only the ones regarding the offshoring of innovation activities. The variable takes the value 1 if the firm has marked the 'availability of specialized knowledge in the host region', the 'availability of qualified human

Table 1. Home region tiers.

Tiers	Description
Tier 1	Stockholm (including Kista and Solna) and Skåne. The Stockholm area employs around 100,000 people in the ICT industry and it is considered a leading region in the EU in ICT. Skåne (together with Copenhagen area – the Oresund region) employ around 93,000 people in ICT. The innovation performance of these two regions is high, according to the regional innovation scoreboard. Furthermore, Skåne is the region in Sweden with the highest number of ICT-related patents
Tier 2	Göteborg. Göteborg grew recently in the ICT industry with Ericsson and Volvo IT driving innovation. There are around 4700 ICT companies with 22,000 employees. The innovation performance of this region is also high, according to the regional innovation scoreboard
Tier 3	Rest

Sources: Hollanders (2009), Transform (2006), Hansen and Serin (2010) and Franzén and Wallgren (2010).

capital at a lower cost than in your own country' or 'access to knowledge infrastructure and services in the host region (R&D infrastructure, technical support services, etc.)' as important factors explaining the decision to offshore innovation.

3.1.3 *Control variables*

Additionally, we include a variable capturing the type of firm (standalone, subsidiary and HQ) and another one for the size of the firm. Of the firms in the sample 15% offshore production or innovation activities, but only 6% offshore at a global level (outside Europe). Regarding collaboration for innovation, 85.3% have established collaboration activities with different organizations, but only 35% collaborate at a global level. Most of the companies in the sample are standalone companies (88%), while subsidiaries and HQs represent only 12%. In terms of the region Tier, 42% of the firms are located in Tier 1, 19% in Tier 2 and 39% in Tier 3 regions. Table 2 provides the descriptive statistics of the variables used in the regression models.

3.2 *The model*

The analysis of the effect of competences on GINs can be analysed with a linear regression model. We estimate two different equations for the types of GINs; thus we have a set of equations for global research collaboration and a second set of equations for global offshoring. For the case of global research collaboration, we differentiate by collaboration within Europe (CEUR$_i$), and global collaboration (excluding Europe) (GC$_i$) and the dependent variables (CEUR$_i$ and GC$_i$) are continuous variables indicating the number of different types of organizations the firm collaborates with. The independent variables (x_i) are a set of dimensions that predict the engagement on global collaboration.

$$CEUR_i = x_i\beta + \varepsilon_i, \tag{1}$$

$$GC_i = x_i\beta + \varepsilon_i. \tag{2}$$

Regarding offshoring, we differentiate by offshoring within Europe (OEUR$_i$) and global offshoring (excluding Europe) (GO$_i$). Thus, we estimate two equations for offshoring. The dependent variables (OEUR$_i$ and GO$_i$) are dummy variables indicating whether or not the firm offshores production or innovation activities. The independent variables (x_{ii}) are a set of dimensions that predict the engagement on global collaboration.

$$OEUR_i = x_{ii}\beta + \varepsilon_i, \tag{3}$$

$$GO_i = x_{ii}\beta + \varepsilon_i. \tag{4}$$

3.3. *Case*

To illustrate the complex relationship between competences and the offshoring of innovation we use a case study in the ICT industry. The firm selection is based on three criteria, namely the firm's global presence (particularly presence in China, India and SA), production and innovation capabilities, innovation leadership and headquartered in Sweden. Due to the request of anonymity of the firm, we use TELEQUIP instead of the real name of the company.

In terms of locations, TELEQUIP has important R&D facilities in European countries North America and China. The research conducted in TELEQUIP R&D centres worldwide can be both

Table 2. Descriptive statistics.

Variable	Type	Obs.	Mean	Std. dev.	Min.	Max.
Dependent variables						
Collaboration Europe	Numerical	171	0.485	0.821	0	4
Collaboration global (excluding Europe)	Numerical	171	0.333	0.553	0	2
Offshoring Europe	Dummy 1 = yes	171	0.047	0.212	0	1
Offshoring global (excluding Europe)	Dummy 1 = yes	170	0.059	0.236	0	1
Independent variables						
(a) Competences as enablers						
Employees with university degree	Dummy 1 = yes	171	0.924	0.266	0	1
Employees with postgraduate degree	Dummy 1 = yes	171	0.468	0.500	0	1
R&D activities	Dummy 1 = yes	166	0.458	0.500	0	1
R&D employees	Numerical	165	5.200	7.420	0	33
Intramural R&D (local, regional, global)	Dummy 1 = yes	171	0.304	0.461	0	1
Service innovation	Categorical 1 = firm level 2 = country level 3 = world level	171	1.035	0.880	0	3
Support innovation	Categorical 1 = firm level 2 = country level 3 = world level	171	0.585	0.734	0	3
Advanced production systems	Numerical	171	1.637	1.458	0	5
OEM	Dummy 1 = yes if OEM > 50	171	0.094	0.292	0	1
ODM	Dummy 1 = yes if ODM > 50	171	0.158	0.366	0	1
OBM	Dummy 1 = yes if OBM > 50	171	0.386	0.488	0	1
Host-region competences	Dummy 1 = yes	171	0.035	0.185	0	1
(b) Competences as drivers						
Region TIER	Categorical 1 = Tier 1 2 = Tier 2 3 = Tier 3	171	1.971	0.904	1	3
Control variables						
Standalone	Dummy 1 = yes	170	0.876	0.330	0	1
Subsidiary	Dummy 1 = yes	170	0.100	0.301	0	1
MNC	Dummy 1 = yes	170	0.024	0.152	0	1
Size	Categorical 1 = less than 10 2 = 10–49 3 = 50–249 4 = 250–999 5 = more than 1000	169	1.840	0.782	1	5

for the development of a completely new product or service for the whole corporation as well as for the adaptation of an existing product to a local market.[3]

Interviews were conducted in 2010 and 2011 with several CEOs of the company in the HQs as well as in the subsidiaries in SA and China: the Vice-president and head of R&D at HQs, the Chief director of TELEQUIP China, the CEO for Commercial management of TELEQUIP sub-Saharan Africa, the Strategy and Marketing director of TELEQUIP sub-Saharan Africa and the CEO of

Innovation and partnering of TELEQUIP sub-Saharan Africa. We used the information collected in the different sites to check the validity of the statements (for example, between the HQs and the subsidiaries). Interviews were semi-structured and lasted 2–3 h. All interviews were recorded and transcribed. A document summarizing the most important issues raised in the interview was also produced within 24 h after the interview. Additional information was collected from the annual reports, website and other public information of the firm.

4. Globalization of innovation and competences in the Swedish ICT industry

4.1 *Results of the survey*

The results of the regression equation given in Table 3 show that both firm-level competences as well as regional competences matter for firms engagement in globalization of innovation, but they relate differently for global research collaboration than for global offshoring.

In the case of global research collaboration, firm-level competences and regional competences seem to matter almost equally, while for the case of offshoring of innovation regional competences seem to matter most. Results are also consistent with the two levels of geographical offshoring analysed in this article (Europe and Global).

Regarding *global collaboration for innovation*, the results confirm that skills and the technological effort are related to research collaboration, both in Europe and globally. Indeed the number of employees with postgraduate degree, the number of employees in R&D and the engagement in intramural R&D activities are positively correlated to global research collaboration in both geographic levels. This result suggests that firms with higher levels of absorptive capacities in terms of their human capital and R&D activities identify and collaborate for innovation with organizations located abroad, which is consistent with Cohen and Levinthal (1990). However, the level of organizational competences is not related to the propensity of the firm to engage in research collaboration neither with geographically close nor distant partners.

The competences available at the regional level in Sweden (captured by the variable Region Tier) are significantly related to research collaboration only within Europe; however, no significant results were found for global research collaboration. This result is consistent with the discussion brought by Chaminade and Plechero (2012), as firms located in Tiers 2 and 3 regions will tend to establish more research collaboration with external partners to compensate for lower level of capabilities in their regions.

The type of firm is also another important determinant. Standalone and MNCs seem to be keener to establish more collaboration networks at both geographic levels than subsidiaries of MNCs. This result was expected, as standalone firms and MNC need to establish extramural collaboration networks with other agents, in order to compensate for knowledge not available in their internal networks (Castellani and Zanfei, 2006; Barnard and Chaminade, 2011).

Interestingly enough, size does not seem to matter for the propensity of Swedish ICT firms to engage in global research collaboration, but it shows to be important in research collaboration within Europe. This result seems to be in line with data from the Swedish innovation survey which also shows a very high proportion of small (and medium-size firms) that report to collaborate for innovation with distant partners such as Indian or Chinese (Eurostat, 2009). The international orientation of the Swedish business sector (Marklund et al., 2004) is also reflected in their propensity to engage in global research collaboration, independent of the firm size or the location of the unit in Sweden.

Both firm-level and regional competences are related to the propensity of Swedish ICT firms to engage in *offshoring of innovation* (offshoring of production and innovation activities). At the

Table 3. Competences as drivers and enablers of GINs.

	Collaboration Europe	Collaboration global	Offshoring Europe	Offshoring global
Competences as enablers				
Human Capital				
Employees with university degree	0.231 (0.263)	0.024 (0.184)	0.033 (0.064)	**−0.099*** (0.076)
Employees with postgraduate degree	**0.316**** (0.129)	**0.139*** (0.090)	−0.006 (0.032)	−0.039 (0.038)
R&D activities				
R&D activities	−0.117 (0.204)	−0.079 (0.143)	**−0.083*** (0.051)	−0.027 (0.061)
R&D employees	**0.025*** (0.014)	**0.015*** (0.010)	**0.005*** (0.003)	0.004 (0.004)
Intramural R&D	**0.276*** (0.158)	**0.191*** (0.111)	0.041 (0.039)	0.001 (0.046)
Other organizational competences				
Service innovation			**0.026*** (0.019)	0.015 (0.022)
Support innovation			0.014 (0.022)	−0.015 (0.026)
Advanced production systems	0.042 (0.044)	0.039 (0.031)	**0.014*** (0.011)	**0.017*** (0.013)
OEM	−0.116 (0.215)	−0.075 (0.151)	−0.054 (0.053)	0.039 (0.062)
ODM	**−0.257*** (0.181)	0.015 (0.127)	**−0.064*** (0.044)	**−0.068*** (0.052)
OBM	−0.040 (0.144)	−0.037 (0.101)	−0.017 (0.035)	0.019 (0.042)
Host-region competences			**0.144*** (0.082)	**0.416***** (0.097)
Competences as drivers (Offshoring)				
Region TIER	**0.107*** (0.072)	0.029 (0.051)	0.004 (0.018)	−0.030* (0.021)
Other firm characteristics				
Standalone	**0.367*** (0.212)	**0.231*** (0.149)		
Subsidiary				
MNC	**0.367*** (0.212)	**0.231*** (0.149)	−0.138* (0.105)	0.006 (0.125)
Size	**0.127*** (0.092)	0.060 (0.064)	−0.014 (0.022)	**0.047*** (0.026)

Note: Standard errors in parenthesis.
*Significance at 10% level.
**Significance at 5% level.
***Significance at 1% level.

firm level, the skills or qualification of human capital, the engagement in R&D activities and the existence of other organizational competences are positively related to offshoring of innovation, although with different degrees in terms of the geography of networks.

The skills of the employees in the firm seem to be relevant only for global offshoring and R&D activities and more specifically, the number of employees performing R&D activities is significant only when the firm offshores in Europe. Organizational competences are important for

Table 4. Competences as enablers and drivers of globalization of innovation in the Swedish ICT industry.

	Competences as enablers	Competences as drivers
Research collaboration in Europe	Employees with postgraduate degree (**) R&D employees (*) Intramural R&D (*) ODM (–) (*) Standalone (*) MNC (*) Size (*)	Region Tier (*)
Global research collaboration	Employees with postgraduate degree (*) R&D employees (*) Intramural R&D (*) Standalone (*) MNC (*)	
Offshoring of innovation in Europe	R&D activities (–) (*) R&D employees (*) Service innovation (*) Advanced production systems (*) ODM (–) (*)	Host region (*)
Global Offshoring of innovation	Employees with university degree (–) (*) Advanced production systems (*) ODM (–) (*) Home region (–) (*)	**Host regions (***)** Region Tier (–) (*)

offshoring, no matter at which geographical level. Our results suggest that firms that have implemented advanced production systems are more prone to engage in European and global offshoring.

The size of firms is an important determinant for global offshoring as could be expected, suggesting that large firms tend to establish routines to coordinate global activities, results consistent with those by Cantwell (1995) and Kogut and Zander (1992).

The results also confirm that regional competences are a very important driver for the offshoring of innovation, particularly for global offshoring. The availability of knowledge in the host region is highly correlated to this form of GIN, and the Region Tier is also correlated in a lesser extent, thus pointing out to the importance of asset seeking strategies in the process of globalization of innovation of Swedish ICT firms. The case presented in the following section will provide some insights into the relationship between host-region competences and the decisions of the firm to offshore innovation activities. Table 4 summarizes the main findings of the econometric analysis for the ICT industry.

4.2 *Host-region competences and the offshoring of innovation to emerging economies: the case of TELEQUIP*

The analysis of the ICT industry in Sweden points out to the importance of the competences in the host region as important drivers for the globalization of innovation activities, particularly offshoring of innovation. When offshoring globally, the skills of the staff and the organizational competences are important enablers while the competences in the host region is the most important factor shaping the decision of the firm to locate innovation activities abroad.

The case of TELEQUIP is interesting to illustrate how different competences accumulated in specific regions in emerging economies are shaping the decision of a multinational company to locate innovation activities.

TELEQUIP is an R&D intensive company. The level of skills of the human capital is also very high. The R&D personnel represent around 22% of the total work force. Of the total R&D employees, 28% are in Sweden, 14% distributed among the five centres in China, 5% in USA, or 2% in India, among others (Ujjual and Tunzelmann, 2011).

In the last decade or so, TELEQUIP has followed a clear strategy of reducing the number of R&D sites worldwide while increasing the size of the remaining sites (less sites but larger ones). This has occurred in parallel with the increasing technological complexity of ICT products and services, which demands a larger variety of skills (from software developers, to radio experts, computer engineers, etc.). While the number of sites in Europe has decreased, the presence in USA remained unchanged while new R&D sites within the emerging economies, like India and China, were opened. The reason for this move towards large Asian economies is related to their proximity to the local market and adaptation of the products to the local demands and standards as would be expected, but the access to competences and more explicitly, the access to 'domain competences'[4] is regarded as the second.

Different subsidiaries play a very different role in the global innovation strategy of the company depending on their competence level. Each of the largest R&D sites of TELEQUIP sites has specialized in a particular knowledge domain. For example, the site in the Silicon Valley (USA) has the R&D site for radio products, as the site in India is strong in IT which is related to TELEQUIP business support systems and the ones in China are providing global solutions in different knowledge domains and for a variety of business segments like networks (radio networks, core networks and service networks), global services (consulting), power modules and consumer and business applications for the multimedia business.

In general, the R&D activities and the most specialized competences (in the internal network) remain concentrated in the sites located in Europe and the USA but, according to the Vice-president R&D China has upgraded rapidly as an important R&D site inside TELEQUIP.

4.2.1 *China*

Accessing domain competences is one of the main drivers for TELEQUIP to locate one of the largest corporate R&D sites in China. In 2009, China represented 14% of the R&D personnel of TELEQUIP. The Chinese R&D labs develop solutions for the whole corporation and not only for China. More than 25% of the employees in the Chinese subsidiaries of TELEQUIP are working on products in different fields and solutions, developing on an average 100–150 products for the global market each year (Ujjual and Tunzelmann, 2011).

The location in particular regions also facilitates close interactions with universities and research centres. The interviewee with the Operation Development Director of TELEQUIP in China regards the large pool of skilled people coming from various Chinese universities as a main reason for locating the R&D sites in this country and in particular regions. For example, the Nanjing centre has been started due to the presence of regional actors, such as universities and colleges, as well as TELEQUIP's biggest manufacturing unit. In his view, there are not many differences between the Chinese market and markets in the rest of the world which makes it easier for the subsidiary to provide solutions for the entire company. In his words:

Our market strategy is to provide global solutions, and solve problems in terms of network smooth and call quality, whether what we face is high-end markets or low-end markets.

The division of labour in terms of innovation between the HQ and the subsidiary is better explained by the CEO of TELEQUIP in Sweden. He indicates that

> For the activities related to Radio based stations the most important innovations are the ones that are developed in Sweden, Canada and China but Sweden does mainly core innovation while in China the activities are mainly related to the implementation of idea. The Chinese subsidiary can be often relevant, for example, for incremental innovation (e.g. reducing cost and adapting the product to the specific profile of Chinese operators). But some of those innovations also have a global effect. An example of incremental innovation with a 'global' effect is the production of a play station adapted to the local context; this idea is starting now to be spread worldwide.

This possibility of the Chinese R&D subsidiaries to develop solutions potentially useful for the entire corporation puts an additional emphasis on the competences in the subsidiaries. They are not merely adapting the products to the local market, but developing products or services (sometimes brand new) that are potentially useful for the entire corporation.

4.2.2   *India*

TELEQUIP has three subsidiaries in India, employing basically 2% of the R&D staff of TELEQUIP. According to the Vice-president R&D the Indian subsidiary can be regarded as an extension of the multimedia business unit at TELEQUIP and strong in IT competences. But the Chinese have a broader range of domain competences in many different areas and thus conduct research for different business of TELEQUIP. R&D in India is narrower than in China not because the Indian market demands fewer or less sophisticated products, but because they do not have all the requisite competences. Especially since TELEQUIP – as a group – benefits from what goes on in its Chinese operation in that it generates knowledge and equipment for global markets, competences rather than market proximity seem to matter more.

So, it is the breadth and depth of skills available in China that makes the Chinese site a more interesting location for R&D for TELEQUIP than India.

4.2.3   *South Africa*

The subsidiary of TELEQUIP in SA aims at adapting TELEQUIP products for the African market. The subsidiary does not have its own R&D department. The interviews done by one of our partners in SA may provide some insights[5] into why this is so. A CEO of TELEQUIP sub-Saharan Africa explains that the reasons behind a lack of R&D site in SA are related to size of market (smaller than that of China and India, for example) and the lack of skilled labour or specific expertise in certain competences. He emphasizes the lack of engineers as a main hindrance for TELEQUIP in SA. Table 5 provides an overview of the enrolment in tertiary education in China, India and SA in comparative perspective. As can be observed, although the proportion of students enrolled in tertiary education in Science and Engineering fields in SA is higher than in India and China, their numbers are way below these two Asian countries.

The Commercial Management of TELEQUIP in sub-Saharan Africa also talks about reasons for choosing India and China as the R&D sites, he mainly refers to the issue of a large pool of skilled labour at a reasonable price. In his words:

> R&D price is still quite high and to do it we have to look at the centres that provide engineering expertise and efficiency. And also at a very low cost. And India and China provide those fundamentals.

Further on he refers to the fact that in the case of China the products can also be supplied at a global level, thus confirming what the interviewee in the HQ said.

Table 5. Enrolment in tertiary education in China, India and SA (total and by field).

Countries	Tertiary education enrolment Gross (%)	Technical enrolment at tertiary level					
		Science		Engineering		Total for science and engineering	
		Number	%	Number	%	Number	%
China	24	128,350	4	1,516,611	5	1,644,961	9
India	16	2,056,675	10	1,490,618	7	3,547,293	17
South Africa	16	135,505	15	71,172	8	206,677	23

Sources: South African statistics from the Department of Higher Education and Training South Africa, Statistic on India from National Indian Bureau Publication 2011 and China data from UNESCO and from National Statistics Bureau of China.

The role of the South African subsidiary in the global strategy of TELEQUIP is related to the adaptation of the products to the African market. For doing so, knowledge of the local languages is essential. As one of the interviewees in SA indicates 'as more and more people get into the mobile arena with handsets and so on, the local languages become more important'. Therefore in order to penetrate the whole of Africa it is a necessity to have skilled people from African regions. He indicates that even though the HQs have the knowledge on networks they need to have a better understanding of the local consumers.

The interviews held in Sweden, China and SA point out to a kind of division of labour of offshoring sites in TELEQUIP according to competences. It also shows the interplay between firm-level competences and regional competences as enablers and drivers of innovation (Table 6).

Core R&D seems to be conducted barely in three sites worldwide in Sweden, USA and China. These centres provide complex R&D solutions for the different business and for the entire corporation which requires a combination of a wide arrange of skills. A second tier of centres are those that provide very specific competences in certain domains, like, for example, the R&D centre in Bangalore which provides very deep expertise in software. They are also global, in the sense that they provide solutions also to the entire company, but only on specific domains. A final tier of centres are those that conduct mainly development for the local markets. Finally, there are locations in which there are not yet any R&D centre, but only production and sales, with small adaptations to local markets.

Table 6. Competences as a *driver* for offshoring of TELEQUIP and the role of different sites in the global innovation strategy of TELEQUIP.

Sites	Competences	Role
Sweden (HQ)	Advanced R&D competences in a variety of domains	Core innovation
China (Beijing)	Broad domain competences in radio communication	Provide solutions for the entire company (e.g. play station) Implementation of core innovations developed at the HQ
India (Bangalore)	Strong competences in internet protocol business (specific competences in certain domain)	Provide solutions for the entire company but only in the specific domain of IP
South Africa (Gauteng)	Local languages	Simple adaptation of services to local market

5. Conclusions

By distinguishing between competences as an enabler and competences as a driver this article contributes to our understanding of the role of firm and regional competences in the globalization of innovation.

For Swedish ICT firms, the level of competences in the region where the firm is located (home region) and the level of the competences in the host region are related to the propensity of the firm to engage in offshoring. The level of competences at the firm level is related to both global research collaboration and global offshoring of innovation. The involvement of the firm in R&D activities is correlated with both global research collaboration and offshoring of innovation, as it increases not only the innovative capability of the firm but also the capacity to tap into and absorb knowledge from external sources (Cohen and Levinthal, 1990). Global research collaboration is also related to organizational competences particularly the level of flexibility and quality of the processes within the firm. Engaging external sources in the innovation process is necessary but also costly. Having advanced production systems in place may help to standardize some of the processes thus reducing the transaction costs involved in open innovation. Thus, firm-level competences are an important *enabler* for the globalization of innovation, particularly offshoring of innovation. Home-regional competences are important for global research collaboration and offshoring of innovation, but in different directions, suggesting that firms located in Tiers 2 and 3 will tend to establish global research collaboration to tap into knowledge produced externally, while firms in Tier 1 regions are more prone to establish global offshoring of innovation.

The results of the survey also confirm that competences accumulated in the host region are an important *driver* for the globalization of innovation and in particular for the offshoring of innovation, as the recent literature on the role of emerging countries in R&D offshoring has pointed out. What the literature has been lacking is a comparison between competences in different locations vis-a-vis the decisions of the multinational company to locate different innovation activities in the different subsidiaries. In other words, the BICS countries are treated more often than not as a relatively homogeneous block of countries.

What the case illustrates is how the breadth and depth of the competences available in three of the BICS countries actually determine the type of innovation activities that the subsidiary performs as well as the role that it plays in the global innovation strategy of the company. While some subsidiaries may be able to play a double role adapting existing products to the local market and developing new solutions for the global markets, others may only play a limited role.

The case of TELEQUIP also points out that there is not one single reason why a company decides to engage in GINs. It is a combination of factors that include firm strategy, firm-level competences and the characteristics of the potential locations in terms of markets and skill supply. In terms of the strategy, TELEQUIP's selection of the sites seems to respond to a double strategy: some of the sites have been selected because they excel in very specific competences (like Bangalore in India) while some others are a combination of the willingness to position themselves in a larger market (also in India) while accessing a broader base of domain competences (Beijing).

It is interesting to see that some of the factors that the literature has traditionally considered as influencing research collaboration and offshoring, like the engagement in R&D activities (Cohen and Levinthal, 1990), are only important when the partners of the collaboration or the destination of the offshoring are in close proximity to regions or countries and presumably with a similar level of technological capabilities. When research collaboration or offshoring takes place at the global level, other factors like organizational competences take over in level of importance, which points out to the challenge of engaging in innovation at a global scale in organizational terms (Barnard and Chaminade, 2011).

Finally, the results of the survey point to some interesting future venues of research. Sweden is a small economy with strong international linkages (Marklund et al., 2004). The innovation system is highly dominated by multinationals which have been the focus of extensive analysis by Swedish researchers in international business. What the analysis presented in this paper suggests is that small and medium-size enterprises are also active players in GINs, particularly in global research collaboration. But these firms are traditionally characterized by limited competences and resources. Understanding the drivers and enablers of these firms to engage in globalization of innovation could provide some insights into the current literature which is highly dominated by MNCs' perspective.

Acknowledgements

Research for this article was partially funded by the European Community's Seventh Framework Programme (Project INGINEUS, Grant Agreement No. 225368, www.ingineus.eu). The authors alone are responsible for its contents which do not necessarily reflect the views or opinions of the European Commission, nor is the European Commission responsible for any use that might be made of the information appearing herein. Additionally, financial support from the Swedish Research Council (Linneaus grant) is acknowledged. We especially thank our partners in South Africa – Tashmia Ismail and Prof. Helena Barnard – from GIBS, University of Pretoria for the interviews they conducted in the subsidiaries of TELEQUIP in South Africa. Lucinda David helped with the data on enrolment in tertiary education in South Africa, China and India. We are thankful to the comments received from two anonymous referees to an earlier version of this article. All errors are exclusively the authors'.

Notes

1. This section is based on Plechero and Chaminade (2010).
2. The distribution of the respondents/non-respondents by size is the following: 5–9 employees (42/40%), 10–49 employees (45/45.9%), 50–199 employees (9.7/10.8%), 200–999 employees (1.5/2.6%) and more than 1000 employees (1/0.5%). The proportion between respondents and non-respondents per sub-industry is 1.8/2.3 for manufacture communication equipment (NACE code 26.30) and 98.2/97.7 for information technology and computer services (NACE code 62.10–62.90).
3. An example of the development of a local solution for local needs could be the development of radio equipment in rural areas in India that would be conducted completely by TELEQUIP India. Another example of a development in which the subsidiaries will be involved could be a technology developed in the USA that needs to be adapted to the standards and requirements of the market in which TELEQUIP is commercializing that technology.
4. Domain competences refer to the skills needed for the supply of different business solutions for the clients, which includes, among others, knowledge on radio networks, core networks, service networks, consultancy, TV and media applications (software development), etc.
5. Interviews were conducted by Tashmia Ismail and Helena Barnard, Gordon Institute of Business Studies, Pretoria University, South Africa. The authors of this article had access to the transcription of the interviews.

References

Altenburg, T., Schmitz, H., and Stamm, A. (2008) Breakthrough? China's and India's transition from production to innovation. *World Development*, 36(2), pp. 325–344.

Amin, A., and Thrift, N. (1994) Living in the global, in: A. Amin and N. Thrift (eds) *Globalization, Institutions, and Regional Development in Europe* (Oxford: Oxford University Press).

Amin, A., and Thrift, N. (1995) *Globalization, Institutions, and Regional Development in Europe* (Oxford: Oxford University Press).

Archibugi, D., and Coco, A. (2004) A new indicator of technological capabilities for developed and developing countries (ArCo). *World Development*, 32(4), pp. 629–654.

Archibugi, D., and Coco, A. (2005) Measuring technological capabilities at the country level: A survey and a menu for choice. *Research Policy*, 34(2), pp. 175–194.

Archibugi, D., and Michie, J. (1995) The globalisation of technology: A new taxonomy. *Cambridge Journal of Economics*, 19(1), pp. 121–140.

Arora, A., and Bagde, S. (2006) The Indian Software Industry: The Human Capital Story. DRUID Conference. Copenhagen, Denmark.

Arora, A., and Gambardella, A. (2004) The globalization of the software industry: Perspective and opportunities for developed and developing countries. *NBER Working Paper Series*. Cambridge, Massachusetts.

Arora, A., and Gambardella, A. (2005) *From Underdogs to Tigers: The rise and growth of the software industry in Brazil, China, India, Ireland, and Israel* (Oxford: Oxford University Press).

Arora, A., Arunachalam, V.S., Asundi, J., and Fernandes, R. (2001) The Indian software industry. *Research Policy*, 30(8), pp. 1267–1287.

Arora, A., Gambardella, A., and Torrisi, S. (2001) In the footsteps of SiliconValley? Indian and Irish software in the international division of labour. SIEPR Discussion Paper No. 00-41. Stanford, Stanford Institute for Economic Policy Research: 38.

Asheim, B.T., and Isaksen, A. (1997) Location, agglomeration and innovation: Towards regional innovation systems in Norway? *European Planning Studies*, 5(3), pp. 299–330.

Asheim, B.T., and Isaksen, A. (2002) Regional innovation system: The integration of local 'sticky' and global 'ubiquitous' knowledge. *Journal of Technology Transfer*, 27(1), pp. 77–86.

Asheim, B., Ebersberger, B., Herstad, S. and Heidenreich, M. (2011) MNCs Between the Global and the Local: Knowledge Bases, Proximity and Globally Distributed Knowledge Networks. Innovation and Institutional Embeddedness of Multinational Companies. Cheltenham: Edward Elgar (in print).

Athreye, S., and Prevezer, M. (2008) R&D offshoring and the domestic science base in India and China. *Working Papers*. Centre for Globalisation Research, University of London.

Audretsch, D.B., and Feldman, M.P. (1996) R&D spillovers and the geography of innovation and production. *The American Economic Review*, 86(3), pp. 630–640.

Audretsch, D.B., and Feldman, M.P. (2004) Knowledge spillovers and the geography of innovation. *Handbook of Regional and Urban Economics*, 4(4), pp. 2713–2739.

Barnard, H. and Chaminade, C. (2011) Global innovation networks: What are they and where can we find them? (Conceptual and empirical issues). *CIRCLE Electronic Working Papers*. Lund University.

Barney, J.B. (1996) The resource-based theory of the firm. *Organization Science*, 7(5), pp. 469–469.

Barney, J., Wright, M., and Ketchen, D.J. (2001) The resource-based view of the firm: Ten years after 1991. *Journal of Management*, 27(6), pp. 625.

Bathelt, H., and Glûckler, J. (2003) Toward a relational economic geography. *Journal of Economic Geography*, 3(2), pp. 117–144.

Bell, M., and Albu, M. (1999) Knowledge systems and technological dynamism in industrial clusters in developing countries. *World Development*, 27(9), pp. 1715–1734.

Bell, M., and Pavitt, K. (1995) The development of technological capabilities, in: I. Haque (ed.) *Trade, Technology and International Competitiveness*, pp. 69–101 (Washington, DC: The World Bank).

Boschma, R.A., and Frenken, K. (2006) Why is economic geography not an evolutionary science? Towards an evolutionary economic geography. *Journal of Economic Geography*, 6(3), pp. 273–302.

Boschma, R.A., and Frenken, K. (2009) Some notes on institutions in evolutionary economic geography. *Economic Geography*, 85(2), pp. 151–158.

Burt, R.S. (1992) *Structural Holes* (Cambridge: Cambridge University Press).

Cantwell, J. (1995) The globalisation of technology: What remains of the product cycle model? *Cambridge Journal of Economics*, 19(1), pp. 155–174.

Cantwell, J., and Piscitello, L. (2005) Annual Conference of the European International Business, Competence-creating vs. competence-exploiting activities of foreign owned MNCs: How interaction with local networks affects their location, (pp. 10–13), Oslo, 10–13 Dec.

Cantwell, J., and Piscitello, L. (2007) Attraction and deterrence in the location of foreign/owned R&D activities: The role of positive and negatives pillovers. *International Journal of Technological Learning, Innovation and Development*, 1(1), pp. 83–111.

Castellacci, F., and Archibugi, D. (2008) The technology clubs: The distribution of knowledge across nations. *Research Policy*, 37(10), pp. 1659–1673.

Castellani, D., and Zanfei, A. (2006) Multinational Firms, Innovation and Productivity. Cheltenham, UK., Edward Elgar.

Chaminade, C. (2009) On the concept of global innovation networks. *CIRCLE Electronic Working Paper 2009/05*. Lund University, Sweden.

Chaminade, C., and Plechero, M. (2012) Do regions make a difference? Exploring the role of different regional innovation systems in global innovation networks in the ICT industry. *CIRCLE Electronic Working Papers*. Lund University Sweden

Chaminade, C., and Vang, J. (2008) Globalisation of knowledge production and regional innovation policy: Supporting specialized hubs in the Bangalore software industry. *Research Policy*, 37(10), pp. 1684–1696.

Coe, N., Dicken, P., and Hess, M. (2004) Global production networks: Realizing the potential. *Journal of Economic Geography*, 8(3), pp. 271–295.

Cohen, W., and Levinthal, D. (1990) Absorptive capacity: A new perspective on learning and innovation. *Administrative Science Quarterly*, 35(1), pp. 128–152.

Cooke, P. (1992) Regional innovation systems: Competitive regulation in the new Europe. *Geoforum*, 23(3), pp. 365–382.

Cooke, P., Gomez-Uranga, M., and Etxebarria, G. (1997) Regional systems of innovation: Institutional and organizational dimensions. *Research Policy*, 26(4–5), pp. 475–491.

Dantas, E., Giuliani, E., and Marin, A. (2007) The persistence of 'capabilities' as a central issue in industrialization strategies: How they relate to MNC spillovers, industrial clusters and knowledge networks. *Asian Journal of Technology Innovation*, 15(2), pp. 19–43.

De Bresson, C., and Amesse, F. (1991) Networks of innovators: A review and introduction to the issue. *Research Policy*, 20(5), pp. 363–379.

Dickens, P. (2007) *Global Shifts: Mapping the changing contours of the world economy* (New York: Guilford).

Dunning, J.H. (1993) *Trade, Location of Economic Activity and the Multinational Enterprise: A search for an eclectic approach* (London: Routledge).

Dunning, J.H. (2001) The eclectic (OLI) paradigm of international production: Past, present and future. *International Journal of the Economics of Business*, 8(2), pp. 173–190.

Dunning, J.H., and Narula, R. (1995) The R&D activities of foreign firms in the United States. *International Studies of Management & Organization*, 25(1/2), pp. 39–74.

Dunning, J.H., van Hoesel, R., and Narula, R. (1996) Explaining the new wave of outward FDI from developing countries: The case of Taiwan and Korea. MERIT working paper, Maastricht University, The Netherlands.

Eisenhardt, K., and Martin, J. (2000) Dynamic capabilities; what are they? *Strategic Management Journal*, 21(9), pp. 1105–1121.

Eurostat (2009) Community innovation survey 2006–2008. http://epp.eurostat.ec.europa.eu/portal/page/portal/microdata/cis

Fifarek, B.J., and Veloso, F.M. (2010) Offshoring and the global geography of innovation. *Journal of Economic Geography*, 10(4), pp. 559–578.

Franzén, E., and Wallgren, D. (2010) Potential for the Green ICT innovation system: A case study from the Gothenburg region. Master of Science Thesis. Chalmers University of Technology, Göteborg.

Freeman, C. (1987) *Technology Policy and Economic Performance: Lessons from Japan* (London: Pinter).

Freeman, C. (1991) Networks of innovators: A synthesis of research issues. *Research Policy*, 20(5), pp. 499–514.

Gereffi, G., Humphrey, J., and Sturgeon, T. (2005) The governance of global value chains. *Review of International Political Economy*, 12(1), pp. 78–104.

Gertler, M.S. (2010) Rules of the game: The place of institutions in regional economic change. *Regional Studies*, 44(1), pp. 1–15.

Giuliani, E. (2007) The selective nature of knowledge networks in clusters: Evidence from the wine industry. *Journal of Economic Geography*, 7(2), pp. 139–168.

Giuliani, E., and Bell, M. (2005a) The micro-determinants of meso-level learning and innovation: Evidence from a Chilean wine cluster. *Research Policy*, 34(1), pp. 47–68.

Giuliani, E., and Bell, M. (2005b) When micro shapes the meso: Learning networks in a Chilean wine cluster. *Research Policy*, 34(1), pp. 47–68.

Grant, R. (1991) The resource-based theory of competitive advantage: Implications for strategy formulation. *California Management Review*, 33(3), pp. 114–135.

Hansen, P. A., and Serin, G. (2010) The European ICT clusters (accessed on 18 June 2011 at http://rucforsk.ruc.dk/site/files/32956338/the_european_ict_clusters_web_0.pdf).

Hollanders, H. (2007) Innovation modes. Evidence on the sector level. Europe Innova, Sectoral Innovation Watch, Deliverable WP4. European Commission, Brussels.

Howells, J. (1990) The internationalization of R & D and the development of global research networks. *Regional Studies*, 24(6), pp. 495–512.

Humphrey, J., and Schmitz, H. (2002) How does insertion in global value chains affect upgrading in industrial clusters? *Regional Studies*, 36(9), pp. 1017–1027.

Knight, G.A., and Cavusgil, S.T. (2004) Innovation, organizational capabilities, and the born-global firm. *Journal of International Business Studies*, 35(2), pp. 124–141.

Kogut, B., and Zander, U. (1992) Knowledge of the firm, combinative capabilities and the replication of technology. *Organization Studies*, 3, pp. 383–397.

Lall, S. (1992) Technological capabilities and industrialization. *World Development*, 20(2), pp. 165–186.

Lall, S., and Pietrobelli, C. (2005) National technology systems in sub-Saharan Africa. *International Journal of Technology and Globalisation*, 1(3/4), pp. 311–342.

Lewin, A.Y., Massini, S., and Peeters, C. (2009) Why are companies offshoring innovation? The emerging global race for talent. *Journal of International Business Studies*, 40(6), pp. 901–925.

Li, J.J., Poppo, L., *et al.* (2010) Relational mechanisms, formal contracts, and local knowledge acquisition by international subsidiaries. *Strategic Management Journal*, 31(4), pp. 349–370.

Lundvall, B.-A. (1988) Innovation as an interactive process: From user–producer interaction to the national system of innovation, in: G.E.A. Dosi (ed.) *Technical Change and Economic Theory*, pp. 349–369 (London: Pinter).

Lundvall, B.-A. (1992) User–producer relationships, national systems of innovation and internalization, in: B.-Ä. Lundvall (ed.) *National Systems of Innovation. Towards a Theory of Innovation and Interactive Learning*, pp. 45–67 (London: Pinter).

March, J.G. (1991) Exploration and exploitation in organizational learning. *Organization Science*, 2(1), pp. 71–87.

Mariani, M. (2002) Next to production or to technological Clusters? The economics and management of R&D location. *Journal of Management and Governance*, 6(2), pp. 131–152.

Marklund, G., Nilsson, R., Sandgren, P., Granat Thorslund, J. and Ullström, J. (2004) The Swedish national Innovation system 1970–2003. A quantitative international bench marking analysis. VINNOVA ANALYSIS VA 2004:1.

Martin, R., and Moodysson, J. (2011) Innovation in symbolic industries: The geography and organization of knowledge sourcing. *European Planning Studies*, 19(7), pp. 1183–1203.

Mol, M.J. (2005) Does being R&D intensive still discourage outsourcing?: Evidence from Dutch manufacturing. *Research Policy*, 34(4), pp. 571–582.

Moodysson, J. (2008) Principles and practices of knowledge creation: On the organization of 'Buzz' and 'Pipelines' in life science communities. *Economic Geography*, 84(4), pp. 449–469.

Moodysson, J., Coenen, L., and Asheim, B. (2008) Explaining spatial patterns of innovation: Analytical and synthetic modes of knowledge creation in the Medicon Valley life-science cluster. *Environment and Planning A*, 40(5), pp. 1040–1056.

Morgan, K. (2007) The learning region: Institutions, innovation and regional renewal. *Regional Studies*, 41(5), pp. 147–159.

Mothe, J.D.L., and Paquet, G. (eds) (1998) *Local and Regional Systems of Innovation* (Norwell: Kluwer Academic Publishers).

Narula, R., and Zanfei, A. (2004) Globalization of innovation: The role of multinational enterprises, in: J. Fagerberg, D. Mowery and R. Nelson (eds) *The Oxford Handbook of Innovation*, pp. 318--347 (Oxford: Oxford University Press).

Nooteboom, B. (2000) Learning by interaction: Absorptive capacity, cognitive distance and governance. *Journal of Management and Governance*, 4(1–2), pp. 69–92.

Nooteboom, B. (2003) Learning and governance in inter-firm relations. ERIM Report Series Research in Management. Erasmus University, Rotterdam.

Nooteboom, B. (2004) *Inter-firm Collaboration, Learning and Networks. An Integrated Approach* (London: Routledge).

Nooteboom, B., Van Haverbeke, W., and Duysters, G. (2007) Optimal cognitive distance and absorptive capacity. *Research Policy*, 36(7), pp. 1016–1034.

Parthasarathy, B., and Aoyama, Y. (2006) From software services to R&D services: Local entrepreneurship in the software industry in Bangalore, India. *Environment and Planning A*, 38(7), pp. 1269–1285.

Penrose, E.G., (1959) *The Theory of the Growth of the Firm* (New York: Wiley).

Plechero, M., and Chaminade, C. (2010) Different competences, different modes in the globalization of innovation? A comparative study of the pune and beijing regions. CIRCLE Electronic Working Papers, Lund University, Sweden.

Powell, W.W., and Grodal, S. (2004) Networks of innovators, in: J. Fagerberg, D. Mowery and R. Nelson (eds) *The Oxford Handbook of Innovation*, pp. 1--29 (Oxford: Oxford University Press).

Sabiola, F., and Zanfei, A. (2009) Multinational firms, global value chains and the organization of knowledge transfer. *Research Policy*, 38(2), pp. 369–381.

Saxenian, A.L. (2001a) Bangalore: The Silicon Valley of Asia? Center for Research on Economic Development and Policy Reform (Berkeley University), California.

Saxenian, A.L. (2001b) Bangalore: The Silicon Valley of Asia? Working Paper. Tanford, Center for Research on Economic Development and Policy Reform: 32.

Sousa, C.M.P., Martínez-López, F.J., and Coelho, F. (2008) The determinants of export performance: A review of the research in the literature between 1998 and 2005. *International Journal of Management Reviews*, 10(4), pp. 343–374.

Teece, D.J. (1980) Economies of scope and the scope of the enterprise. *Journal of Economic Behavior and Organization*, 1(3), pp. 223–247.

Tödtling, F., Lengaver, L., and Höglinger, C. (2011) Knowledge sourcing and innovation in 'Thick' and 'Thin' regional innovation systems. Comparing ICT firms in two Austrian regions. *European Planning Studies*, 19(7), pp. 1245–1276.

Transform (2006). Benchmarking and Fostering Transformative Use of ICTs in the EU Regions (accessed on 4 November 2011 at http://www.transform-eu.org/).

Ujjual, V. and Tunzelmann, N.V. (2011) The R&D Organisation, R&D Management and R&D Strategies of MNEs undertaking International R&D, INGINEUS internal reports, www.ingineus.eu.

UNCTAD (2006) World Investment Report. FDI from Developing and Transition Economies: Implications for Development. United Nations, Geneva.

Verspagen, B., and Schoenmakers, W. (2004) The spatial dimension of patenting by multinational firms in Europe. *Journal of Economic Geography*, 4(1), pp. 23–42.

Wernefelt, B. (1984) A resource-based view of the firm. *Strategic Management Journal*, 5(10), pp. 171–180.

Zander, I. (1999) How do you mean [] global'? An empirical investigation of innovation networks in the multinational corporation. *Research Policy*, 28(2–3), pp. 195–213.

Zanfei, A. (2000) Transnational firms and the changing organisation of innovative activities. *Cambridge Journal of Economics*, 24(5), pp. 515–542.

The globalization of innovation in the Danish food industry: exploitation and exploration of emerging markets[†]

Stine Jessen Haakonsson

Department of Business and Politics, Copenhagen Business School, Denmark

The internationalization of innovation in the food industry is becoming increasingly oriented towards emerging markets. Innovative lead firms express a need for 'tapping into knowledge' by collaborating with research facilities, customers and suppliers in these new locations. European firms experience a push towards market expansion and knowledge generation directed at emerging markets. This results in new network constructs: global innovation networks. The aim of this paper is twofold. First, it identifies and outlines the determining factors behind the internationalization of innovation due to the need to access new markets and knowledge. This unfolds through strategies of exploitation and exploration. Second, it investigates the extent to which these strategies connect to position in the value chain and factors in the host economy. In this, the potential impact at the receiving end of the offshore equation is also addressed. Through an analysis of the Danish food industry, the paper concludes that the internationalization of innovation is an emergent phenomenon predominantly associated with exploration strategies. As much as exploitation may neither rely on nor develop local technological capabilities, exploration seeks and engages with local capabilities in the host economy.

1. Introduction: innovation beyond the home country

The Danish food industry is one of the strongest and most innovative in Europe and is well embedded in the national innovation system. Recently, new network constructs have emerged. Due to the fact that the home market is limited and the knowledge base highly integrated, and therefore relatively homogeneous, large companies increasingly search for markets and knowledge elsewhere. Consequently, there is a growing push towards internationalization among lead firms in the Danish food industry. This push generates corresponding new strategies for the internationalization of markets, production and, increasingly, innovation. However, little is known about internationalization of innovation in the food industry and the impact of these processes on the broader economy.

The research leading to these results benefitted from funding under the European Union's Seventh Framework Programme [FP7/2007–2013], grant agreement no. 225368 (INGINEUS, Impact of Networks, Globalisation and their Interaction with EU Strategies). I am very grateful to my colleagues from the UK and South Africa (Susana, Jo, Vandana, Michael, Glenda and Luke) in the INGINEUS team for their fantastic work in conducting interviews for the case studies in India and South Africa.

This paper explores which strategies apply to the internationalization of innovation in the food industry, and how position in the global value chain, along with the capabilities in the host economy, determines the type of engagement in *global* networks. As large Danish food companies are highly integrated in innovation networks in their home economy, one would expect them to also engage in similar networks abroad, in what has been termed global innovation networks (GINs). Moreover, the capabilities available in a location are also likely to impact the type of local engagement by lead firms and thereby the transfer of knowledge to the host economy. The aim of this paper is to reveal whether lead firms in different segments of the food value chain follow different strategies in the construction of GINs. The paper addresses two main questions: first, how can we understand the impact of push factors in the home economy *and* pull factors in the host economies on the way large companies restructure innovation activities within GINs? And secondly, to what extent is this related to the position of the lead firm in the global value chain?

The paper is structured as follows. In order to create a conceptual framework to understand the current changes in the organization of innovation in the food industry, the following section presents a literature review of the internationalization of innovation into GINs. This involves analysis of how network constructs relate to the strategies of exploitation and exploration of innovation abroad. The methodology deployed is outlined at the end of this section. Section three identifies the push factors facing lead firms in the Danish food industry, focusing on network embeddedness in the home economy and the national innovation system within which the industry is placed. Hence, the aim of Section 3 is to establish an understanding of the push factors experienced at the industry level. In Section 4, the focus narrows to the company level via a presentation of four case studies and analysis of their respective GIN constructs. The case studies are divided into two types on the basis of the distinction between knowledge exploration and exploitation strategies, in order to identify the possible link between network construction and strategy for the internationalization on innovation. The two types of internationalization of innovation identified also relate to the value chain segment in which the companies are situated. Exploiters tend to be firms catering for the end consumer, whereas explorers are feeding technology into downstream globalized buyers. This will be discussed in Section 5. The final section concludes on the push and pull factors identified in relation to the strategies, exploitation and exploration and identifies possible implications in relation to capability building in the host economies.

2. The internationalization of innovation: GINs

Innovation is becoming progressively more globalized and today many companies are undergoing a process of reorganizing innovation, herein research and development (R&D), to produce what has been coined 'GINs' (Ernst, 2006; Chaminade, 2009). These networks are characterized as encompassing substantially more actors than earlier innovation constructs and being of a much wider geographical reach. The actors found in GINs challenge existing theoretical frameworks addressing the internal and external organization of innovation. These networks span across continents and consist of a wide variety of actors including headquarters, subsidiaries, suppliers, customers, competitors, research institutions, universities and others (Archibugi and Iammarino, 2002; Ernst, 2002, 2006; Narula, 2003; UNCTAD, 2005, 2009; Coe et al., 2008).

The new network configurations, the GINs, can be observed from multiple entry points. One is the type of networks lead firms engage in (Ernst and Kim, 2002). Second are the strategies behind them. Here there is a distinction between knowledge exploiting and knowledge exploring/augmenting strategies (Kuemmerle, 1999b). Thirdly, locational approaches address questions of why and on what premises companies experience push and pull factors in the global economy

(Buckley and Ghauri, 2004; Graf and Mudambi, 2005; Haakonsson et al., 2012; Dunning, 2009). Fourthly, the changing roles of subsidiaries have been analysed focusing on the evolutionary drivers of subsidiaries and on internal competition between subsidiaries in a process of 'decentralized centralization' (Birkinshaw and Morrison, 1995; Birkinshaw and Hood, 1998). So far, little attention has been paid to the type of networks different lead firms engage in and how this relates to push factors and pull factors at home and abroad. Moreover, the home economy has not been seen as a determinant of lead firms' reconfiguration of innovation.

Despite the emergence of a conceptual framework for GINs, the constructs remain at the nascent stage and some even contest their existence. Some authors have shown that multinational corporations (MNCs) in general tend to concentrate core activities such as R&D in their home national innovation system (Narula, 2002; Rugman, 2005). Others analyse managerial challenges in outsourcing innovation (Grimpe and Kaiser, 2010; Stanko and Calantone, 2010). The literature similarly focuses on the role of the host economy in terms of the attractiveness of competence clusters and available talents at the firm level (Florida, 1997; Cantwell and Piscitello, 2005; Bardhan, 2006; Nieto and Rodríguez, 2011). This implies that new locations are increasingly gaining attention from MNCs. Over the past decade, the emerging markets of China, India, Brazil and South Africa stand out as new highly attractive locations for innovation activities (London and Hart, 2004; Demirbag and Glaister, 2010). This points towards the need for an approach which incorporates location, in addition to a time dimension through an evolutionary perspective (Lewin et al., 1999).

In order to conceptualize the globalization or internationalization of innovation, Archibugi and Michie (1995) developed a taxonomy, which includes three main types of internationalized innovation. These are not necessarily mutually exclusive but are understood to emerge in successive stages (Archibugi and Michie, 1995; Archibugi and Iammarino, 1999). Moreover, the model provides an evolutionary understanding of the development of innovation networks from the point of view of the MNCs engaged in the internationalization of innovation.

The first stage is *international exploitation*. International exploitation implies the marketing of nationally produced innovations beyond the company's home market, i.e. through exports, licensing and the offshoring of production. The second stage is *global generation of innovation*. This entails corporations reorganizing their activities beyond their home economy and (re)locating R&D and other innovative activities both within the home country *and* in host countries. This could, for example, be intra-firm offshoring of R&D (foreign direct investments (FDIs) in R&D) in order to adjust products to local conditions, tastes or government regulations. The third stage is *global techno-scientific collaboration*. In this stage, companies and universities collaborate in joint scientific projects and innovation networks across countries and continents. This regards cutting-edge innovation. Among the lead firms in the Danish food industry, some examples are second generation bio-fuels and genomics.

In reality, MNCs may engage in all three types of internationalization of innovation and their engagement varies according to different factors: intra-firm factors (size, products, innovations) (Meyer and Peng, 2005), features in the host economy (location attractiveness) (Kuemmerle, 1999b; Graf and Mudambi, 2005; Mudambi, 2008), and the home country of the MNC (Edquist and Hommen, 2008). Deploying an evolutionary perspective to analyse the development of new network constructs is apposite and fruitful, particularly in the context of emerging markets (Lewin et al., 2009). At the firm level, the three types of internationalization of innovation relate to the MNC strategies of offshoring and outsourcing R&D through knowledge exploitation and knowledge augmenting/exploration strategies, as proposed by Kuemmerle (1999a, 1999b). Identifying what determines the shift from exploiting to exploring strategies is highly relevant for the host economy. However, extant evidence suggests that this shift is mostly driven by the competitive strengths of the MNC (Cantwell and Mudambi, 2005).

Emerging economies are also emerging as locations for the internationalization of innovation. In this context, issues of existing absorptive capacity (Lall, 2001), and any potential contribution to technological capabilities in the host country (Teece et al., 1997; Archibugi and Coco, 2005; Morrison et al., 2008), have attracted attention to the host side of the offshoring equation. When innovation networks encompass emerging markets and span across world regions they can be validly termed 'global' (see definition by Rugman and Verbeke, 2005). Although the literature has explored push factors which lead MNCs to internationalize their activities, such as the need for larger markets to recover the costs of R&D (exploitation), the need to access specialized knowledge not available at home (exploration), or something in between, such as accessing cheaper human resources in low-cost locations (exploitation and/or exploration), this has not been directly connected to the pull factors in the host economies. Such factors may include the availability of skilled personnel, research institutions, the national regulative framework and infrastructure. Similarly, spill-over effects of different strategies and distance to the location are largely ignored (with few exceptions, see Cantwell and Piscitello, 2005).

In order to operationalize these issues in the emerging GIN literature it is useful to distinguish between strong and weak forms of GINs. Hence, the degree of the three parameters – globalization, innovation and network – needs to be established at the lead firm level as these are the drivers of GINs (Chaminade, 2009). Hence, GINs are highly global, spanning across world regions, or internationalized within Europe in this case (Rugman, 2005; Haakonsson and Thompson, 2010). With regard to innovation taking place in the network, this can be highly innovative in that it targets complementary knowledge via knowledge exploration or more market-oriented and based on knowledge exploiting strategies. Finally, MNCs may be highly networked, engaging with many different types of actors for innovation purposes or internalize innovation activities (Chaminade, 2009).

In order to understand the push and pull mechanisms motivating MNCs to engage or not engage with different GIN constructs, this paper investigates the globalization of innovation in the food industry as exemplified by Danish lead firms. The paper is based on in-depth case studies in four of the largest and most knowledge-intensive Danish lead firms in the food industry, each of which have developed into MNCs with global market reach and internationalized production and markets. Two of the companies have specialized in the production of intermediates such as ingredients and are among the world leaders in their field. Both of these companies have a strong foothold in Denmark and Europe but supply ingredients to food producers globally. The other two companies are also knowledge-intensive and engaged in R&D. However, they produce final products for direct consumption. Exploring the internationalization strategies of lead firms in two different segments of the value chain will reveal why lead firms engage in different types of internationalization of innovation.

Methodologically, the paper is based on findings from the EU FP7 project 'Impacts of Networks, Globalisation, and their Interaction with EU Strategies' (INGINEUS). This project included three pillars of empirical data collection. The first pillar is constituted by a large number of case studies, including four on innovation networks in the Danish food industry, which are used in this paper. The case studies were conducted in and around the food industry in 2010 and 2011. The companies selected represent the most internationalized companies. A total of 25 qualitative interviews were conducted at the four companies, of which 20 were in Denmark, 2 in South Africa, 1 in India and 2 in China. The interviewees were innovation managers and researchers involved in global innovation projects at home and abroad. The list of company interviewees can be found in Appendix 1. Due to confidentiality agreements, the names of the companies and interviewees cannot be disclosed. In addition to the company interviews, interviews were conducted with six experts in the Danish food industry, representatives of the Danish Ministry of Food, Agriculture and Fisheries, two universities and two research institutions.

The second pillar of the INGINEUS project involved a survey across three sectors and seven countries. The aim of the survey was to map emerging GINs along the three parameters of degree of globalization, type of innovation and network density. The survey included all firms with more than five employees. Of the 200 Danish companies that received the questionnaire, 48 companies responded, giving an overall response rate of 24%. The third pillar was a desk study of relevant secondary data from national and international statistics databases. This is based on sources from the national statistical office, Statistics Denmark, to which companies are required to report their activities annually. In addition, data were collected from Eurostat, the OECD and relevant Danish ministries.

3. The Danish food industry and the home economy: a rationale for exploiting and exploring new locations?

The Danish economy has developed on the foundation of a high level of activities within the agricultural sector which have led to the development of a strong and innovative food industry (Hansen, 2009; European Cluster Observatory, 2010). As most products are fresh, have limited shelf-lives and food preferences vary greatly over geographical regions, the products are predominantly sold within Europe. The industry accounts for approximately 20% of Danish exports, of which 64% is sold within Europe. Also at the European level, agro-processing is one of the largest and most important manufacturing sectors. It accounts for 14.5% of total European manufacturing turnover (€917 billion for the EU-27) and 14% of total employment in manufacturing (Eurostat, 2011).

One of the main characteristics of the European, and within the context of this study the Danish, food industry is that it contains a very large number of small- and medium-sized enterprises and few large-scale MNCs. The larger companies are more engaged in innovation as well as internationalization and thus the case studies in this paper were selected from the largest Danish food companies, the MNCs. The industry is strong in innovation. At the national level, there are 3512 people employed in food-related R&D in Denmark, of which approximately 60% work in the private sector. A total of 246 Danish food companies engage in R&D. The Danish Government maintains a strong focus on this sector and aims to develop the national food industry into an 'Agro Food Valley' by the year 2022 (Ministry of Food, Agriculture and Fisheries, 2009). The rationale behind the creation of the Agro Food Valley is based on the overall vision that Denmark should remain a lead location for agro-food innovation in Europe and increase the competitiveness of the industry. One recent initiative is the establishment of an Agro Food Science Park outside Århus in 2009. This park is designed to host between 40 and 50 companies and facilitates collaboration and knowledge sharing along and across the value chains within the Danish food industry. It is located close to the country's second largest university and some of the large Danish food companies. Two of these, Danisco and Arla, are among the leading Danish food producers, and together these two have more than 500 people in R&D in this region.

The Danish national innovation system has a tradition of collaboration, with strong networks among public and private actors (Lundvall, 1999). Accordingly, home conditions for innovation networks of Danish companies are good and the economy is an attractive location for Danish as well as foreign companies. Further, the Danish economy is small and open which demands a greater degree of company internationalization than in the case of larger economies (Katzenstein, 1985). Consequently, in order to cover the costs of innovation in introducing new products, companies need to reach beyond their national market. For this reason, Danish companies are highly

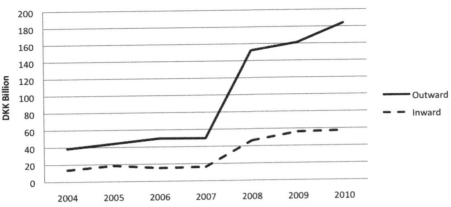

Figure 1.   FDI in the Danish food industry (FDI stock, DKK billion). Source: Statistics Denmark (2012).

'Europeanized' (Haakonsson and Thompson, 2010; Thompson and Kaspersen, 2012). However, the internationalization of food companies has recently expanded geographically in terms of market, and therefore also in terms of production and innovation.

FDI is one measure of internationalization. Danish companies' outward FDI is orientated towards destinations within the European Union. However, while Europe dominates FDI from Denmark, investments into Asia and the Americas have increased over the past decade. The FDI stock invested in Asia has almost tripled from DKK 21.5 billion in 1999 to 60.0 billion in 2010. Danish investments in the Americas have more than doubled in the same period from DKK 66.6 billion to 145.9 billion (Statistics Denmark, 2012). Africa has increased the most proportionately, rising from DKK 2.8 billion in 2000 to 10.6 billion in 2010 (Statistics Denmark, 2012). More specifically, Danish food industry FDI levels follow the general upward trend, although the level of outward investment compared to inward investment is high in this sector (Figure 1). The figure indicates huge growth in FDI activities in the food industry.

FDI flows only tell us about the direct investments in the industry (e.g. the setting up of property, plants, laboratories, and sales offices abroad), and hence do not show other network relationships such as outsourcing, contracting and innovation collaborations. According to the INGINEUS survey, most of the small- and medium-sized enterprises' collaboration on innovation is with customers, consultancies and suppliers. Furthermore, these customers, consultancies and suppliers are predominantly located in Denmark and Western Europe. The survey revealed that when it comes to innovation, small- and medium-sized enterprises tend to have a narrow geographical focus, which predominantly relates to upstream and downstream actors in their value chain and is supplemented by national consultancy companies. However, large companies report innovation beyond Europe. This is the focus of the case studies below. Notably, the importance of this industry in the home economy has decreased both in terms of the number of companies and employment (Table 1). Over the past decade, more than 17,000 jobs have been lost and approximately 230 companies have closed or merged.

The Danish food industry is currently the third largest food cluster by employment in the EU according to the European Cluster Observatory (ECO, 2010). More importantly, the industry is perceived to be the most innovative and export oriented among the large food clusters in the European Union (Table 2).

The national innovation system is characterized by a high level of available competencies. According to OECD Stat (2010), the percentage of the Danish population graduating from tertiary education was 47.3% in 2007 (up from 37.3% in 2000). In comparison to the EU average,

Table 1.   Companies and employment in agro-food 2000–2009.

	2000	2001	2002	2003	2004	2005	2006	2007	2008	2009
Danish food companies (total)	1886	1845	1837	1757	1774	1792	1777	1727	1717	1647
Employees (in food industry)	69,917	69,194	68,377	68,000	64,952	61,570	59,908	60,131	59,564	52,246

Source: Statistics Denmark (2012).

Table 2.   The three largest agro-food clusters in the European Union.

Cluster	Employment	Innovation	Export
Lombardia (Milan), Italy	107,806	Medium	Strong
Cataluña (Barcelona), Spain	103,066	Medium	Strong
Denmark	76,203	High	Very strong

Source: European Cluster Observatory (2010).

Table 3.   Higher education and life-long learning enrolment in Denmark and EU-27.

Enabler	EU-27 (%)	Denmark (%)
Tertiary education (enrolled per 100 population aged 25–64)	24.3	34.5
Life-long learning (enrolled per 100 population aged 25–64)	9.6	30.2

Source: Innovation Scoreboard, European Commission (2010).

Denmark has a highly ranked education system and a strong tradition of life-long learning with high levels of enrolment (Table 3).

The companies' operations are embedded in a variety of more or less formalized networks at the national level (Katzenstein, 1985; Maskell, 2004; Borrás and Haakonsson, 2011). However, since the home market is small, being a successful player implies a high level of internationalization. In the food industry, the large Danish companies that have developed into lead firms have also developed into strong international players within innovation. A big political concern is the consequences of outsourcing for the home economy, particularly any associated loss of jobs. According to the companies in the Danish survey, job losses in the Danish workforce are very limited. Those jobs moving abroad are mainly low-skilled. Meanwhile, the jobs created in Denmark as a result of the international sourcing activities of the enterprises were, to a large extent, reported to be highly skilled. Likewise, research shows a mobilizing effect of internationalized innovation on innovation networks at home (Borrás and Haakonsson, 2011).

Over the past 10 years, the amount spent on R&D per capita in Denmark has doubled, indicating that jobs staying in or being created in Denmark are more knowledge-intensive than those leaving. At the national level, R&D expenditure as a percentage of GDP has increased, particularly in the private sector (Figure 2). This figure is relatively high and, as discussed below, it is particularly high in the food sector.

Three universities are the most active in R&D within the food sector: the University of Copenhagen, the University of Århus and the Technical University of Denmark. All three institutions collaborate with companies. Compared with the average research spend, the share of applied research is higher in the food industry (61%) than in other research areas (42%). The total

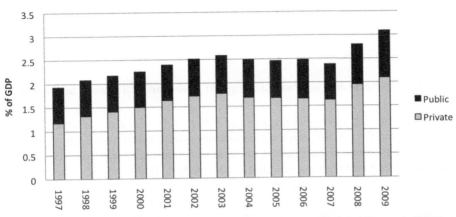

Figure 2.   R&D at the national level as a percentage of GDP. Source: Statistics Denmark (2012).

Table 4.   Patents by companies in the Danish food industry.

Company (food-related division)	Patents 2004–2008
Novozymes	62
Danisco	39
Novo Nordisk	32
Slagteriernes Forskningsinstitut	19
Aasted-Mikroverk	15
Gumlink A/S incl. Dandy A/S	15
Chr. Hansen	12
CP Kelco	9
Rhodia Chimie	6
Neurosearch	6
Egebjerg Maskinfabrik	6

Source: Ministry of Science, Innovation and Higher Education (2010).

amount spent by companies on R&D is approximately DKK 2.1 billion (Borrás and Haakonsson, 2011). Ninety percent of this was provided by the companies while 10% came from other sources (Ministry of Science, Innovation and Higher Education, 2010). Denmark ranks third in OECD in terms of food patenting (by population size). In 2008, 116 patent applications were generated from the Danish food industry and research institutions, while 63 patents were granted by the European Patent Organisation in the same year. A few companies are extremely dominant in this group: 11 companies were awarded more than five food-related patents between 2004 and 2008 (Table 4).

The most problematic factors related to doing business in Denmark do not concern available competencies, innovativeness or network readiness. On the contrary, push factors motivating Danish companies to shift innovation activities abroad must be explained by other means. The explanation cannot rest on the availability of qualified labour, although the size of the home economy remains a relevant factor.

In the next section, we explore R&D sourcing undertaken by large Danish companies through the internationalization of production and innovation. As a location for global leaders, networking companies and universities that extensively collaborate internationally, the national innovation system in Denmark is highly supportive. However, as we will see in the following section, some of the lead firms increasingly orientate R&D beyond this. For these firms, access to new markets and/or specialized knowledge are important determining factors.

4.   Innovation as R&D and internationalization: push and pull factors in the food industry

Before investigating the internationalization of R&D, it is necessary to make a distinction between the 'R' and the 'D'. *Research* in this industry relates to innovation and the introduction of new products, processes and services. *Development* is innovation applied to existing products or innovation related to selling these products in new markets. Within regard to the introduction of new products and core *research*, the case companies report that they seek supplementary skills and specialists. This means they engage in exploration (hereafter 'exploring') strategies targeting complementary research capacity. Two of the companies reorganized their R&D into 'global operations' in which projects are led by the most specialized in the particular field and often span several R&D locations/sites.

With regards to *development*, companies look for new markets. While internationalizing their market, companies also need to engage in *development*, adjusting their products to local markets, local raw materials, and local conditions (e.g. tastes, textures, raw produce and quality). This combines a market access strategy with an exploiting strategy (hereafter: 'exploiting') involving global development activities. All four case companies are engaged in the *development* of products within emerging markets. One example is the investment by one of the companies in the use of yeast for low-quality wheat flour in South Africa. This is a strategy aimed at the African market in the longer term. Although yeast is already produced by the company, in order to use it in emerging markets, the product requires adaptation. These adaptations may eventually feed back into products sold in existing markets.

Knowledge-intensive activities are increasingly taking place across national boundaries and involve more and more actors. This is the case for the large Danish food companies. The four case companies are all among the most research-intensive companies in the Danish food industry. All have externalized and/or internationalized R&D and other innovation activities. Consequently, innovation is increasingly networked. These companies' emerging GINs are generally constructed through company subsidiaries linked into local research environments in emerging markets (e.g. in Bangalore or Beijing). However, while most of the off-shored R&D activities are kept in-house for various reasons, the companies expressed a need and desire to link into local knowledge for two main reasons: exploitation and augmentation/exploration.

Exploitation is used as a strategy to adapt current products to local tastes, raw materials and markets (e.g. the use of ingredients for pasta in noodles). For this type of internationalization, customers are important. Locally present global customers and intermediate suppliers are often important partners in the innovation network for MNCs in upstream segments of the value chain. Exploration strategies are used to tap into knowledge which the companies cannot access elsewhere or which is better or cheaper abroad. For this type of internationalization, exploration strategies dominate and involve local institutions, competitors, universities, etc. Moreover, local technological capabilities constitute important determinants of pull factors. These two models of innovation internationalization are not mutually exclusive. Often both strategies help explain a company's presence in a location and form part of its location strategy.

To gain a more in-depth understanding of the processes at play when Danish food companies internationalize innovation, the paper now turns to the four case studies. The first two companies (the explorers) specialize in the production of ingredients and additives, i.e. they are situated upstream in the value chains. The other two (the exploiters) make more traditional products which are developed in Denmark but continuously adjusted to local tastes. They are producers of finished products.

Accordingly, two models of GIN involvement were identified: (1) the globalization of innovation through *exploration* and (2) the internationalization of innovation through *exploitation*. The former implies a reorganization of innovation processes at the global scale, involving techno-scientific networks of specialized knowledge actors in R&D. The latter implies product development in collaboration with actors upstream in the companies' value chains.

4.1 Explorers and the globalization of innovation

Companies 1 and 2 are both engaged in making highly innovative products. In fact, knowledge is their main product, as they both deliver ingredient solutions to customers. These companies develop recipes which include their products as ingredients and improve customer products in terms of, for instance, preservation, flavour and quality. In other words, they face an urgent need to be ahead in solving the problems raised by the globalization of food chains.

R&D is high priority. Company 1 spends about 5% of turnover on R&D which is predominantly carried out in five large R&D platforms near their core markets, in addition to some supplementary small research units. Ten percent of R&D spending is placed outside the company and this often involves collaboration with universities. There are 870 people working in R&D, of which 67% have a university degree. Company 2 spends about 15% of its turnover on R&D and also has R&D sites in locations with significant sales and where they can identify an interesting and high-quality research environment. Although both companies have a strong need for specialized knowledge at all levels, and therefore are engaged in exploration, their innovation designs are very different.

Company 1 mainly collaborates with customers for *development*. While researching ingredients, the company recruits many employees from the food sector. They come from specialized segments of the food industry. Food tastes are different around the world, and even for the same products, the company requires local varieties. In order to remain a key supplier for global food producers, the company encourages a willingness to take risks, curiosity, freedom, trust, networks, room for all, open-mindedness, experimenting at all levels and entrepreneurship among employees. To facilitate the realization of ideas from within the company, the company has nominated some researchers in-house as 'Cre-actors'. The Cre-actors are professional internal consultants who support people who come up with 'a good idea' to develop it further in the company. Innovation as *research* is coordinated by an internal committee, ensuring that the same structure and innovation management exists across the different locations. 'Operations are specialized and we have developed a system of exchanging knowledge so that a problem in the bread industry in South America may be solved by our specialized team in Canada'. Innovation, although internationalized, remains centrally coordinated.

The two main reasons for offshoring R&D are (1) it is cheaper and (2) it promotes adaptation to the market. China has recently received a lot of attention with regards to R&D. One Innovation Manager explained: 'China produces a number of highly qualified PhDs every year. This area is really exciting for our business. Some of our people in the US have spent 3–6 months at the China site to help [with] developing the culture, etc.' (interview 14-04-2010, Innovation Manager). Representatives from the company also pointed out: 'In addition to having access to highly educated staff and first class universities, we also find a mature bio-technology network in China, which we can use to continually enhance our advantages' (interview 31-03-2011, Vice President for R&D). Moreover, the extant global production network of Company 1 developed into the GIN this company is part of today. Except for a takeover of a US company, R&D centres have been established nearby existing production facilities. Since R&D often takes place in collaboration with customers, there is good reason to locate R&D and innovation near new markets. Company 1 moved from exporting products to adapting products to the local market and engaging with local technological capabilities. As such, the company followed the evolutionary development suggested by the internationalization of innovation typology (Archibughi and Michie, 1995).

Prior to the internationalization of innovation, the company faced several barriers to expanding R&D activities at home. One Innovation Manager elaborated on push factors in Denmark: 'At the national level in Denmark we need more support for networking. We also need more flexibility for getting foreign employees to Denmark, for example tax holidays for foreign researchers' (interview 15-04-2011, Innovation Manager). Due to the relatively long history of the food industry and related research in Denmark, there are many opportunities for food production and research at home. Many of the required knowledge workers come from the Danish food industry. However, in order to meet the requirements of new markets and explore ideas not available at home, the company reconfigured its innovation network at the global level. China and Brazil are the main new locations, but the company also established an innovation centre in South Africa.

Company 2 manages all of its R&D projects internationally. In this company, there is a policy that only 20% of a project team should be located near to the project leader. Researchers are based at different sites so they can engage with the people there: 'Practically, it is easier to talk with people in Beijing if we have researchers placed there' (interview 06-01-2011). Today research centres are located in the USA, Japan, Brazil, Denmark, China, Switzerland, India, the UK and Australia.

The R&D site in China was established in the mid-1990s after the company had been in the Chinese market for more than 20 years. The original strategy behind this was to develop into a key player in the booming Chinese economy, rather than to access low-cost labour or knowledge. Today, the company holds a strong position in the Chinese market for enzymes and has developed partnerships with state-owned enterprises. This is only possible due to their local presence and the prolonged history of the company in China. From being a site of development, applying the company's products to the Chinese market, the R&D site has developed into being a part of the global R&D operations. In fact, 80% of the research carried out in China today contributes to the company's global R&D projects. The company invested in upgrading a variety of skills of Chinese staff, including linguistic capabilities to enable staff to take part in global operations. This had the effect of making the company more attractive as an employer. According to the company, there is not so much a low-cost incentive for offshoring R&D to China as a market incentive: '… costs are really not the issue. In China, salaries have increased a lot recently also because there is a shortage of English speaking researchers' (interview 23-10-2009). In China, Company 2 followed the evolution from exploitation to techno-scientific collaborations over a period of 20 years.

In India, the evolutionary process unfolded in the reverse direction. The company took over a local specialized, knowledge-intensive company, its R&D facilities and 150 employees. The company went directly into technological collaborations through a brown field investment. The acquisition added to the company's global product portfolio as the new site is highly specialized in a technology field supplementary to the existing global R&D facilities. The resulting products are now only made in Bangalore and sold worldwide. In India, the company tapped into appropriately qualified people and networks needed to meet international standards. The Indian Institutes of Technology and Science (IIT and IIS) are renowned in the company's product area and perform world class research. One manager explained: 'it is easier to tap into these resources if you have local presence' (interview 14-04-2010).

Company 2 understands that competitiveness is about being present globally – and 'you look more serious if you have local R&D'. Still, the company has no plans to cut down on its activities at home: 'We are not moving R&D out from Denmark – approximately half of R&D is located in Denmark and more people are hired there every year'. However, the proportion of researchers located in Denmark is diminishing. 'One interesting question here is whether we can find the qualified people we need at all, which is problematic', likewise, 'it is easier to attract US personnel to our US site than to Denmark' (interview 11-06-2011, Innovation Manager). For the development of products for new markets a local presence is crucial: 'sitting in Denmark thinking about what would work for preserving juice from fruits in India may not be the most brilliant thing to do'. Regarding collaborations in Africa: 'their bread is different and has a different look which is important to acknowledge when developing our products'.

4.2 *Exploiters and internationalization in traditional food companies*

For Companies 3 and 4, the key current tendencies are: (1) they collaborate more with academics, suppliers and customers than previously; (2) they keep in-house R&D in Denmark; (3) some of the R&D is supplemented with smaller operations – either specialized or market-oriented – in foreign locations and (4) R&D activities focus on improving existing products and processes. The core explanation for these is that the companies produce for end consumers.

Company 3 aims to become the largest producer of their products globally. Hence, the company strategy focuses on the growth of production and market share. Consequently, R&D focuses on products and sustainability: a central issue is how to keep the products fresh. However, all R&D activities are centred at the headquarters in Copenhagen. The R&D Manager explained: 'Our corporate R&D focus is no longer linked to the supply chain, but to the marketing process and the end customer' (interview 23-05-2011).

Company 3 has strong historical research ties with two of the largest universities in Denmark. Seven full-time internal professors within very specialized research areas are employed in the company. In addition to this, there are 40 PhDs and post-doctoral staff on the payroll. The researchers tend to move on, as was stated by the Innovation Manager: 'most of them continue their careers elsewhere – and by doing so they create a foundation for further research collaboration'. There is some internationalized research into developing inputs, mostly in collecting samples of raw material.

Products do not change radically, but the company engages in development as a number of adaptations and incremental changes take place both in the production process (focusing on making the products last longer, extending the shelf-time) and in marketing (targeting other customer groups). In addition to this, there is a 'front-end unit' for each market in charge of identifying the needs in the particular markets. The front-end units, whose role, among others, is to identify future needs for innovation in terms of product development, are also located in the HQ. Company 3 has so far not internationalized innovation beyond mere exploitation. However the company has plans to establish a research facility in Hong Kong. A company manager expressed interest in more open innovation models.

Company 4 focuses on fresh products. R&D activities target ingredients and nutrition and are predominantly market-oriented. The company has experienced a degree of Europeanization and today has six R&D centres in Europe, of which two are in Denmark and one each in Sweden, Finland, the Netherlands and the UK. Collaboration is important in their R&D set-up as many research projects involve public funding and university partners. Ten to fifteen percent of R&D expenditure is used on external cooperation. Most knowledge is produced in Denmark. The Vice-Director of R&D explained that this is because 'Denmark has a strong tradition for agro-food. Danish research in the agro-food sector is very specialized, as knowledge competences at Danish universities are very good, deep and specialized in some specific areas' (interview

06-04-2011). In addition to their core products, Company 4 is engaged in basic research on geno-mics for which they collaborate with the whole network of genome research in Denmark.

At the international level, collaboration happens mostly when this company purchases very specific R&D services: 'We buy this research or knowledge in universities where we know there are special instruments or special knowledge competences' (interview 05-04-2011). For Company 4, internationalization of R&D is part of a strategy of moving closer to market – and also in terms of proximity and access to authorities who approve products, which is a big issue for this company. According to the manager, the company certainly engages in more international collaboration today than 10 years ago. The plan is to establish more permanent collaboration fra-meworks in place of the *ad hoc* collaboration structure of today. The company also expressed concern about recent trends in the Danish food industry: 'The Danish agro-food research sector is under pressure. The problem is that some of the competences we need are diminishing' (interview 24-04-2011, R&D Manager). Hence, this company increasingly faces push factors for the internationalization of innovation, but so far has not internationalized beyond Europe.

5.   GIN formations in the Danish food industry

As illustrated by the case studies above, two different types of constructs of GINs were identified in the Danish food industry: the explorers and the exploiters. Table 5 shows the main character-istics of these two constructs.

The explorers category was illustrated by Companies 1 and 2. This is a model in which we can identify core innovation activities across a range of countries and even continents. The companies rely on constant innovation and operate in networks across national boundaries. As a conse-quence, both are engaged in developing communication tools for sharing information with and among subsidiaries. For some products, they engage in techno-scientific collaboration with uni-versities specialized internationally within specific research areas, either to accrue knowledge or to recruit. The internationalization of innovation is global, provides new-to-the-world innovation and includes partners beyond the global value chain.

The exploiter category was identified in Companies 3 and 4. These companies concentrate R&D at home. However, products are increasingly sold beyond the Danish market as this market is small. Some products are produced and sold globally, with minor local adaptations

Table 5.   Two types of internationalization of innovation in the Danish food industry.

	Global	Innovation	Network
The explorers			
Company 1	Globalized R&D platforms	Future-oriented *research*, new-to-the-world innovation	Development activities with customers
Company 2	Managing R&D projects globally R&D across several continents	Significant proportion of turnover into R&D	More than 10% of R&D funding in universities University collaborations: China, India, USA, Denmark
The exploiters			
Company 3	R&D at headquarters in Denmark	*Development* into keeping products fresh	Collaboration with local university partners
Company 4	Some R&D in Europe	Marketing-driven research Focus on end customer	Public research funding Domestic network

Table 6.   Push and pull factors in the internationalization of innovation in the Danish food industry.

	Internationalization of innovation	
	Exploitation	Exploration
Push factors	Companies 1–4 Limited home market Facing competition	Companies 1 and 2 Innovation at home not enough Difficult to attract knowledgeable workers Access to networks outside home economy Limited knowledge regarding new markets
Pull factors	Emerging new markets, growth economies Location of core consumer groups Development into tastes and durability	Market/knowledge of local market Cutting-edge research environment Specialized technical knowledge Tapping into mature knowledge networks

to products made at local production facilities. So for these companies, R&D remains nationally based, and to some extent European. These GINs are very weak, but the firms are nevertheless highly networked.

Another interesting aspect of these four cases is that for the explorers, the GINs seem to have developed within their previously established global production networks – in places where they already have significant production and sales – except in specific cases where the company in question has merged with an existing research-intensive company, as was the case for Company 1 in the USA and Company 2 in India. This bolsters the argument for an evolutionary approach. Reasons for establishing R&D outside Denmark were pinpointed in the following two statements: 'not all good knowledge can be produced in Denmark' and 'it is difficult to attract key foreign researchers to our R&D sites in Denmark'. In other words, these two companies increasingly face push factors for establishing outside their home economy. The exploiters are considering offshoring research but are highly embedded in the Danish (and to some extent European) national innovation system.

In sum, strategies for the internationalization of innovation by explorers or exploiters can be understood to be determined by both push factors emanating from prior network constructs and pull factors in the new location (Table 6).

Table 6 shows the linkages between push and pull factors. All four companies are internationalizing the use of innovative products through a market-seeking strategy of exploitation. For those companies whose products are intermediates for other lead firms, this has led to a globalization of innovation and a strategy of exploration. Meanwhile, the pull factors determining location attractiveness, for instance, of emerging markets, differ according to the type of innovation activity internationalized. China and India are both perceived as important locations by these companies, mainly because these countries have both a growing market and large research communities, at least at a regional level. The explorers seek technological capabilities and supplementary specialized technological knowledge in the host country. Targets might include localized knowledge regarding taste, ingredients and produce, participation in complementary research environments and specialized knowledge, particularly regarding researchers who are difficult to attract to Denmark.

6.   Conclusion

The Danish food industry is well embedded in the national innovation system and among the most internationalized and innovative in Europe. Due to a small home economy and high levels of investment in innovation activities, large companies experience a need to move beyond the home market. In some cases, this is for innovation purposes. The size of the home market and the internationalization of lead customers constitute the push factors behind this process. So far, the push factors are only mirrored in the innovation strategies of large players in the industry. Initially, the companies engaging in the internationalization of innovation use exploitation strategies, they become 'Exploiters'. However, two case companies positioned upstream in value chains had more recently also engaged in innovation outside Europe, for which reason they are 'Explorers'. Explorers maintain their position as turnkey suppliers by tapping into new knowledge within their technological fields. They are creating strong GINs.

The strength of pull factors experienced in regard to this development is a condition of whether host economies can provide technological capabilities supplementary to those readily available in extant networks. These pull factors are strengthening in emerging economies. China, Brazil and India have been on the companies' radars for a decade, but recently the choice of location is broadening beyond these 'usual suspects'. One of the exploring companies has engaged in innovation in South Africa. As Africa seems to host newly emergent markets, companies positioned upstream in value chains need to collaborate in order to match intermediates to raw materials in this region. For exploiters, it is a different story. Downstream companies producing directly for consumers seek to expand into emerging markets predominantly because of market potential and the prospect of economic growth. These companies have not engaged beyond mere production in new locations. Generally, the internationalization of innovation by these companies is at a very low level.

The theoretical contribution is threefold. First, the position in the global value chain impacts the configuration of the GIN, mainly along two lines, the extent of globalization and the role of innovation. Secondly, the development of GINs is at a very nascent stage and therefore rightly remains contested. However, from the perspective of Northern lead firms there is an emerging pattern of some lead firms restructuring innovation internationally in new locations. Thirdly, the strong GINs identified in this study belong to the group of large companies. Small- and medium-sized enterprises only access GINs as network partners of the large companies.

While this has not been the main focus of this paper, there are certain lessons to be learned about the impact of these processes in host economies. Exploring companies seek and contribute to domestic technological capabilities, whereas exploiting companies do not. For countries seeking to attract exploring companies' innovation, the availability of knowledge is highly relevant. However, this knowledge needs to be specialized, for instance, in local raw materials and local food culture or highly technical within a certain field, as was the case with Company 2 in India. Today, lead firms strengthening their GINs target complementary specialized technological capabilities more than lower costs of innovation. The benefit for an emerging economy of providing this is that the national innovation system can be augmented by upgrading and knowledge transfer. Furthermore, domestic actors (private as well as public) may gain access to the established networks the lead firm has at home.

There is huge potential in establishing an attractive location for companies with exploration strategies as the establishment of networks may generate mobilizing effects in the host economy. For the food industry in particular, there is scope for upgrading local industry to international standards via the specialities and taste varieties available in the location. Hence, there is potential for upgrading innovation networks at home by linking to larger or more specialized ones abroad. Access to innovation networks abroad for actors in emerging markets is an issue that certainly requires further research. Likewise, in policy terms, this research would suggest that governments need to generate locations attractive for GINs. These must be strong research environments with a 'local flavour' which are complementary to existing ones elsewhere. The findings may ameliorate some of the concern in Europe based on the notion that knowledge tasks are moving to low-cost locations. This is not the case. The four case studies show that lead firms' need to tap into complementary knowledge does not negatively affect home-based networks.

References

Archibugi, D., and Coco, A. (2005) Measuring technological capabilities at the country level: A survey and a menu for choice. *Research Policy*, 34(2), pp. 175–194.

Archibugi, D., and Iammarino, S. (1999) The policy implications of globalisation of innovation, in: D. Achibugi, J. Howells and J. Michie (eds) *Innovation policy in a global economy*, pp. 242–71 (Cambridge: Cambridge University Press).

Archibugi, D., and Iammarino, S. (2002) The globalization of technological innovation: Definition and evidence. *Review of International Political Economy*, 9(1), pp. 98–122.

Archibugi, D., and Michie, J. (1995) The globalization of technology: A new taxonomy. *Cambridge Journal of Economics*, 19(1), pp. 121–140.

Bardhan, A.D. (2006) Managing globalization of R&D: Organizing for offshoring innovation. *Human Systems Management*, 25(2), pp. 103–114.

Birkinshaw, J., and Hood, N. (1998) Multinational subsidiary evolution: Capability and charter change in foreign-owned subsidiary companies. *The Academy of Management Review*, 23(4), pp. 773–795.

Birkinshaw, J.M., and Morrison, A.J. (1995) Configurations of strategy and structure in subsidiaries of multinational corporations. *Journal of International Business Studies*, 26(4), pp. 729–753.

Borrás, S., and Haakonsson, S. (2011) The impact of global innovation networks on national systems. The case of the Danish Food Industry. *INGINEUS Deliverable D10.1: 'Comprehensive research paper on Global Innovation Networks: challenges and opportunities for policy'*, available at: www.ingineus.eu

Buckley, P.J., and Ghauri, P.N. (2004) Globalisation, economic geography and the strategy of multinational enterprises. *Journal of International Business Studies*, 35(2), pp. 81–98.

Cantwell, J., and Mudambi, R. (2005) MNE competence-creating subsidiary mandates. *Strategic Management Journal*, 26(12), pp. 1109–1128.

Cantwell, J., and Piscitello, L. (2005) The recent location of foreign-owned R&D activities by large MNCs in the European regions: the role of spillovers and externalities. *Regional Studies*, 39(1), pp. 1–16.

Chaminade, C. (2009) On the concept of global innovation networks. *Electronic Working Paper*. CIRCLE, Lund University, Lund, Sweden.

Coe, N.M., Dicken, P., and Hess, M. (2008) Global production networks: Realizing the potential. *Journal of Economic Geography*, 8(3), pp. 271–295.

Demirbag, M., and Glaister, K.W. (2010) Factors determining offshore location choice for R&D projects: A comparative study of developed and emerging regions. *Journal of Management Studies*, 47(8), pp. 1534–1560.

Dunning, J.H. (2009) Location and the multinational enterprise: A neglected factor? *Journal of International Business Studies*, 40(1), pp. 5–19.

Edquist, C., and Hommen, L. (2008) *Small country innovation systems. Globalization, change and policy in Asia and Europe* (Cheltenham: Edward Elgar).

Ernst, D. (2002) Global production networks and the changing geography of innovation systems. Implications for developing countries. *Economics of Innovation and New Technology*, 11(6), pp. 497–523.

Ernst, D. (2006) Innovation offshoring. Asia's emerging role in global innovation networks. *Working Paper*. East-West Center, Honolulu, Hawaii.

Ernst, D., and Kim, L. (2002) Global production networks, knowledge diffusion, and local capability formation. *Research Policy*, 31(8–9), pp. 1417–1429.

European Cluster Observatory. (2010) *Europe Innova*. Official European cluster mapping tool. Financed under the Competitiveness and Innovation Framework Programme (CIP) by the European Commission. Available on: www.clusterobservatory.eu (27 February 2012).

European Commission. 2010. Innovation Scoreboard. Pro-inno. Available on: www.proinno-europe.eu (27 February 2012).

Eurostat. (2011) Various tables on industry and innovation, available on: http://epp.eurostat.ec.europa.eu

Florida, R. (1997) The globalization of R&D: Results of a survey of foreign-affiliated R&D laboratories in the USA. *Research Policy*, 26(2), pp. 85–103.

Graf, M., and Mudambi, S.M. (2005) The outsourcing of IT-enabled business processes: A conceptual model of the location decision. *Journal of International Management*, 11(8), pp. 253–268.

Grimpe, C., and Kaiser, U. (2010) Balancing internal and external knowledge aquisition: The gains and pains from R&D outsourcing. *Journal of Management Studies*, 47(8), pp. 1483–1509.

Haakonsson, S.J., Jensen, P.Ø., and Mudambi, S. (2012) A co-evolutionary perspective on the drivers of international sourcing of pharmaceutical R&D to India. *Journal of Economic Geography*, doi: 10.1093/jeg/lbs018.

Haakonsson, S. and Thompson, G.F. (2010) Myten om de store danske virksomheder i globaliseringen. *Offentligt eller Privat? Historiske og aktuelle udfordringer i politik og økonomi* (Jurist- og økonomforbundets forlag: København).

Hansen, H.O. (2009) Status for fødevareklyngen i Danmark. Paper presented at the *Danmark som Agro-Food Valley* 5, February 2009.

Katzenstein, P. (1985) *Small states in world market. Industrial policy in Europe* (New York: Cornell University Press).

Kuemmerle, W. (1999a) The drivers of foreign direct investment into research and development: An empirical investigation. *Journal of International Business Studies*, 30(1), pp. 1–24.

Kuemmerle, W. (1999b) Foreign direct investment in industrial research in the pharmaceutical and electronics industries – results from a survey of multinational firms. *Research Policy*, 28(2–3), pp. 179–93.

Lall, S. (2001) *Competitiveness, technology and skills* (Cheltenham: Edward Elgar).

Lewin, A.Y., Long, C.P., and Carroll, T.N. (1999) The coevolution of new organizational forms. *Organization Science*, 10(5), pp. 535–550.

Lewin, A.Y., Massini, S., and Peeters, C. (2009) Why are companies offshoring innovation? The emerging global race for talent. *Journal of International Business Studies*, 40(6), pp. 901–925.

London, T., and Hart, S.L. (2004) Reinventing strategies for emerging markets: Beyond the transnational model. *Journal of International Business Studies*, 35(5), pp. 350–370.

Lundvall, B.-Å. (1999). *Det danske innovationssystem – et forskningsbaseret debatoplæg om innovationspolitiske udfordringer og handlemuligheder. DISKO-projektet: Sammenfattende Rapport*. Erhvervsfremme Styrelsen. Erhvervsministeriet.

Maskell, P. (2004) Learning in the village economy of Denmark. The role of institutions and policy in sustaining competitiveness, in: P. Cooke, M. Heidenreich and H.J. Braczyk (eds) *Regional innovation systems,* pp. 154–85 (2nd ed.). (London: Rutledge).

Meyer, K.E., and Peng, M.W. (2005) Probing theoretically into central and Eastern Europe: Transactions, resources, and institutions. *Journal of International Business Studies*, 36(6), pp. 600–621.

Ministry of Food, Agriculture and Fisheries. (2009) Danmark som en Agro Food Valley. Proceedings from a conference organized by the Danish Ministry of Food, Agriculture and Fisheries on 5 February 2009, available on: www.agrifish.dk

Ministry of Science, Innovation and Higher Education. (2010) Kortlægning af dansk fødevareforskning. *Forskning: Analyse og Evaluering 4/2010.*

Morrison, A., Pietrobelli, C., and Rabelotti, R. (2008) Global value chains and technological capabilities: A framework to study learning and innovation in developing countries. *Oxford Development Studies*, 36(1), pp. 39–58.

Mudambi, R. (2008) Location, control and innovation in knowledge-intensive industries. *Journal of Economic Geography*, 8(5), pp. 699–725.

Narula, R. (2002) Innovation systems and 'inertia' in R&D location: Norwegian firms and the role of systemic lock-in. *Research Policy*, 31(5), pp. 795–816.

Narula, R. (2003) *Globalization and technology* (Cambridge: Polity Press).

Nieto, M.J., and Rodríguez, A. (2011) Offshoring of R&D: Looking abroad to improve innovation performance. *Journal of International Business Studies*, 42(3), pp. 345–361.

Rugman, A.M. (2005) *The regional multinationals* (Cambridge: Cambridge University Press).

Rugman, A.M., and Verbeke, A. (2005) Towards a theory of regional multinationals: A transaction cost economics approach. *Management International Review*, 45(1), pp. 5–17.

Stanko, M.A., and Calantone, R.J. (2010) Controversy in innovation outsourcing research: Review, synthesis and future directions. *R&D Management*, 41(1), pp. 8–20.

Statistics Denmark (2008) *International sourcing: Moving business functions abroad* (Copenhagen: Statistics Denmark).

Statistics Denmark. (2012) Various tables, available on: www.statistikbanken.dk (27 February 2012).

Teece, D.J., Pisano, G., and Shuen, A. (1997) Dynamic capabilities and strategic management. *Strategic Management Journal*, 18(7), pp. 509–533.

Thompson, G., and Kaspersen, L.B. (2012) The globalization of the business sector in a small open economy: The case of Denmark and its wider implications. *Socio-Economic Review*, 10(1), pp. 1–27.

UNCTAD (2005) *World investment report – transnational corporations and the internationalization of R&D* (New York: UNCTAD).

UNCTAD (2009) *World investment report – transnational corporations, agricultural production and development* (New York: UNCTAD).

Appendix 1. List of interviews in the four case companies

Company 1
Manager of global innovation
Assistant product manager
Professor at the Technical University of Denmark
Professor at the biology faculty, Copenhagen University
Research manager in China
Innovation manager in South African affiliate
Innovation manager in South African laboratory

Company 2
Director organizational development
Business development manager
Vice-president of organization
Senior director protein optimization
Senior finance, IT and legal director in China
Head of R&D in India

Company 3
Director IT solutions for innovation projects
Communications director
Vice-president for R&D
Innovation Manager

Company 4
Senior director of corporate research and innovation
Vice-director R&D
Business area manager – nutrition
Head of corporate nutrition
Innovation director
Senior manager, R&D ingredients
Research manager – innovation centre
Innovation manager – ingredients

Building capabilities through global innovation networks: case studies from the Brazilian automotive industry

Ana Valéria Carneiro Dias[a], Maria Cecília Pereira[a] and Gustavo Britto[b]

[a]Department of Production Engineering, Universidade Federal de Minas Gerais, Av. Antonio Carlos, Belo Horizonte, Brazil; [b]Centro de Desenvolvimento e Planejamento Regional - Cedeplar, Belo Horizonte, Brazil

Internationalization of R&D towards developing countries has created innovation network configurations that are truly global. These global innovation networks (GINs) are set up in developing countries for technological or market reasons. Sometimes firms in a country are integrated for market reasons, and are responsible only for the adaptation of products for local conditions, but over time, the very fact of being part of a GIN increases their technological capabilities and they start conducting more significant innovation. In order to examine how this local innovation capability may evolve and what new capabilities are built in the process, we investigated the Brazilian automotive industry. We conducted case studies in subsidiaries of one large European automotive original equipment manufacturer and four automotive systems suppliers. Results confirmed that due to specificies of the local technological learning process, becoming part of a GIN has significantly contributed to enhance local innovation capabilities.

Introduction

The determinants of internationalization of production and of R&D activities have been a widely investigated within economic literature. For pioneering the field or putting forward novel perspectives, some studies have gained vintage status (Cantwell, 1989; Dunning, 1993). More recently, however, with the rise of a handful of newly industrialized countries to the fore of economic debate, a new wave of studies have sought to shed further light on the subject in general and on the issues of internationalization of innovative activities in particular (Chiesa, 2000; Calabrese, 2001; von Zedwitz and Gassmann, 2002; UNCTAD, 2005; Cantwell and Mudambi, 2005; Gammeltoft, 2006; Dunning and Lundan, 2008).

From the perspective of developing countries, the internationalization of innovation activities may be seen as a way to accelerate the building of local technological capabilities, through their integration into global innovation networks (GINs). Such networks may be composed of local companies, headquarters or local branches of multinational corporations (MNCs), universities and research centres located in different countries. Within these networks, the transfer of explicit and especially tacit knowledge between the actors is believed to be significantly enhanced (Chaminade, 2009).

Explanations of why R&D is internationalized and, therefore, why a GIN is established frequently mention two main drivers. The first is linked to technological sourcing, i.e. companies would search for a technology, a competence or a skill that is not available in their home country (Archibugi and Michie, 1995). The second driver is market proximity, given that local innovation activities facilitate the process of adaptation of centrally (externally) developed products to local conditions. In some cases, a company inserted in a GIN experiences an upgrade in its innovation structure: once set up for adaptation activities, local engineering eventually becomes a source of new technology within the GIN. This indicates that a learning process has taken place and that local innovation capabilities have been increased at a faster pace within a GIN than otherwise would have been the case.

However, the process of GINs formation involves a myriad of factors. From a broader perspective, it is determined to a large extent by firms' growth strategies, which in turn depend on their pool of competences and capabilities (Teece, 1980). Second, given a set of possible strategies, innovation will depend on firms' ability to take part and make use of interactions with other firms and organizations (Bell and Pavitt, 1995). Finally, the process of internationalization of both production and R&D will be closely associated with firms' past trajectories. This includes key factors such as existing connections with the corporate network, which may be crucial to local and international collaboration, as well as previous knowledge of international markets (Dunning and Narula, 1995; Dunning et al., 1996).

The importance of firms' competences and capabilities inevitably directs attention to other firm-level aspects related to human capital, broadly defined, educational background, managerial and organizational competences (Cohen and Levinthal, 1990; Sousa et al., 2008; Von Tunzelmann, 2009; Plechero and Chaminade, 2010).

Not surprisingly, many of the studies of the new geography of production and innovation have focused on experiences specific to Asian counties, such as India (Arora et al., 2001) and China (Altenburg et al., 2008), and on firms and sectors related to information and communications technology (ICT) (Castellacci and Archibugi, 2008; Chaminade and Vang, 2008). At the same time, given recent economic trends, there has been increasing attention diverted to fast growing large developing countries, loosely grouped under the BRICS label.

The aim of this paper is to contribute to the literature on GIN formation by a closer examination in relation to firm-level competence and capability-building. However, unlike the eastern, ICT-oriented existing studies, the paper looks south at the mature, highly internationalized automotive sector. The process of capability building in the automotive industry differs from that in the ICT industry, as tacit knowledge is much more important in the automotive sector; innovation in ICT is more related to explicit knowledge (Sturgeon et al., 2008). Furthermore, while the global ICT industry is organized in a modular value chain, the global automotive industry is organized in relational value chains (Gereffi et al., 2005; Sturgeon et al., 2008). Therefore, our aim was to investigate how GIN affiliation may contribute to enhance firm competences and capabilities, providing new empirical evidence to technological learning theory in the context of developing countries and mature, tacit-knowledge dependent industries.

In order to do so, we carried out five case studies to examine the trajectory of the innovation capabilities of original equipment manufacturers (OEMs) and suppliers, all subsidiaries of MNCs, in the automotive industry in Brazil. The Brazilian automotive industry has been trailing a trajectory of technological capability building from adaptation of products to local conditions to the development of new-to-the-world technologies. The investigation then focused on which factors were present in the process of learning and developing new skills in the industry, as well as on what new competences and skills are currently being developed within the companies.

The paper is structured as follows. In the next section, the theoretical framework is briefly presented, focusing on concepts such as GINs, factors that motivate internationalization of R&D, and aspects that influence technological learning by firms in developing countries. The following section presents the methodology and describes the case studies. Finally, we argue that recent trends of the automotive industry in Brazil may be used to illustrate how firms in developing countries can profit from GIN participation by enhancing their technological capabilities.

Global innovation networks, learning and local capabilities

In this paper, we examine the internationalization of R&D using the concept of GINs. GINs are defined as networks of firms and other organizations in which innovative activities are accomplished by pulling resources from partners and different regions and countries, including developing ones (Barnard and Chaminade, 2011; Gastrow et al., 2011). MNCs that once established global production networks (GPNs) are one of the main drivers of GINs as they expand activities overseas, adding engineering and R&D activities to production (Ernst and Kim, 2002; Ernst, 2006). In this sense, GINs may be considered as an evolution of GPNs. Hence, MNCs play a key role in the development of GINs.

The process of internationalization of MNCs' innovation activities occurs for a number of reasons (Dunning, 1993; Florida, 1997; Kuemmerle, 1997; Reddy, 1997; Gassmann and von Zedtwitz, 1999; Patel and Vega, 1999; Chiesa, 2000; von Zedwitz and Gassmann, 2002). The first is market-related: including foreign subsidiaries in innovation networks should make it easier to reflect local preferences, enabling higher product penetration in these markets. The second reason is technology-related: to gain access to technologies that the main development centre is not aware of. According to Kuemmerle (1997), market-related factors would lead to the establishment of a local R&D structure mainly directed at exploiting innovation developed in the home country (home-base exploiting site), whilst technology-related reasons would lead to local R&D structures aimed at enhancing the firm's technological capabilities (home-base augmenting site). Other reasons, such as lower labour cost outside the most developed countries, and even time zone differences, which could turn product development into an around the clock process, thus accelerating time to market, have also been mentioned in the literature (Florida, 1997; Reddy, 1997; Chiesa, 2000; Miotti and Sachwald, 2001; Gammeltoft, 2006).

Another set of drivers of internationalization of R&D is related specifically to the role of human capital. Gastrow et al. (2011) argue that it is possible to conceptualize human capital's influence in terms of pull and push factors. Pull factors relate to the phenomenon of attraction of R&D by the host country due to specific local assets. Push factors are present when a deficiency in terms of human capital availability in the home country drives innovative activities abroad.

A local R&D unit originally set up to fulfil a specific task within the MNC may evolve over time to perform a different role. In other words, a subsidiary could shift from a home-base-exploiting R&D unit to a home-base-augmenting one. Cantwell (1999) analysed this trajectory for the case of MNCs from the USA that operated in the UK. UK subsidiaries of US firms have shifted their focus on innovation from industries in which they were strong in their home country, such as electrical equipment, to industries in which UK companies were expert, such as chemicals and pharmaceuticals. In this case, the transformation of home-base exploiting to home-base-augmenting R&D happened in the context of a developed country, with well-established local technological capabilities, which is not necessarily the case for developing countries.

Ernst and Kim (2002) drew attention to the fact that GPNs can be seen as organizational configurations that favour knowledge transfer; therefore, developing countries could take advantage of their integration into global networks in order to increase their technological capabilities. Given that integration of local firms into GINs requires a minimum level of capabilities, the participation in such networks would boost knowledge transfer because global firms that integrate (or even coordinate) the networks are compelled to transfer technical and managerial knowledge to local firms or subsidiaries. GPNs also act as mediators of local capability building by promoting many forms of tacit and explicit knowledge conversion processes – socialization, combination, externalization and internalization (Nonaka and Takeuchi, 1995).

Lall (2001) examined features of technological learning that should be taken into account by research policy-makers in developing countries. For instance, the learning curve for a given technology is not uniform or predictable; there are differences in learning that arise from different levels of development between the countries. Nor is it possible to determine exactly how a firm should learn, as there are differences among firms due to characteristics of the technology (modern or traditional, speed of change, similarity to the firm's knowledge base); thus learning has to be learned and firms learn by developing organizational routines.

Indeed, learning is path and context dependent. The learning process is also technology specific as some technologies are more explicit-knowledge based while others are much more tacit. Automotive technologies are mentioned by Lall (2001) as examples of 'engineering technologies', considered to be more dependent on tacit than on codified elements.

Another feature of technological learning is the dependence of some technologies on external sources of knowledge or information such as other firms, technology institutions or capital goods suppliers. This dependence might lead to the establishment of networks in order to gain access to knowledge which is fragmented by nature. In addition, even if the R&D function may be one of the most important to increase capabilities, as innovation is in itself a process of learning, it is not the only place where learning occurs within the firm. Learning and capability building can take place at any organizational level such as the shop-floor, quality management, maintenance, procurement, logistics, as well as through interactions with external partners (Lall, 2001). Finally, there may be different depths of technological development. While know-how or operational capability must be present in order to perform any activity, know-why is representative of a deeper form of capability, which leads workers to understand the principles of the technology and thus may enhance more autonomous innovative capabilities.

To sum up, in order to profit from networks to increase local capabilities, firms and countries should first present technology or market reasons to be integrated in the networks (pull factors). Once part of a GPN, they should analyse the aspects related to technological learning and create routines, strategies or policies which take these aspects into account in order to foster learning and eventually become part of a GIN.

What is important to note is that the process described here could be conceived with the explicit aim of capability building. For instance, developing countries or local firms can deploy a specific set of policies to develop local skills aiming at addressing a perceived deficiency in skills elsewhere, thus building a combination of pull (local skills) plus push (lack of skills in central countries) factors.

Case studies and the automotive sector in Brazil

In order to examine the process of capability building, we carried out in-depth case studies. In total, five companies were chosen, one OEM and four autoparts makers. The OEM is a subsidiary of a European MNC. It is ranked amongst the 10 largest OEMs in the world, amongst the 5 largest in Europe, and it is one of the market leaders in Brazil. The autoparts companies are all direct suppliers of this manufacturer, and are also subsidiaries of MNCs; all autoparts firms also supply the OEM outside Brazil.

In other words, they are part of a GPN and, as discussed below, of a GIN. All suppliers are engaged in technological activities in Brazil, although each presents distinct local capabilities. In addition, we have chosen suppliers that have been operating in Brazil for different periods of time. Suppliers 3 and 4 had set up their facilities in Brazil during the 1950s, when the first

OEMs plants were established. Suppliers 1 and 2 are latecomers, set up during the 1990s, after the Brazilian market was opened and federal government incentive policies promoted FDI aimed at the local and regional markets. In terms of affiliation to production networks, Suppliers 1 and 2 have always operated in Brazil within a GPN. Suppliers 3 and 4, in turn, became part of GPNs during the 1990s. Therefore, it is possible to examine the evolution of a GPN towards a GIN.

Three of the autoparts makers have headquarters in the same country as the manufacturer. Supplier 1 is a spin-off of the OEM. Supplier 2 inaugurated its Brazilian facilities to respond to a request from the OEM in a follow sourcing scheme, as it already was one of OEM's main supplier in Europe. Supplier 3 used to be an important local company that was acquired by an MNC during the 1990s. Supplier 4 has been present in Brazil since the 1950s as a subsidiary of a traditional US company. Table 1 summarizes the characteristics of the selected companies.

In each company, semi-structured interviews were carried out. Interviewees were either product engineers, engineering managers, or human relations managers or directors. In one case, an innovation manager was interviewed. The interviews were guided by a script conceived within the INGINEUS – Impact of Networks, Globalisation and their Interaction with EU Strategies – project. Questions were related to the technological and skills development trajectory of the unit, considering different actors directly involved with knowledge intensive activities – shop floor workers, supervisors, technicians, engineers, as well as marketing and innovation managers. Questions also referred to the existence of linkages with training institutions, universities, and research centres in Brazil or abroad.

A secondary source of data was desk research, which focused on information on foreign direct investment in the Brazilian automotive industry, the Brazilian education system, and local training systems. This contributed to build a general panorama of competence and skill building and availability in Brazil. Additional data, mainly on the Brazilian automotive industry, were drawn from the Brazilian Automotive Industry Yearbook (ANFAVEA, 2009, 2010, 2011) and the Brazilian Autoparts Manufacturers Association (*Sindicato Nacional das Empresas de Autopeças* – Sindipeças), as well as from several studies on the Brazilian automotive industry, in particular, those

Table 1. Case studies.

Company	Product	Capital origin	Time in Brazil	Interviewees
OEM	Vehicles	Europe	More than 30 years	Innovation manager HR director Product engineering manager
Supplier 1	Power train systems	Europe	10 years as an independent company	HR manager Product engineering manager
Supplier 2	Stamped parts and bodies	Europe	11 years	HR manager Product engineer
Supplier 3	Suspension systems	Europe	More than 50 years	HR manager Product engineering manager
Supplier 4	Transmissions and engine parts	USA	More than 50 years	Product engineer Product engineering manager

presented at the GERPISA (*Groupe d'Études et Recherches Permanent sur l'Industrie et les Salariés de l'Automobile*) international research network. It is also worth mentioning that the OEM, Supplier 1, Supplier 3 and Supplier 4 have been the subject of thorough academic studies in the last 10 years.

Automotive sector

Established in Brazil during the second half of the 1950s, the automotive industry experienced continuous growth until the late 1970s. During the 1980s, the sector suffered a strong contraction. In the 1990s, following the process of trade liberalization and monetary stabilization, the production of vehicles experienced a marked recovery. Pushed by competition from foreign markets and by the growth of the local market, a strong investment cycle took place. From 1990 to 2000, OEMs invested over US 15 billion, while the autoparts companies invested close to US 11 billion. From 2001 to 2010 OEM's investments increased to over US 19 billion, whereas autoparts numbers stayed close to US 11 billion. By the early 2000s, six OEMs that were not operating in Brazil at that time had announced or inaugurated new plants in the country. At the same time, all OEMs that already operated Brazilian plants had announced new investments to increase production capacity (ANFAVEA, 2011). The result can be seen in Table 2, a fourfold increase in production capacity from 1990 to 2010.

The continuous growth during the 1990s and the new investments in the 2000s meant a significant increase of the automotive industry's share in the GDP. From 1990 to 2010, the share rose from 9.2% to 19.5% (ANFAVEA, 2011).

The trend observed in total investment was mirrored by spending on innovative effort. Table 3 shows the relative weight of the automotive sector relative to total manufacturing in terms of sales revenue and innovative effort in 2003 and 2008. The automotive sector's share of total spending on innovative activities is larger than that of sales revenue. In 2008, the automotive sector accounted directly for over 16% of the total expenditure on innovation of the country's manufacturing industry. Not only that, the share increased significantly in the period both for OEMs and autoparts makers. Another important aspect during this time is the sharp increase in internal R&D, close to four-fold for the automotive sector.

These investments brought an increase in innovative efforts, in terms of both product and process. The new plants followed lean production flexibility criteria, adopting multi-tier or hierarchical supply chains for components and parts (Salerno et al., 2009).

Table 2. Number of vehicles produced, licensed, exported and imported[a].

Year	Production	Licensing	Exports	Imports
1990	914,466	712,741	187,311	115
1995	1,629,008	1,728,380	263,044	369,048
2000	1,691,240	1,489,481	371,299	174,178
2005	2,530,840	1,714,644	897,144	87,961
2006	2,612,329	1,927,738	842,837	142,366
2007	2,980,108	2,462,728	789,371	277,083
2008	3,215,976	2,820,350	734,583	375,150
2009	3,182,923	3,141,240	475,325	488,874
2010	3,646,133	3,515,100	767,432	551,872

Source: ANFAVEA (2011).
[a]Sum of total automobiles, light commercial vehicles, lorries, and buses.

Table 3.   Firms sales and spending on innovative activities.

| Sectors | Sales | | Spending on innovative activities | | | |
| | | | Total | | Internal R&D | |
2003	Total	(%)	Total	(%)	Total	(%)
Total manufacturing	721,098.4	100	17,863.6	100.0	3,932.1	100.0
Motor vehicles, trailers, and semi-trailers	65,580.9	9.09	2,566.2	14.4	429.9	26.0
Motor vehicles	42,270.0	5.86	1,988.6	11.1	880.3	22.4
Bodies (coachwork)	3,499.4	0.49	80.2	0.5	17.1	0.4
Parts and accessories for motor vehicles	19,811.5	2.75	497.4	2.8	125.2	3.2
Other transport equipment	12,919.6	1.79	1,112.5	6.2	527.9	13.4
2008						
Total manufacturing	903,532.6	100.0	23,501.9	100.0	5,781.3	100.0
Motor vehicles, trailers, and semi-trailers	111,638.7	12.4	3,879.0	16.5	1,684.0	29.1
Motor vehicles	67,229.8	7.4	2,823.8	12.0	1,352.4	23.4
Bodies (coachwork)	5,609.2	0.6	140.6	0.6	44.3	0.8
Parts and accessories for motor vehicles	38,799.7	4.3	914.6	3.9	287.4	5.0
Other transport equipment	17,515.5	1.9	890.9	3.8	353.9	6.1

Sources: IBGE (2008).
Notes: Values are in US Dollars (million). Activities classified according to the statistical classification of products by activity (CPA).

In relation to the autoparts industry, the investments, although high, were smaller than those observed for manufacturers. This difference is due to the high growth of autoparts imports during the whole period. Another characteristic of the investments in these activities was the intense process of mergers and acquisitions (M&A) that took place in the late 1990s and the beginning of the 2000s. This process led to the denationalization and concentration of the Brazilian autoparts industry during this period.

After the financial crisis in Asia, in 1998, the Brazilian automotive industry experienced a period of instability and uncertainty that lasted until 2003. From this year onwards, its production and sales once more presented a strong trend of growth, with the production capacity nearly reaching its limit. During this time, a recovery of investments could also be observed (from 2006/2007), having been only momentarily slowed down by the international financial crisis. Current trends, however, point to an increase of production and new investments. Projections indicate that production capacity, which went from 2.0 to 3.5 million vehicles with the investments of the 1995/2001 period, will reach 6 million in 2013 (ANFAVEA, 2010). It is, therefore, a mature and important industry, with OEMs responsible for almost a fifth of the country's industrial GDP (ANFAVEA, 2010). There is a striking presence of MNCs in the sector, including in local competence-building.

During the 1990s, following a trend observed for the manufacturing industry as a whole, the automotive sector when through a deep process of production restructuring. MNCs subsidiaries and local suppliers replicated practices based on the Toyota Production System (TPS), which had been adopted at their headquarters. This process modified the profile of the workforce, especially of the operational, technical and supervisory workers. From the 2000s onwards, the headquarters shifted strategies of local subsidiaries, leading to the configuration of new GPNs (Fleury, 1999).

In tandem with the deep process of production restructuring observed over the past 15 years – ownership changes, strategies shifts, capacity modernization, and increase – innovation, as well as engineering activities in general, has evolved, following a distinctive path. It begins with the adaptation of products developed abroad to the conditions of the local market after the installation of the MNCs. The next step is the development of local products broadly based on those produced at the headquarters. Finally, in some cases, the possibility of developing products for other markets (other developing countries, or, more rarely, developed countries) arises.

However, for companies operating in Brazil, this evolution suffered a major setback during the 1990s. As part of a process of generalized restructuring of production under fierce competition, caused by both tariff reduction and the overvalued currency, companies reduced the installed capacity of engineering activities (following the initial concepts of what a 'global product' should be). This trend was reverted during the 2000s, with the reintegration of the Brazilian subsidiaries into the global strategies of the MNCs (Fleury, 1999).

The new strategies of the MNCs included the possibility of a new international division of knowledge-intensive activities. In this division, the Brazilian subsidiaries would be responsible for the development of certain products or technologies, directed to local, regional or, in some exceptional cases, global markets. Alternative fuel engines, robust suspension systems, and light, low cost vehicles are examples of technologies which led to a selective decentralization of engineering activities towards Brazil (Dias and Salerno, 2004).

As a consequence, GINs have emerged, albeit incipiently. Nevertheless, it is important to highlight that the Brazilian subsidiaries are usually responsible for the development of technologies related to specificities of the local market (such as alternative fuels for internal combustion motors or more robust suspension systems). Significant innovation activities related to more advanced technologies (e.g. electrical motors or new materials) have not been observed. Hence, it can be argued that, in the Brazilian automotive sector, basic research is almost inexistent – applied research and product development are the norm.

Case 1: OEM

The OEM is a subsidiary of a European MNC which has been operating in Brazil for more than 30 years. It is the largest subsidiary outside its home country (in terms of production volumes and sales), and it is considered a strategic branch inside the corporation. The building of local competences is a consequence of the trajectory of the subsidiary, which is typical of the Brazilian automotive industry: innovation related activities have evolved from adaptation, or 'tropicalization', to product development. No significant basic research activities exist in this subsidiary, only applied research – more specifically, product and process development. The Brazilian unit is formally responsible for adapting products which were developed in the headquarters to emergent markets, in particular Brazil, as well as for developing new products on centrally designed platforms.

As a whole, it is possible to say that workers' formal qualifications have been increasing at the OEM over the years at all organizational levels. For instance, 12% of shop floor workers have college degrees or are enrolled in college – in Brazil 36% of the population of tertiary age are in tertiary education (UNESCO, 2009). Currently, the lowest admission requirement is a high school degree. The workers who fail to meet the standard are stimulated to qualify themselves, either through partnerships the company has established with local educational institutions, or by means of an internal incentive for minimal qualifications (e.g. general education development courses).

The company has established partnerships with educational institutions, consultancies, and training institutes associated with the manufacturer. Partnerships with public institutions for operational level qualifications were not mentioned. The company stressed the importance of training in management tools, especially tools from the TPS. It is worth mentioning that this is a corporate policy and all firms of the group (OEM, Supplier 1 among others) must implement it. The company also trains its workers to allow for broader comprehension of how the production processes work. There are training programmes aimed at developing competences related to continuous improvement (kaizen) and to methods of analysing and solving problems. The OEM also has a programme of financial incentives to workers who propose innovative ideas to improve products or processes, including operational level workers. The programme can foster the search of new knowledge by the workers and by the company as a whole.

The case studies demonstrated, in all companies investigated, a growth trend for the local engineering sectors and their workers' competences. Basic research occurs fundamentally at the headquarters, and collaboration is more intense with the latter's laboratories. Nevertheless, in the last 7 years, the company has set up new local laboratories that made local development projects possible. This trend became stronger with tax incentives provided by nationwide policies to foster innovation.

However, the fact that the OEM presents important capabilities related to the development of products aiming at emerging countries – low cost, medium performance products – also helped to reposition the local branch within the broader network. These capabilities were built along the trajectory of the company, from local adaptation to local development. For instance, in the 1980s, when the Brazilian federal government consolidated its research programme on ethanol as a biofuel, the company developed and launched the first ethanol engine in the Brazilian market. In the 1990s, it was the first company to introduce a vehicle equipped with a 1000 cc engine to comply with the public policy of decreasing federal taxes on small sized vehicles (locally known as popular vehicles), in order to stimulate sales. At the end of the 1990s, the Brazilian unit was part of the global team that developed a car destined for emerging markets (Dias and Salerno, 2004).

The engineering department grew from 400 employees in 2005 to approximately 850 in 2010. The sector of product development is structured as at the headquarters; this makes the relationship with the headquarters easier, as each Brazilian engineer has a European counterpart. Whenever a technical matter emerges, they are able to meet, thus enhancing an international network. According to the company, engineers still lack a background in technical areas. Once in the company, they must undergo training programmes in product development management (amongst others, quality and reliability), as well as technical training (in automotive engineering). The company also has formal incentive programmes for specialization, Master's and PhD courses. Training programmes in a research centre at the headquarters are also frequent.

Following sector standards, OEM's interaction with research institutes and local laboratories is not very intense. On the other hand, the relationships between the OEM and suppliers are of extreme relevance in the Brazilian automotive industry – which is also a pattern observed worldwide. Co-design i.e. joint development of products or processes by the manufacturer and the suppliers is a common practise in the industry. The OEM is in charge of directing co-design activities in the network, with this type of interaction being part of the company's history. There are four types of suppliers: suppliers that co-develop the products; suppliers that develop the product given the specifications; suppliers that only manufacture the product according to the specifications; and the more simple 'commodities' suppliers.

Case 2: Supplier 1

Supplier 1, which was previously a powertrain department inside the organizational structure of a European car assembler, was created in the beginning of the 2000s. Its headquarters are located in the same European country as the car assembler. At the time of our investigation, the company was carrying out an internal programme to promote innovation in its products and processes.

Due to its trajectory, despite its existence as an independent company for less than 10 years, it has profited from the 30-year Brazilian experience of the car assembler from which it split. Many of its workers were previously workers of the car assembler; and its organizational structure and procedures are still very similar to the car assembler. Some of its workers were responsible for the development of important local innovations such as the small engines and the ethanol fuelled engines that were mentioned above. These competences, which arose from the path followed by the OEM, are being consolidated at present, for instance, with the development of flex-fuel technologies. Indeed, the company faces on-going changes, towards greater local technological competence regarding new local and global products (alternative fuels), as well as competences related to large production, due to TPS. It is thus necessary for the employees – operators, technicians, and engineers as well – to constantly upgrade their skills. Supplier 1 requires a minimum of secondary education for shop floor workers, who have also been trained in TPS tools – especially quality control, problem-solving methods, autonomous maintenance and continuous improvement. Supplier 1 recognizes the importance of the worker 'having a notion of innovation', according to one HR manager. Similar to the OEM, Supplier 1 has benefit programmes for workers who propose innovation and improvement ideas.

The impact of being inserted in a global network is evident in the development of competences at the engineering and innovation levels. The relationship with the headquarters is very important, as can be seen in Supplier 1's slogan 'one product, one engineering'. The practice of sending Brazilian engineers to the headquarters to undertake training programmes is common in Supplier 1. In this company, the subsidiary also hosts engineers from abroad, for them to, for example, familiarize themselves with the flex-fuel engine technology – a case of locally developed technology that may be exported to other markets. The company is studying the implementation of a prize for engineers who publish academic papers on innovation ideas. The company's engineers possess specialized knowledge, but they develop flexible abilities in multidisciplinary teams. In the Supplier 1 engineering department, there are about 300 employees, 56% of whom are engineers.

Co-design is also a strategy for Supplier 1. Besides carrying out the development of products with the OEM, some of the main locally developed products involved decisive participation of suppliers. For example, recently a new device aimed at enhancing the performance of flex fuel and ethanol engines was developed in Supplier 1, together with a company which belongs to the same group as Supplier 3. This device was granted a Brazilian and a European patent. The development of this device is strongly related to the competences of engineers of Supplier 1, developed over 20 years of the Brazilian ethanol programme. These competences were not developed initially because of GINs, but they might be enhanced within a GIN.

Another example concerns an important local innovation introduced in a transmission system, developed along with Supplier 4 in response to a demand from the OEM for a system that could improve the performance of its small off-road vehicle (developed in Brazil) in low adherence road conditions. Supplier 1 started conceptual research on technologies available for traction, presented by the headquarters as well as by other suppliers. Since final product price could not be increased, given the characteristics of the Brazilian emerging market, it was necessary to create a low-cost solution. Finally, the idea for a device was borrowed from the agricultural machinery market and seemed to present the best cost-benefit-viability scenario. However, a specialist supplier to implement this in a first prototype was needed, as integrating the new mechanism in a small front transversal transmission represented a new-to-the-world challenge. So, after dealing with potential suppliers in a more focused stage of definitions, Supplier 4, which presented the application of an electro-mechanical locker differential system, was finally chosen. A product development team was created with manufacturing engineers, production engineers, purchasing engineers, testing engineers, and technicians as well as engineers from Supplier 4, in Brazil and in the USA. The new product called for new production processes, because the new transmission would aggregate fragile electric components (Bagno et al., 2008) – something challenging for a traditional gearbox assembly line. Shop floor workers were trained in the new process.

This case illustrates how engineering worked through transversal processes with other departments such as process and manufacturing engineering, service, legislative council, clients, and others. Management of complementary capabilities among Supplier 1 internal teams, OEM and

Supplier 4 was important. It can thus be said that an innovation network emerged, and that the overall competence level of the network (or, of the actors involved in the network) was increased. Since some of the competences needed to develop the new device were not present in the Brazilian subsidiary of Supplier 4, engineers from the USA development centre were integrated into the team.

Case 3: Supplier 2

Supplier 2 is a subsidiary of a European TNC company operating in Brazil for less than 10 years, following a demand posed by its main client, the OEM. Therefore, its very presence in Brazil is a consequence of being inserted in a global network which operates with follow sourcing policies, since Supplier 2 is a main supplier of the OEM in Europe. It produces stamped parts and car bodies and its whole production is destined to the OEM.

The company adopted TPS techniques in its production lines, driven by the OEM. Indeed, in the automotive industry, car assemblers drive the value chain and it is not uncommon that they compel their suppliers to adopt specific production methods and techniques. In Supplier 2, with the introduction of TPS, the company realized that it was necessary to require an elementary school degree for shop floor workers – it is paramount that workers understand the production process, have better control over the production, and know how to use TPS management tools. An increase in the qualifications of the technical and supervisory positions is evident as well. For supervisory levels, a high school degree is required, preferably in technical courses, and a college degree is desired. For the technical level, a high school degree in a technical course is demanded. Supplier 2, as the OEM and Supplier 1, also presents a kaizen programme, in order to enhance continuous improvement.

The engineering department of Supplier 2 has a significantly higher proportion of technicians in relation to engineers. The area comprises approximately 120 persons, 30% of them engineers and 70% technicians (basically CAD operators). The engineering works are arranged according to the automobile parts projected, in a functional structure very similar to the OEM, its main client. When a project involves more than one area, a multidisciplinary team is formed including engineers and technicians of all relevant areas. Most CAD operators are taking engineering courses.

The company has no partnerships with research institutes or local universities. A respondent explained that the company is not engaged in many market-driven innovations, as most of their products and project services are the property of the client. The European headquarters has the engineering competences that the Brazilian branch relies on, especially regarding projects on vehicle bodies. On the other hand, the headquarters does not possess a structural calculation competence, carried out only by the Brazilian branch, to support the company worldwide. Innovation projects in the company tend to be internal and process-related, but even in these cases Supplier 2 does not use research results or research institutes for the improvement of its processes.

Some of the CAD operators are subcontracted. Such interaction does not lead to innovation for the company. On the other hand, the company has pursued partnerships with suppliers to start innovation projects for their benefit, and not the client. As an example, a North-American supplier performed structural calculations for a bus body, a product for which the company did not possess know-how, with transfer of the structural calculation technologies to the Brazilian company. Typically, the OEM chooses most of the suppliers that participate in product development, and formally establishes the interaction between Supplier 2 and its suppliers.

Case 4: Supplier 3

Supplier 3 is a former Brazilian company acquired by a multinational group in the 1990s, during the period of restructuring of the Brazilian automotive industry. It was one of the largest Brazilian autoparts firms and had followed a path of technological development in Brazil. When the acquisition occurred, many questions were raised concerning the risk of reduction of engineering and innovation activities in the company. Indeed, to a certain extent, some of the engineering activities the firm carried out in Brazil were centralized in the European headquarters, but others, more related to local products, were kept in the country. In the case of technologies related to suspension systems, due to local conditions, vehicle suspension in Brazil must be much more robust than European ones. Competences linked to the development and testing of these robust, low-cost suspensions were developed in the company.

The company demands a minimum of secondary education for shop floor workers. Currently, the lowest admission requirement is a high school degree. There is increasing demand in terms of education and labour skills. The workers who do not meet the standard are stimulated to qualify themselves, either through partnerships the company establishes or by means of an internal incentive for minimal qualification (e.g. general education development courses). The company has incentive programmes for the minimum qualification and development. They also offer training for understanding how the production processes work.

Increasing the minimum requirement for qualification for production workers (high school) is related to the trajectory of technology and innovation of the company, as well as the characteristic transformation of the company's history over the past year. In 1990, after the acquisition, it began to incorporate more complex technologies and new ways of managing processes such as quality and cost reduction programmes. The profile of the shop floor workers was also changed. Production workers must be prepared for the correct interpretation and use of quality tools in place, as the TPS, for example. There are also incentives to promote the application of better practices, through a programme of suggesting innovation and improvement ideas.

At present, there are engineers with specialized knowledge, as well as the organization of multidisciplinary teams conjugating flexible abilities related to product and process design, quality management, reliability engineering, and cost engineering. These teams are mainly in the product development centre, located in its own premises, which are equipped with laboratories for testing new products. Engineers of Supplier 3 directly interact with the suppliers and subcontracted companies, in co-design activities, as well as in qualification and training programmes.

Case 5: Supplier 4

Supplier 4 is a subsidiary of a USA multinational group, which has been operating in Brazil since the 1950s. It produces transmissions and engine parts for cars, trucks, and bus manufacturers. Most of its products are sold to manufacturers and around 25% is destined for the aftermarket. During the 1970s, the company started a policy of local adaptation of its products, which evolved to local development in the 1980s, thus consolidating its local engineering, which is specialized in transmission and clutch components for small pickup vehicles (a type of vehicle which is not present in USA); other competences are centralized in the headquarters.

Supplier 4 confirmed evidence of the tendency for higher qualifications and instruction amongst technicians and supervisors. Most of its supervisors currently possess higher education, while its technicians possess secondary education and technical degrees. The main reason identified was the greater scope of abilities demanded of the direct workers, and, consequently, of supervisors and technicians as well. Improvement suggestion systems (kaizen) extensive to all employees were also verified in Supplier 4. In this company, multi-functional groups design the improvement projects. They hold regular meetings in order to accompany the evolution of the project, observing the methodologies of the TPS.

The engineering department makes use of multidisciplinary teams for the development of products for local or world markets (the headquarters consider Supplier 4 a competence centre for certain products). The engineers of Supplier 4 are currently presented with goals regarding innovation and submission of patent proposals. There are incentives for innovators, via internal prizes. The company also possesses a centre for the development of new products, equipped with a laboratory for testing materials and for mechanical tests. The tests the company cannot internally perform are carried out at the USA headquarters, at the facilities of the clients, at research institutes or at universities.

Discussion

The evolution of competences, knowledge, and skills displayed by the workers of the Brazilian automotive sector is closely related to the industry's trajectory over the past 20 years. Even though all the companies set up their facilities in Brazil in order to gain access to local (plus regional) markets and not for technological reasons, all of them have enhanced their local innovation structures, although at different levels. Competences related to engineering and to technological development have grown in pace with the increase of innovation-related activities, especially the development of local products, which occurred largely during the 2000s.

The relationship between the increase of competences and the greater responsibility of the firms is bidirectional. There is, on the one hand, an effort to increase local competences due to changes in the technological profile of the unit determined by the headquarters (which leads to offering qualification and training programmes inside the companies, through partnerships with local institutions or by local governments). At the same time, such an increase enables the Brazilian subsidiaries to demand from their headquarters the allocation of time to perform activities with greater technological content, configuring a virtuous cycle that combines pull and push factors (Gastrow et al., 2011). The Brazilian professionals actively seek higher qualifications and experience, while the companies are also in a process of acquiring autonomy in R&D.

The product development process in the automotive industry has for some time profited from external sources of knowledge, notably suppliers. Incipient partnerships are attempted with local universities, aimed at technological development, mostly within the OEM. Co-design is a widespread practice within this industry, confirmed by all the case studies; the two new-to-the-world technologies developed by Supplier 1 were created in co-design with two other suppliers, in Brazil and abroad. The transfer of competences and knowledge for product development activities occurs in an informal and contextual manner, consistent with the predominance of tacit knowledge in the automotive industry (Lall, 2001).

In this sense, a 'global network' or 'global chain' configuration can be identified in the competence-building process of local branches of MNCs. This process involves the unit, the headquarters and its suppliers and clients (multinational and local), universities and local training or qualification institutions. Knowledge and technology transfers occur locally and globally.

The main force in the internal dynamics of this network is the OEM (the headquarters and the subsidiary company). The (bidirectional) relationship between the headquarters and the subsidiary determines which competences must be locally developed, at operational as well as at management and engineering levels. The local development needs of the OEM determine partnerships with the education institutions and the universities. They also determine the competence development needs of suppliers, especially those participating in co-design. Co-design practises themselves create an engineering network in which there is a daily exchange of experiences and knowledge, especially tacit knowledge, increasing the competences of the network as a whole, as predicted by Ernst and Kim (2002).

At the global scale, knowledge transfers occur mainly between the headquarters and the subsidiary. In the case studies, a distinctive demand for increased autonomy in relation to the headquarters could be observed. Interviewees were eager to have more room to develop new technologies locally – in other words, to create pull factors. If at present cases of new-to-the-world locally developed technologies are still rare, there is a possibility that in the future the number of major local innovations will increase.

This reasoning is supported by the fact that the level of formal education has shown an upward trend in all five companies, that is, not only know-how but also know-why is being encouraged. As Lall (2001) indicates, the presence of know-why competences in general means that deeper capability exists, which supports more technological autonomy. Indeed, in the staff departments and at the technical and engineering levels, professionals have consistently shown the intention of acquiring the competences necessary for a career in innovation in the automotive sector. This movement is still emergent in Brazil, and can be seen in the growth of professionals with technical level qualifications (with knowledge of specific software for product development, especially CAD and simulation or laboratorial ones) and higher education (business and engineering courses).

In addition, in engineering areas, there is important interaction between the companies and local research institutes or universities, both public and private, through the investment in specialization, Master's or PhD courses – although there are relatively few PhDs in the sector. However, the market still is short of qualified and experienced professionals, particularly specialists in the technical and engineering areas. This can be explained by the very recent nature of research in the sector, intensified only from the 2000s (Dias et al., 2011).

An equally important way of developing engineering competences is the transfer of local engineers to training programmes at the headquarters of MNCs. There are cases in which local subsidiaries send engineers abroad with the explicit purpose of training at the headquarters' research centres, plants or training centres. Finally, the fact that the OEM trains engineers, technicians, and managers of the suppliers is relevant.

An attempt to standardize production management models between the OEM headquarters, the OEM, and the suppliers was detected, led by the OEM headquarters. The production management model chosen is based on the TPS, and presents characteristics such as: adoption of quality tools (statistical process control, PDCA, structured problem-solving methods), continuous improvement (kaizen) performed in a structured manner, multifunctional capabilities and an increase in the demand for holistic knowledge (comprehending the whole production, being able to deal with eventualities, amongst others). Hence, there have been efforts to improve the qualifications of shop floor workers, materialized, fundamentally, in the form of (internal and external) training in the new management tools adopted. This trend provides empirical support for Lall's (2001) proposition that technological capabilities are developed at all organizational levels.

Taking all these factors into consideration, it can be argued that participation in a global network, albeit incomplete, has led to an increase of the local competences in the Brazilian automotive sector. A process of technological learning occurred within the network, and local subsidiaries have evolved from home-base-exploiting units to home-base-augmenting ones. This occurs via internal development (internal training, knowledge transfer between the headquarters and the branch or between the client and the supplier) as well as via the development of competences through the establishment of partnerships with local supplier, clients, and education and research institutions.

However, it is important to note that, with the exception of the technologies related to ethanol fuelled engines, local capabilities have been developed by the Brazilian units over the years in an informal way. These competences are related to local market characteristics, such as conditions of usage and customers' preferences and lower income levels. To the extent that some of these characteristics are also present in similar, important developing markets (such as South Africa or India) these competences were recognized by the headquarters, local engineering infrastructure was enhanced and its procedures and local capability development were formalized, over the last decade.

Final remarks

This paper investigated how the integration of firms in a GIN affects the demand for local skills and eventually leads to an increase in local innovation capabilities. The analysis showed that demand for higher-level competences, in particular of engineering positions, is closely tied to the configuration of the local GIN. The Brazilian GIN under investigation is in the automotive industry, which has been subject to important qualitative changes in terms of innovative activities in the last decade. From mere processes of adaptation of products developed elsewhere to local markets, local branches have gained increasing degrees of autonomy to develop new products for the local market, which can eventually be selected by the headquarters to serve other countries.

The degree of autonomy is related to a higher degree of integration of the OEM's local subsidiary to the MNC's global activities. In this sense, it seems that emergence of GINs is associated with improvements in the configuration of a GPN. The position of the local subsidiary in its headquarters' global division of innovative labour is highly path dependent. Local capabilities have been built progressively during the past two decades, and accelerated in the past 10 years. Acceleration was possible due to policies companies adopted to foster learning: training programmes, incentives for employees to increase their formal education and thus their know-why, new organizational routines such as kaizen programmes at all organizational levels, teamwork, and formal external linkages with universities. An important managerial implication that follows from this trend is that the process of technological learning and capability building is not necessarily only top-down, that is, determined by the headquarters, but may be promoted by local managers. Through the creation of local pull factors, these managers could contribute to shift a firm's role in the MNC's international division of labour to encompass R&D, encouraging a virtual cycle of local capability building.

The quality of linkages between firms in the production network also contributed to build new capabilities and to the emergence of a GIN as it made knowledge transfer inside co-design processes possible. Thus, firms in developing countries can enhance their technological capabilities when integrating into a GIN. Finally, it must be stressed that in the Brazilian case, this has happened in spite of the fact that linkages between firms and universities are very weak, and that there are few public policies explicitly aiming at promoting local innovation in the automotive industry. Therefore, there is plenty of room for further improvement of local capabilities if initiatives within companies are coupled with sound, sector specific policies that strengthen pull and push factors.

Acknowledgments

Research for this paper was partially funded by the European Community's Seventh Framework Programme (Project INGINEUS, Grant Agreement No. 225368, www.ingineus.eu). The authors alone are responsible for its contents which do not necessarily reflect the views or opinions of the European Commission, nor is the European Commission responsible for any use that might be made of the information appearing herein.

References

Altenburg, T., Schmitz, T.H., and Stamm, A. (2008) Breakthrough? China's and India's transition from production to innovation. *World Development*, 36(2).

ANFAVEA (Brazilian Automotive Industry Association) (2009) *Anuário Estatístico [Brazilian Automotive Industry Yearbook]*, pp. 1–182 (Sao Paulo: Anfavea).

ANFAVEA (Brazilian Automotive Industry Association) (2010) *Anuário Estatístico [Brazilian Automotive Industry Yearbook]*, pp. 1–188 (Sao Paulo: Anfavea).

ANFAVEA (Brazilian Automotive Industry Association) (2011) *Anuário Estatístico [Brazilian Automotive Industry Yearbook]*, pp. 1–155 (Sao Paulo: Anfavea).

Archibugi, D., and Michie, J. (1995) The globalisation of technology: A new taxonomy. *Cambridge Journal of Economics*, 19(1), pp. 121–140.

Arora, A., Arunachalam, V.S., Asundi, J., and Fernandes, R. (2001) The Indian software industry. *Research Policy*, 20(8), pp. 1267–1287.

Bagno, R.B., Machado, G.A.A. and Fratta, C.L. (2008) Global Cooperation and Innovation: A case study about the development of the world's first application of an electronic locker differential integrated to a front transversal transmission. XVII Congresso e Exposição Internacionais da Tecnologia da Mobilidade, 7–9 October, São Paulo, Brazil.

Barnard, H. and Chaminade, C. (2011) Global Innovation Networks: What are they and where can we find them? (Conceptual and Empirical issues). Proceedings of the GLOBELICS Conference, Buenos Aires.

Bell, M., and Pavitt, K. (1995) The development of technological capabilities, in: I.U. Haque (ed) *Trade, Technology and International Competitiveness* (Washington: World Bank), pp. 69–101.

Calabrese, G. (2001) R&D globalization in the car industry. *International Journal of Automotive Technology and Management*, 1(1), pp. 145–159.

Cantwell, J. (1989) *Technological Innovation and Multinational Corporations* (Oxford: Basil Blackwell).

Cantwell, J. (1999) From the early internationalization of corporate technology to global technology sourcing. *Transnational Corporations*, 8(2), pp. 71–92.

Cantwell, J., and Mudambi, R. (2005) MNE competence-creating subsidiary mandates. *Strategic Management Journal*, 26(12), pp. 1109–1128.

Castellacci, F., and Archibugi, D. (2008) The technology clubs: The distribution of knowledge across nations. *Research Policy*, 37(10), pp. 1659–1673.

Chaminade, C. (2009) On the concept of global innovation networks. *CIRCLE Electronic Working Paper 2009/05* (Lund, Sweden: Centre for Innovation, Research and Competence in the Learning Economy (CIRCLE)).

Chaminade, C., and Vang, J. (2008) Globalisation of knowledge production and regional innovation policy: Supporting specialized hubs in the Bangalore software industry. *Research Policy*, 37(10), pp. 1684–1696.

Chiesa, V. (2000) Global R&D project management and organization: A taxonomy. *Journal of Product Innovation Management*, 17(5), pp. 341–359.

Cohen, W., and Levinthal, D. (1990) Absorptive capacity: A new perspective on learning and innovation. *Administrative Science Quarterly*, 35, pp. 128–152.

Dias, A.V.C., Bagno, R.B., Camargo, O., Pereira, M.C., and Britto, G. (2011), Recent evolutions in R&D activities in the Brazilian automotive industry. Proceedings of the 19th International GERPISA Colloquium, Paris, available at: http://gerpisa.org/en/node/1273.

Dias, A.V.C., and Salerno, M. (2004) International division of labour in product development activities: Towards a selective decentralisation? *International Journal of Automotive Technology and Management*, 4(2–3), pp. 223–239.

Dunning, J.H. (1993) *Multinational Enterprises and the Global Economy* (Harlow: Addison-Wesley).

Dunning, J.H., Hoesel, R., and Narula, R. (1997) Explaining the 'new' wave of outward FDI from developing countries: The case of Taiwan and Korea. Research Memoranda 009 (Maastricht: MERIT, Maastricht Economic Research Institute on Innovation and Technology).

Dunning, J.H., and Lundan, S.M. (2008) *Multinational Enterprises and the Global Economy,* 2nd Edition (Cheltenham: Edward Elgar).

Dunning, J.H., and Narula, R. (1995) The R&D activities of foreign firms in the United States. *International Studies of Management & Organization*, 25(1/2), pp. 39–74.

Ernst, D. (2006) Innovation offshoring: Asia's emerging role in global innovation networks. *East West Center Special Reports*, 10, pp. 1–48. Available at http://scholarspace.manoa.hawaii.edu/bitstream/handle/10125/12531/SR010.pdf?sequence=1.

Ernst, D., and Kim, L. (2002) Global production networks, knowledge diffusion, and local capability formation. *Research Policy*, 31(8–9), pp. 1417–1429.

Fleury, A. (1999) The changing pattern of operations management in developing countries: The case of Brazil. *International Journal of Operations and Production Management*, 19(5/6), pp. 552–564.

Florida, R. (1997) The globalization of R&D: Results of a survey of foreign-affiliated R&D laboratories in the USA. *Research Policy*, 26(1), pp. 85–103.

Gammeltoft, P. (2006) Internationalisation of R&D: Trends, drivers and managerial challenges. *International Journal of Technology and Globalisation*, 2(1–2), pp. 177–199.

Gassmann, O., and von Zedtwitz, M. (1999) New concepts and trends in international R&D organization. *Research Policy*, 28(2–3), pp. 231–250.

Gastrow, M., Kruss, G., Muller, L., and Roodt, J. (2011) Impact of networks, globalisation and their interaction with EU strategies (INGINEUS project): Research papers on 'fragmentation of GINs and capacity building in the automotive, ICT and agro-processing industries'. Commissioned by the European Commission within the Seventh Framework Programme. http://www.ingineus.eu/UserFiles/INGINEU S_D6.1(1)(2).pdf, accessed 4 April 2012.

Gereffi, G., Humphrey, J., and Sturgeon, T. (2005) The governance of global value chains. *Review of International Political Economy*, 12(1), pp. 78–104.

IBGE (2008) 'Pesquisa de Inovação Tecnológica 2008', Instituto Brasileiro de Geografia e Estatística (IBGE), available at: http://www.pintec.ibge.gov.br/downloads/PUBLICACAO/Publicacao%20PINTE C%202008.pdf, accessed 2 April 2012.

Kuemmerle, W. (1997) Building effective R&D capabilities abroad. *Harvard Business Review*, 72(2), pp. 61–70.

Lall, S. (2001) *Competitiveness, Technology and Skills* (Cheltenham: Edward Elgar).

Miotti, L. and Sachwald, F. (2001) Patterns of R&D cooperation by European firms: Cost-economizing versus technology-seeking. AITEG WORKSHOP-Annals, Madrid, 25–26 May.

Nonaka, I., and Takeuchi, H. (1995) *The Knowledge-Creating Company* (Oxford: Oxford University Press).

Patel, P., and Vega, M. (1999) Patterns of internationalization of corporate technology: Location vs home country advantages. *Research Policy*, 28(2), pp. 145–155.

Plechero, M. and Chaminade, C. (2010) Different competences, different modes in the globalization of innovation? A comparative study of the Pune and Beijing regions. *CIRCLE Electronic Working Papers* 2010/3, Lund University.

Reddy, P. (1997) New trends in globalization of corporate R&D and implications for innovation capability in host countries: A survey from India. *World Development*, 25(11), pp. 1821–1837.

Salerno, M., Marx, R., Zilbovicius, M., and Dias, A.V.C. (2009) The importance of locally commanded design for the consolidation of local supply chain: The concept of design headquarters. *International Journal of Manufacturing Technology and Management*, 16(4), pp. 361–376.

Sousa, C.M.P., Martínez-López, F.J., and Coelho, F. (2008) The determinants of export performance: A review of the research in the literature between 1998 and 2005. *International Journal of Management Reviews*, 10(4), pp. 343–374.

Sturgeon, T., Van Biesebroeck, J., and Gereffi, G. (2008) Value chains, networks, and clusters: Reframing the global automotive industry. *Journal of Economic Geography*, 8(3), pp. 297–321.

Teece, D. (1980) Economies of scope and the scope of the enterprise. *Journal of Economic Behavior and Organization*, 1(3), pp. 223–247.

Von Tunzelmann, N. (2009) Competencies versus capabilities: A reassessment. *Economia Politica*, 26(3), pp. 435–464.

UNCTAD (2005) *World Investment Report* (Geneva: UNCTAD).

UNESCO (2009) UIS statistics in brief: Education (all levels) profile – Brazil, UIS, 2009, available at: http://stats.uis.unesco.org/unesco/TableViewer/document.aspx?ReportId=121&IF_Language=eng&BR_Country=760&BR_Region=40520

von Zedtwitz, M., and Gassmann, O. (2002) Market versus technology drive in R&D internationalization: Four different patterns of managing research and development. *Research Policy*, 31(4), pp. 569–588.

Multinational strategies, local human capital, and global innovation networks in the automotive industry: case studies from Germany and South Africa

Jo Lorentzen and Michael Gastrow

Human Sciences Research Council

This paper focuses on the relationship between strategies of Northern and Southern firms, mostly multinational enterprises (MNEs), and human capital in Southern host countries in the automotive supply industry and the implications of this relationship both for the management of technological change and for the constitution of global innovation networks (GINs). Using a case-study approach drawing on firm-level interviews in both the home country (Germany) and the host country (South Africa), we find that the offshoring of knowledge-intensive activities is beginning to appear in an industry that is known more than others for centralizing most such activity close to headquarter locations and always in developed economies. It is also evident that the extension of GINs is not just based on Northern MNEs taking advantage of advanced capabilities in developing countries. Firms from the South, too, *in*shore the relevant knowledge through the acquisition of strategic assets in the North.

1. Introduction

This paper focuses on the relationship between strategies of Northern and Southern firms, mostly multinational enterprises (MNEs), and human capital in Southern host countries in the automotive supply industry and the implications of this relationship both for the management of technological change and for the constitution of global innovation networks (GINs). We define GINs as global networks in which some knowledge-intensive activities are based in developing countries. They differ qualitatively from the better-known global production networks (GPNs) where Northern MNEs traditionally control the key technological assets while outsourcing the supply of parts and components or assembly to contract manufacturers. In particular, we use firm-level case studies to explore the micro-determinants affecting the evolution of GINs (which can evolve and be nested within GPNs).

GINs are a result of the emerging geography of knowledge-intensive activities in the global economy. On the one hand, the increasing complexity of knowledge required for global competitiveness, shorter innovation and product cycles, and the associated cost pressures have led MNEs to offshore and outsource R&D (Archibugi and Iammarino, 2002; Wooldridge, 2010). On the other hand, the spread of technological capabilities in a number of emerging economies such as China and India has opened opportunities for design, applied development, and even basic research (UNCTAD, 2005). What is new is not the offshoring or outsourcing of R&D *per se*

(OECD, 2007), but the gradual involvement of firms and other actors such as universities and research laboratories from a few developing countries in what until a decade or so ago played itself out exclusively among the advanced Triad economies plus a few latecomers from East Asia, notably Korea and Taiwan.

The evidence concerning GINs is not comprehensive. To date, it is primarily based on indications of CEOs or R&D managers of important Northern MNEs who participated in surveys (UNCTAD, 2005; Dilk et al., 2006) or on descriptions of individual examples of such GINs, often in the business press (Wooldridge 2010). However, the INGINEUS project has made available a new source of international firm-level data. This 2010 survey included 1215 companies in six European countries and in Brazil, China, India and South Africa in three industries (agro-food, automotive, and ICT). It revealed that 25% offshored either production or R&D and that, next to market access, the availability of specialized competencies at lower cost than in the home region and access to knowledge infrastructure and services in the host region were the most important location-specific advantages. Between 5 and 6% additionally reported that subsidiaries in developing countries were responsible for strategic management, product development, and technology and process development (see Appendix 1 for more information about the survey).

While the existence of GINs is not in doubt, their evolution is less clear. We do not know much about the micro-determinants shaping the formation of GINs that are anchored within GPNs. Dutrénit (2004) pointed out that the literature on technological upgrading in developing countries had only ever asked how firms graduated from simpler to more sophisticated capabilities, without looking at subsequent trajectories that would bring them closer to the global technological frontier (see also Lorentzen, 2009). To some extent, this simply reflected an empirical reality, namely that the majority of developing country firms did not 'innovate' in the sense of pushing the frontier.

Yet apart from the fact that there were important Southern firms that did not fit the idea of 'innovation' only as 'adaptation' (Kim, 1997; Hobday et al., 2004) – Samsung's overtaking of Sony is but one example (Chang, 2008) – the small size of this phenomenon does not justify the neglect of the conceptual and theoretical treatment afforded to the evolving technological trajectories of developing country firms towards new-to-the-world activities. Apart from the fact that it was always unlikely to remain small, it is incumbent upon researchers to recognize the limitations of the existing literature and think more systematically about how developing country firms master the hardly trivial process of moving from excellence in execution to more creative activities in which knowledge plays an increasing role.

This paper is an attempt to contribute to a better understanding of the micro-determinants of GINs, with a focus on the role of human capital in developing countries. Lall (2001) analysed the relationship between education and skill systems and technological trajectories in East Asia. He showed how education and skill strategies must anticipate technical change in order for host economies to not only become and remain attractive locations for multinational investment, but also exploit the associated knowledge transfer and spillover in support of economy-wide upgrading. Yet he did not look at R&D capabilities.

This paper extends Lall's analytical framework to include R&D and innovation activities. Against a background of data describing host country absorptive capacities (with a focus on education and skill data and foreign direct investment (FDI) data) and a review of current dynamics in the automotive sector, we analyse a set of case studies from a European car-producing economy (Germany), whose assemblers and suppliers have investments in important advanced developing countries (South Africa). We also look at some South African firms that invested in Europe to access knowledge from more advanced suppliers. These case studies aim to illustrate how sectoral dynamics and local human capital conditioned the embedding of South African automotive manufacturers into (sometimes incipient) GINs.

The automotive sector is suitable for this analysis because it includes a range of different technologies, which illustrate different technological learning trajectories. The sector also offers clear delineations between skill levels in the organization (worker, supervisor, engineer, management, scientist, etc.), which facilitates an analysis according to Lall's understanding of technological upgrading being reliant on upgrading at all skill levels. The firm locations in Germany and South Africa illustrate North–South relationships; although there are unique aspects to these countries, they nonetheless have value as illustrative cases of a developed and a developing country. In this context, our analysis of the case studies focuses on specific instances of technical change, how they were supported by human capital upgrading, what difference this made (or not) for the control of technological progress within each value chain, and how all these influenced the evolution of GINs from GPNs.

2. Conceptual framework: MNEs, human capital, and technological learning in developing countries

The unit of analysis for this paper is people and the skills, competencies, and capabilities that they embody. We make distinctions between these terms based on the work of Van Tunzelmann (2009). Here, we refer to *competencies* as specific sets of skills and knowledge which are usually generated outside the firm, for example, through education institutions, but can also be generated inside a firm, for example, through internal training programmes. When a Northern firm is investigating the possibility of investing in a developing country, the availability of the required competencies is a key factor. On the other hand, *capabilities* refers to the functional capacity of (people inside) a firm to complete specific tasks required for its role as a supplier, a producer, or a consumer. Capabilities are usually built up from inside a firm, for example, through experience, the gaining of tacit knowledge, and organizational innovation. If a Northern firm is seeking to purchase a Southern firm, it is the capabilities embodied in that firm that offer value.

MNEs thus embody certain capabilities while at the same time looking for new ones in a few advanced developing countries. In the South, education and training systems are an essential element of high absorptive capacities, which in turn are a prerequisite for GINs. The relationship between FDI and local human capital is two-way. On the one hand, educational achievements attract inward direct investment (see also Dunning, 1993; Noorbakhsh et al., 2001; te Velde, 2005). On the other hand, MNEs exert influence over education and training systems after entry, both directly (Tan and Batra, 1995; Borensztein et al., 1998; Spar, 1998; Lall and Narula, 2004; Lorentzen, 2007) and because they increase competition (Grossman and Helpman, 1991; Moran, 1998; Chuang, 2000), while accelerating skill-biased technological change (te Velde and Xenogiani, 2007).

Lall analysed dynamic upgrading (2001, esp. Chapters 5 and 7) by linking the capability approach with an analysis of human capital. The important elements of firm-level capabilities and, hence, learning include the following. First, since technologies make different demands on learning requirements, the learning process is technology-specific. What works in an electronics plant where an essentially codified new technology may be embodied in a new piece of capital equipment is not necessarily relevant for an automotive supplier facility where an emerging technology may be a lot more tacit (Jung and Lee, 2010). This also means that when tacit knowledge is important, the role of geographic proximity rises. The breadth of skills and knowledge required to master new technologies also differs, as does the time to take them on.

Second, different technologies depend to differing degrees on external sources of information. In the extreme case, one might think of an almost self-contained cluster as opposed to a global technology network to which different firms and research institutes or migrating knowledge workers contribute. Third, relevant human capital inside the firm includes everybody from the shop-floor workers to senior management. The design of a new product may primarily be in the hands of a few R&D engineers. Yet whether their research leads to a commercially successful innovation also depends on the efficiency and quality with which workers turn prototypes into products. Thus, our analysis of skill availability in host countries includes specific foci on the level of the worker, supervisor, technical, engineering, management, and scientist.

Fourth, technological trajectories cannot be successful by relying exclusively on the mastery of operational know-how. It is also necessary to understand 'know-why', a term which implies deeper capabilities that include an understanding of the principles of the technology. This is especially important in the context of GINs as opposed to GPNs; for the latter, the exclusive pursuit of operational know-how may be a feasible strategy, but know-why is critical to GIN formation. Fifth, technological learning takes place in an environment characterized by externalities and linkages, which in turn depend on institutional characteristics. Education and training institutions are among those that matter prominently.

In looking at the specific linkages between MNEs and local human capital, it is pertinent to distinguish between internalized and externalized transfers of technology. When an MNC chooses to keep (proprietary) technology to itself, the transfer of know-why (but not typically of know-how) may suffer, unless local R&D capabilities are already high (which in developing countries, they of course often are not). Either way, local firms must develop the skills and the knowledge to master the tacit elements of whatever it is that is being transferred.

Much as the early and later stages of catch-up require different kinds of skills and competencies, there are presumably differences in terms of the level of sophistication at which latecomer countries, regions, firms, or other actors get involved in GINs. These differences may play out within the very same country – for example, whereas a university may be involved in basic research that feeds into the design part of a GIN, a firm may contribute productive activities that are mere assembly. So although the terminology of *national* technological capabilities is a useful way of thinking about the technological trajectories of countries, it of course does not mean that entire countries get slotted into GINs at specific levels of (high or low) technological sophistication, but rather at a range of activities (see also Hobday et al., 2004). Undoubtedly, however, the emergence of GINs implies that education and training systems can, on average, no longer provide a merely literate and numerate workforce, as they may have done at the very beginning of technological capability-building.

3. Methodology

In order to identify the effects of firm strategies and local absorptive capacities on the nature and quality of technical change, we first selected German first-tier supplier MNEs with investments in South Africa. Research teams in each of these countries contacted their respective firms and arranged interviews with managers in charge of R&D, technology, or innovation as well as of human capital. This rendered matched case studies where the teams interviewed both headquarters and subsidiary. These cases were supplemented by interviews with South African firms that had invested in subsidiaries in Europe. These 'South–North' cases were complementary, in that they illustrated the formation of GINs from Southern origin and perspective.

We compiled profiles for each firm, based largely on trade magazines and other specialist literature. The interviews were semi-structured and focused on upgrading and location strategies, human capital, and the management of technological change. In line with Lall's observation that skills at all levels matter in processes of dynamic upgrading, the human capital dimension of the interview included questions about all skill levels of the workforce, from shop-floor workers to scientists. Within each case, we then focused on a specific instance of technological change that required upgrading across some or all skill levels of the firms' workforce and identified the requisite learning as well as the actual form this upgrading took.

These instances of technological change were then analysed within Lall's conceptual framework and against the backdrop of sectoral dynamics and the availability of local competencies. These rich cases provide concrete illustrations of the array of factors that shape the emergence and evolution of GINs, both from North to South and from South to North, with a focus on the role of human capital availability. We set out to establish to what extent GINs are emerging from GPNs, what their technological trajectories are, and how these are influenced by contextual factors. Our case studies examine how the various pressures within the automotive sector articulate with local human capital availability to inform firm strategies with regard to technological trajectories and GIN formation. The strategies of both German MNE and South African originated firms were explored, with a focus on how they manage technological upgrading, both through accessing technology transfer from outside the firms and through internal knowledge production such as R&D.

Face-to-face interviews took place in the second half of 2010 and lasted up to 2 h. As part of a global team, the researchers conducted interviews in their own country (the authors were part of the South African research team and conducted all the South African interviews). The interview notes and case-study analyses were later integrated under the rubric of the INGINEUS project. After the interviews, the researchers produced a synthesis of the conversation which they submitted to the interviewees for the vetting of accuracy. The firms were assured confidentiality. The case studies include five firms, of which three are German MNCs with subsidiaries in South Africa and two are smaller South African firms with subsidiaries in Europe and other developed countries (see Table 1).

4. Sectoral dynamics: trends in the global automotive manufacturing industry and their effects on innovation

4.1. Global growth and the market shift from West to East (and North to South)

Global vehicle production more than doubled between 1975 and 2007, coinciding with rapid globalization and the re-structuring of global automotive value chains. The relative weight of

Table 1. Case-study description

Firm	Turnover 2009	Locations	Product range	Interviews conducted
Drivetraincomp	€5–10 bn	Global: 180 locations in 50 countries	Clutches and bearings	South Africa
Exhaustcomp	€1–5 bn	Global: locations in more than 20 countries	Exhaust systems and heating systems	Germany and South Africa
Tempcomp	€1–5 bn	Global: 22 production locations, 11 development centres, and 2 fully equipped R&D centres	Heating and cooling systems	Germany and South Africa
Elecsys1	€0–1 bn	HQ and manufacturing in South Africa; sales and R&D centres in the UK and USA	Electronic components	South Africa
Elecsys2	€0–1 bn	HQ in South Africa; subsidiaries in the UK and Australia	Electronic security systems	South Africa

Note: Turnover is given in ranges to protect anonymity.

developing countries, especially India and China, in vehicle output has increased, whereas production and sales have shrunk in Western Europe and North America (Sturgeon et al., 2009). Between 2007 and 2009, the share of developing country original equipment manufacturers (OEMs) in global production increased from 1.9% to 7.5%, largely due to growth in China. The onset of the world financial crisis in 2008 accelerated this trend (Wad, 2010).

4.2. *Global value chain re-structuring*

Value chains in the automotive industry are producer-driven (Gereffi, 2005), which means that lead firms, namely the OEMs and a few large global suppliers, all of which are still located in developed countries, account for the bulk of innovation activity, the production of most engines and transmissions, and almost all vehicle assembly functions (Birchall et al., 2001; Becker, 2006; Chanaron and Rennard, 2007; Wad, 2010). In the re-structuring of global value chains in the 1990s and 2000s, MNEs took majority control of many joint-venture assembly operations. Suppliers from the OEMs' home regions set up operations in proximity of foreign locations of the assemblers, a process referred to as follow-source. In addition, domestic suppliers were largely relegated to the second or the third tier or were taken over (Humphrey et al., 1998; Barnes and Kaplinsky, 2000; Humphrey and Memedovic, 2003; Barnes and Morris, 2008; Rutherford and Holmes, 2008). The financial crisis increased cost pressures on the industry, turned up the heat on OEMs, and accelerated supplier consolidation (Maxton and Womald, 2004; Barnes and Morris, 2008; Osterman and Neal, 2009).

4.3. *Innovation and upgrading*

Market changes and value chain dynamics strongly influence innovation drivers in the sector, which in turn is likely to impact on the role of human capital in the formation of GINs. First, the concentration of power within a few lead firms has implications for the structure of innovation. Innovation takes place at large firms – OEMs such as Ford and Daimler are consistently among the top spenders on R&D worldwide (Dehoff and Jaruzelski, 2009) – and moves in a top-down fashion. Assemblers create unique standards and specifications, necessitated by the high level of inter-relationships in the performance characteristics of components that differ for every model. Together with the absence of open industry-wide standards, this undermines value chain modularity and makes supplier investments relationship-specific. This creates a consistent demand for R&D among the large firms in the sector, particularly among assemblers and first-tier suppliers, but it also acts as a centripetal force that concentrates R&D within the highest tiers and largest firms. Since barriers to entry are raised by investment requirements and by the top-down direction of design specifications, the scope for innovation among smaller firms is further reduced. The close collaboration between suppliers and assemblers also leads to agglomerations of firms near the headquarters of assemblers and large first-tier suppliers, further concentrating innovation in these clusters. The industry effect is a limit to economies of scale in production and of scope in design.

However, vehicle and component R&D has achieved greater global integration than production, as firms have sought to leverage their design functions across multiple products and end markets, a process referred to as follow-design, while eventually adapting each model to its specific market conditions (Humphrey and Memedovic, 2003; Sturgeon et al., 2009). This also creates high barriers to entry and limits prospects for upgrading by smaller firms and firms in developing countries.

At the same time, contrasting dynamics are influencing the conduct of innovation in the industry. Very large and growing markets such as Brazil, China, and India make it profitable for assemblers to adapt existing or even to produce specific models (Brandt and Van Biesebroeck, 2008). OEMs thus establish regional headquarters as well as regional design and innovation centres. In turn, this creates pressure for lead suppliers to follow suit and to source inputs from local second-tier suppliers which might end up supplying assemblers directly. Similarly, OEMs use advanced developing countries, whose markets do not justify specific models but are large enough to warrant local assembly, as regional production hubs. In countries such as South Africa, Thailand, and Turkey, this opens opportunities for local suppliers, including for export. By contrast, developing countries that are close to and can supply on a just in time (JIT) basis to a regional trade block (e.g. Morocco, Mexico, or Turkey) tend to specialize in labour-intensive components. If capability upgrading occurs, opportunities may arise for the production of capital-intensive parts and even assembly (Lorentzen et al., 2003; Carrillo, 2004).

In sum, technological trajectories depend on the interplay between both Northern and Southern MNE strategies and local absorptive capacities, mediated by geography (cf. Sturgeon and Van Biesebroeck, 2010). Some trajectories depend more on external sources of knowledge and technology, while others have a greater role for internal sources such as R&D. The most straightforward channel for technology transfer is internally from MNEs to their subsidiaries (Ivarsson and Alvstam, 2005). Such transfer can, but need not, take place in joint ventures (Sadoi, 2008; Nam, 2010). Technological upgrading can also take place when a Northern supplier transfers technology to a Southern assembly plant or when a Southern assembler acquires the competencies of a Northern firm, a strategy followed by Chinese OEMs Sichuan Tengzhong Heavy Industrial Machinery Company, Geely, and Beijing Automotive Company (BAIC), with their purchases of Hummer from General Motors, Volvo from Ford, and rights to Saab styling and technology, respectively, or Indian OEM Tata's acquisition of Jaguar and Land Rover.

Of course, none of these strategies are guaranteed short-term success in terms of transfer, especially in the absence of the tacit knowledge that would allow the Southern firms to bridge existing technology gaps. Firm strategies are also mediated by the availability of skills at different levels (Lall, 2001). The establishment of production facilities as part of a GPN may require skills mostly at the lower levels (worker, supervisors, and technicians), while the establishment or growth of innovation activities or an R&D centre will require skills at the higher levels of engineering and management. The availability of these skills in host countries may act as a determinant of technological trajectories and the evolution of GINs within GPNs.

4.4. *Global innovation networks?*

By comparison to other industries, notably electronics, it is evident that GINs do not (yet) characterize the automotive sector. The most important OEMs and suppliers continue to be located in a few regions in a few developed countries. They control a very hierarchical value chain, based on follow-design and follow-source, and centralize (most) R&D. Due to the nature of automotive technology, investments are often asset-specific and closely tie suppliers to system integrators and assemblers. Finally, the industry is already highly concentrated and this is likely to increase further. The general consensus in the literature is that the combined effect of these characteristics is to curtail opportunities for new-to-world innovation for Southern firms.

However, it is also evident that the industry is changing. Markets in Asia are outgrowing the automotive heartlands in the Triad economies. The design of specific new models as well as adaptations of existing models relies in part on local design and innovation centres that create demand for R&D. At the same time, two decades of production of cars for global markets by developing country producers have raised their technological capabilities. Some of these firms are sufficiently confident to acquire Northern assets to advance their upgrading yet further towards the frontier. In addition, cost pressures on the industry make it irrational to neglect stronger absorptive capacities in developing countries, including in R&D. Taken together, this does not mean that the emergence of GINs is a foregone conclusion. But it does mean that the literature is wrong to neglect or dismiss powerful economic arguments in favour of R&D offshoring and outsourcing and advance an interpretation of automotive industry dynamics based more on the past than on a consideration of possible future developments, as well as incipient instances of knowledge-intensive activities in the South that point to a gradually evolving, different landscape.

In sum, trends in the automotive industry do not all point in the same direction (see Table 2). Features that have been characterizing the industry since the early 1990s – hierarchy, knowledge architecture, and consolidation – do not on balance favour the evolution of GINs. On the other hand, cost pressures, which have been around for decades but which the global financial crisis has exacerbated, bringing a few OEMs to the brink of bankruptcy, and the eastward shift of markets both for production and for sales open up opportunities for firms in countries such as Brazil, China, and India. They can combine their advanced capabilities with market-seeking investments by OEMs to work on adaptation as well as dedicated new vehicle models. OEMs and lead suppliers, in turn, can adjust to cost pressures by exploiting high-level capabilities in R&D that firms and research institutes in these countries offer at more competitive prices.

5. Automotive FDI, competence availability, and absorptive capacity in South Africa

Cohen and Levinthal (1989, 1990) define absorptive capacity as the extent to which external knowledge can be internalized. A key factor in the allocation of knowledge-intensive activities to developing countries is the capacity of firms to absorb new technologies from the North. The characteristics of local absorptive capacity can be gauged by examining previous FDI patterns (as historical indicators of absorptive capacity) and educational output data (as indicators of the availabilities of the required competencies).

Table 2.   Characteristics of the automotive industry.

Feature	Does not favour GINs	Favours GINs
Value chain hierarchy	A few OEMs and system integrators in the North control all activity. Unique standards and specifications require asset-specific investments. OEMs insist on follow-design	
Value chain knowledge architecture	Division of labour in R&D between OEMs and lead suppliers leads to agglomerations in the North and to follow-source	Follow-source in large emerging markets involves local second-tier suppliers that can move up the hierarchy
Consolidation	Raises barriers to entry for small and developing country firms	
Cost pressures		Opens opportunities for high-level capabilities in traditionally high-cost activities from lower-cost sources in developing countries
Market size and growth		Production and sales in Brazil, China, and India are catching up on automotive heartlands. Adaptation of existing and design of new dedicated models create demand for R&D

Due to South Africa's history of unequal development, the country suffers from severe skill constraints, within which are nested pockets of higher level competencies and capabilities. Although the country spends massively on education and achieves comparatively high enrolment rates, in many indicators the education system ranks at the bottom of international league tables, especially in math and science education and the availability of scientists and engineers. Brain drain is also a problem. At the same time, the country has relatively good public research organizations, business schools, and university–industry linkages (see Appendix 2 for key indicators comparing South Africa with other developing countries and with Germany).

But these are average assessments. More important is how skill constraints affect automotive firms and how firms address them and with what effect. Historically, the skills required for the growth of South African firms and their integration into competitive GPNs have been available, through competences developed both externally and within firms. Until the early 1990s, the South African automotive industry, which included most large OEMs, was largely cut off from international competition, investment, and value chain relationships. It primarily supplied the domestic market and was not internationally competitive. Following political changes in the country in 1994, the OEMs returned to South Africa and reacquired their assets. They were attracted by market liberalization and the Motor Industry Development Plan (MIDP), an industrial policy aimed at attracting inward direct investment and featuring an import–export complementation scheme, by which component and vehicle exporters could earn credits to offset import duties (Barnes and Kaplinsky, 2000).

Just as in other developing and transition economies, component producers followed suit. Between 1997 and 2003, sourcing from domestic multinational subsidiaries increased from 26% to 37.5% of the supply base, while the use of local firms with local technologies declined from 25.8% to only 10% (Lorentzen and Barnes, 2004). Between 1997 and 2008, investments by assemblers amounted to ZAR31.2bn, of which 8% was devoted to R&D and engineering (Gastrow and Gordon, 2010). This paled in comparison to investments undertaken in Brazil, Mexico, China, Thailand, and Central Europe (Black, 2009). However, BMW, Daimler, and VW positioned their South African operations as a key element in their globalization strategies of the 3-series, the C-Class, and the Golf GTI, respectively, seeking not only greater production efficiencies but also export capabilities, and invested accordingly. Between 1995 and 2008, South Africa's production increased from 278,000 to 563,000 units, largely driven by export growth (Gastrow and Gordon, 2010).

The result of investment in plant and human capital upgrading was that the local industry significantly improved its performance to reach world-class levels (Barnes and Morris, 2008), and the performance of local subsidiaries such as the BMW plant in Roslyn occasionally exceeds that of their parent operation in Germany (Goldstein, 2003, quoting the JD Powers Gold Quality Awards, 2002). In sum, the technological and organizational performance of the industry as a whole and the capabilities of its human capital improved over the last decade and a half. In contrast to data describing national skill availability, the availability of mid- and high-level skills was largely sufficient for the industry's upgrading and growth trajectory (Black, 2009). OEMs played a major role in upgrading unskilled and semi-skilled workers as well (e.g. Lorentzen, 2007). This suggests that automotive firms had established means of creating or harnessing the skills they needed to grow technologically.

Thus, human capital in South Africa has historically been sufficient for integration into GPNs. There have also been pockets of innovation activity and R&D, usually focused on adaptation for the local market, and occasionally the design of new models for the local market. Previous research has described these activities (Gastrow, 2008; Gastrow and Gordon, 2010). It was found that assemblers and component suppliers could find sufficient skills to undertake niche R&D activities, mostly related to adaptation for the local market, and occasionally design for the local market. However, the marginal availability of local skills is small, and this was found to be a constraint on increased R&D activity at these firms.

6. Case studies

Each of our case studies represents a specific case of movement along a technological trajectory. Within this, there is a focus on specific instances of technological upgrading. Each of these reflects a strategic decision to undertake a process or product change in a specific location, and each of these strategic decisions is influenced by the availability of the requisite human capital (among other factors). *Ceteris paribus*, the closer the change is to R&D as opposed to other forms of upgrading, and the more it takes place in South Africa as opposed to Germany, the more evidence there is of a (potentially) evolving GIN.

R&D strategies of the case firms range from no to complete offshoring. The German MNEs are more or less reluctant R&D offshorers. Exhaustcomp and Tempcomp undertake very little innovation activity in South Africa. Their South African subsidiaries can be described as being at the very incipient stages of integration into a GIN that is emerging from within a GPN. Both of these case studies explore the role of human capital at this early stage of GIN development, and both also compare innovation at the South African firms to innovation centres that have been established in India by the same MNEs. Drivetraincomp undertakes small pockets of development activity for the South African market and is somewhat more evolved. This case study focuses on the role of local market adaptation in stimulating innovation in the host country.

The smaller South African firms illustrate GIN formation originating in the South. Elecsys2 undertakes its R&D in South Africa. Elecsys1 undertakes its entire R&D abroad, following the purchase of a knowledge-intensive firm based in Europe and the USA. These cases illustrate how human capital and the search for it shape the formation of GINs not just extending South from the developed world, but also extending North from the developing world.

6.1. *German MNEs with subsidiaries in South Africa*

The three German MNE case-study firms are all 'mittlestand' firms that originated in Germany in the late nineteenth century or early twentieth century and have grown to become global suppliers to the automotive sector on the back of continuous R&D. Drivetraincomp, in addition to its headquarters and operations in Germany, has an additional 180 locations in 50 countries. The group manufactures a broad range of products and is a major supplier to global OEMs. The South African subsidiary was established in the 1950s and focuses on the production of clutches and related components. This subsidiary has consistently supplied several of the OEMs with assembly operations in South Africa and also supplies the aftermarket. Exhaustcomp is also headquartered in Germany and has subsidiaries in over 20 countries. The firm produces exhaust systems and related products for OEMs across global markets. The South African subsidiary was established to supply local OEMs and also to export back to Europe to earn import complementation credits according to South Africa's automotive development policy scheme. Tempcomp provides heating and cooling systems to global OEMs. The firm has a global footprint of 9 development sites, 22 production sites, and 10 joint ventures worldwide. There are three production facilities in South Africa, supplying mostly domestic customers.

All interviews at the German-owned firms reported that skill availability in the home country is sufficient to support the core R&D functions of the firms, usually located in proximity to the headquarters. In Germany, the excellent education system and vocational training system produce large quantities of high-level skills, and moreover the recent contraction of the sector has resulted in floating skills being available in the labour market. Thus, human capital availability is not a 'push' factor for outsourcing innovation activity from Germany to other countries; rather, it is a pull factor that influences these decisions. One important push factor is the availability of the requisite skills and absorptive capacities at a lower cost; another is proximity to large final markets, where adaptation to local tastes and conditions might be a preferred strategy for growing market share. The contrasting cases of India and South Africa illustrate how differences in these pull factors lead to different outcomes in terms of the allocation of knowledge-intensive activity and the trajectories of technological upgrading.

R&D is part of Drivetraincomp's strategy since its origin in the late nineteenth century and has played a major role in establishing its global market position. The group traditionally conducts basic R&D as well as pre- and product development at its headquarters and centrally coordinates global innovation activity. This is typical of the sector in Germany. It invested in a new R&D centre in the USA in the early 2000s and more recently in China, both of these being responses to market opportunities and the need to be geographically and otherwise closer to their customers in these markets. The South African subsidiary only undertakes applied development. For example, Drivetraincomp SA designed a specific drivetrain component for a Japanese OEM. For this contract, it interacted directly, not via the parent, with the customer. Its knowledge of local road surface and load conditions allowed it to develop an adaptation of an existing component to the much tougher requirements faced by commercial vehicles in developing countries. Its technology was subsequently passed on to the Brazilian subsidiary. This example illustrates how pressures to adapt products to domestic markets create opportunities for innovation in developing countries.

These opportunities, however, can only be grasped if the required capabilities exist. Despite skill shortages at the aggregate national level, Drivetraincomp's South African subsidiary reportedly can access most of the competencies required for applied development, and over time the firm had built up development capabilities. While the average literacy and numeracy levels in the country are low, an unequal education system appears to produce sufficient high-level skills to meet the firm's engineering and innovation needs, although the interview reported that the small size of this pool acted as a constraint on the growth of knowledge-intensive activities, particularly with regard to engineering. Where skill gaps occur, local engineers make use of the group intranet to access the requisite skills from colleagues in Germany or other countries. For example, they consult with mathematicians and physicists based in Germany with regard to basic research issues, or they can consult with specialists based in Brazil if there is a particular matter of applicability to developing country conditions. Communication is horizontal and does not go through headquarters. Thus, in this case, an organizationally 'flat' GIN is nested within a deeply hierarchical global value chain.

Similarly to Drivetraincomp, Exhaustcomp's and Tempcomp's principal R&D facilities are located in Germany. This reflects high local R&D capabilities and the need for proximity to OEM customers – as indicated in the literature and as reported in the interviews. Both companies have established development centres in other countries where market size and characteristics warrant and demand adaptation of existing products. Exhaustcomp has 4 such centres and Tempcomp has 11 in different parts of the world. Both companies opened R&D facilities in Pune, India, during the last decade – a move in line with the sectoral dynamics of increased cost pressures and market shifts. These centres now undertake work that either used to be done only by their parent companies themselves or was outsourced to specialized engineering service firms in Germany. Although some of the offshored work consists of standardized tasks, in both cases, this is a departure from their previous practice to retain complex R&D tasks exclusively in Germany and entails an advancing technological trajectory among their Indian subsidiaries.

The Indian subsidiaries illustrate how MNEs respond to large developing markets with available human capital. In the South African case, a different set of conditions have rendered a contrasting set of responses. While Drivetraincomp's South African subsidiary undertakes some product development for the local market, the Exhaustcomp and Tempcomp subsidiaries conduct almost no product innovation and are limited to a narrow scope of process innovation. In both cases, the headquarters give the South African subsidiary little leeway in influencing process innovations, although local managers claim that they have the necessary capabilities. For example, the South African Exhaustcomp plant reported a reject rate of 60 to 80 parts per million, compared with about 200 in the equivalent German plant. Because of the large finished goods stock held in the logistical pipeline to their international customers, the South African subsidiary suffers far higher costs from production rejects. It thus modified its production processes to lower reject rates to below that of the German plant. In the interpretation of the South African management, the existing division of innovation labour is due to group internal hierarchies rather than a reflection of lack of capabilities on their part.

Exhaustcomp also has some product innovation capabilities. Where OEM customers request components for vehicles that are marketed exclusively in South Africa, the subsidiary is involved in product innovation for those vehicles, in partnership with the OEM and suppliers. However, it is not involved in development activities for any other products produced by the group. It thus appears that a major constraint on innovation activity at the subsidiary level is related to the firm strategy of 'reluctant outsourcing', rather than being dominated by issues of human capital availability.

In the cases of South African subsidiaries, the strategic reasons for retaining R&D in Germany (centralized control, proximity to customers, and lower co-ordination costs) outweigh the benefits of allocating R&D to the subsidiary (lower labour costs and adaptation capabilities for local markets) – with some exceptions. This leaves limited process innovation and niche areas of product innovation for local market design and adaptation in the hands of the South African subsidiaries. By contrast, the Indian market offers sufficient incentives to MNCs for them to allocate R&D activities to their subsidiaries in the country: a plentiful supply of skills and a large and growing market.

6.2. South African firms

Elecsys1 used to be a South African company that produced electronic components for OEMs, with a focus on customized engine management systems. After the market liberalization and value chain changes that took place after 1994, the firm was in danger of being substituted by a follow-source supplier – its domestic customers were re-aligning their value chains with the agreements their groups were reaching with their global suppliers. In order to retain access to the OEM market in the long term, Elecsys1 needed a development facility that was recognized for its capabilities, specifically to design the components required by the OEMs. The firm could not find the requisite domain competencies locally; in addition, since global value chain re-alignment favoured suppliers based near the headquarters of OEMs, it was imperative that the firm establish a foothold near its customers. Thus, in the mid-2000s, the firm acquired an engineering services consultancy based in Europe, previously owned by an OEM. The acquisition gave it access to one R&D centre each in the European and North American markets. Much like the purchase by Chinese firms of developed country assets such as Jaguar, MG, and parts of Volvo, the company bought assets that were technologically more advanced than its own.

This established the basis of an emerging GIN, in which knowledge began to flow between the Southern headquarters and the newly purchased Northern subsidiaries. However, this does not imply immediate technological upgrading; the division of labour remains similar, in that the developed country operations undertake R&D, while the South African operation focuses on manufacturing, using the designs originating in the subsidiaries. However, the locus of control is now in South Africa, and the developed country operations have become a tool for access to customers and product development to meet their needs. The company now supplies very advanced engine management systems for upmarket vehicles that it develops in-house. This R&D-based product innovation would not be possible without the acquisition. In combination with the advantages of flexibility that characterize the South African manufacturing operation (which is small and labour-intensive, and therefore more flexible), the enlarged firm is carving out a niche as a non-Triad first-tier supplier to global OEM customers.

Elecsys2 manufactures electronic security systems for OEMs and the aftermarket. Although it exports to global markets, the firm develops many of its products in South Africa. All R&D is conducted internally. It owns a subsidiary in Australia, where R&D is performed to adapt the firm's products to the Australian market, while the South African headquarters provide technical support and training. It does not do basic research, but undertakes applied development on the basis of high-tech components that it sources globally. For example, the firm imported breathalyzers from the UK and integrated the technology into an automotive application (an immobilizer). When the market for breathalyzers grew and the UK company was not in a position to meet the increasing quality standards and higher volumes, Elecsys2 re-engineered the product. At the assembly level, this required very little adaptation because it is essentially a standard process. Components may vary in size and so on, but operators familiar with electronics assembly can easily be trained to make a breathalyzer instead. This is a capital-intensive process that minimizes human error. Hence, changes in competencies are more relevant at the level of engineers, and it is typically they who drive the change in the first place. That is, they suggest a new application and then design the requisite process to produce it. This is essentially an engineering solution to a human capital problem: the firm struggles to find sufficient shop-floor skills, so it limits the locus of technological change to the engineering level, where it can find skills – particularly because it has a close relationship with a local university, from which it routinely recruits graduates.

6.3. *Technological upgrading, technology transfer, and R&D*

From a certain level of technological capability, most firms not only do either upgrade or innovate, but do both (Hobday et al., 2004). In some areas, they still re-engineer or adapt, while in others they already engage in new product or process design. But it is possible to distinguish between firms – or their subsidiaries – with new-to-the-world activities, and those that operate at a considerable distance from the frontier.

The South African operations of Drivetraincomp and Elecsys2 undertake knowledge-intensive activities, and Elecsys2 has significantly increased its research intensity over the past decade. Yet both companies engage essentially in applied development, recombining complex sources of knowledge to design components and systems. Neither engages in basic R&D; nor are they likely to do so in the future. Hence, their technological trajectory merely confirms the larger story of upgraded supplier competencies in the automotive industries of developing countries over the past two decades. Neither firm faces insurmountable skill constraints, and both have developed a variety of strategies to deal with these constraints.

For example, faced with low skill levels on the shop floor, when Elecsys2 develops a new product, the primary skill requirement is at the engineering level. At the assembly level, new products require very little adaptation because the electronic components they produce essentially employ a standard, capital-intensive assembly process that minimizes human error as much as possible. Hence, skill is less important at the shop-floor level and more important at the engineering level, where the firm manages to find adequate skills.

Another example is the development by Drivetraincomp of a clutch for a major Japanese assembler. The primary purpose of this development was to modify the existing design to cope with the rougher and more varied driving conditions in South Africa; in addition, the South African designed product was also produced by the group's subsidiary in Brazil. In this instance, Drivetraincomp had access to the necessary skills to develop the product and successfully bring it to market in South Africa. This access was secured through a variety of means: contact with the local university, attendance at internal group technical conferences, participation in internalized knowledge networks, and active recruitment of senior management and engineering staff.

By contrast, Elecsys1 and the two other German MNEs engage in activities that are qualitatively different from merely reaching world quality standards. Human capital influences these strategies in opposite ways. In the case of Elecsys1, R&D offshoring to Europe is the result of the local absence of the requisite capabilities. In the case of Tempcomp and Exhaustcomp, R&D offshoring to India is manifestly not the local absence of such capabilities in Germany, but their presence abroad at a much more competitive price. In both cases, human capital thus acts as a pull factor. In the South African subsidiaries of the German firms, pockets of limited process innovation and niche opportunities for product adaptation for the local market need to be supported by sufficient skills. These skills can be accessed through similar means to Drivetraincomp. However, these is not much room for manoeuvre: current skill availability is sufficient for current needs, but not sufficient to support substantially larger-scale or more advanced R&D – so skill supply is not an operational constraint, but is a constraint on the firms' technological trajectories and participation in GINs.

6.4. *The management of tacit knowledge*

R&D offshoring presupposes the existence of advanced capabilities in the destination country. But in an industry in which tacit knowledge plays a major role in technological progress, the existence of highly qualified engineers and scientists is not sufficient – what also needs to happen is the management of this knowledge across large distances, time zones, languages, and cultural divides.

While cultural divides were not reported to be a major concern in the German MNEs' South African operations, interviews in Germany and South Africa reported that the Indian subsidiaries, including the new R&D centres, faced significant challenges in these areas. In response, the German firms use cross-cultural communication and the migration of knowledge workers to address this problem. When Exhaustcomp opened an R&D facility in India, the manager was appointed in India and then transferred to the headquarters in Germany, where he remained for over a year. There his experience and training included the absorption of tacit knowledge by collaborating in different departments and getting to know the 'mindsets' of the researchers at the headquarters. In India, he had to reconcile this experience with local processes. He therefore acts as a knowledge bridge between India and Germany. This organization of learning is used across the group. At the headquarters, there are engineers from several countries where the firm is present, some undergoing training before they return to their home countries, others permanently appointed in Germany to be the contact point for the related subsidiary abroad.

Tempcomp faced similar challenges of knowledge transfer between Germany and India and in response commissioned a knowledge management expert from within the company to investigate possible responses. This formed part of an 'action-oriented' PhD project. Their aim was to improve opportunities to relocate design tasks from the German R&D centre to the Indian centre through means of knowledge management, including information technology, the organization of activities, the content of communication, and interpersonal communication. Their findings suggested five main sets of measures. First, one of the main problem areas was identified as intercultural communication. A training course on intercultural communication for German and Indian engineers, hosted by a Tempcomp employee with cultural ties to both countries, was developed and undertaken in both Germany and India. Second was an attempt to codify the tacit knowledge held in Germany for the benefit of Indian staff. This included IT-based guidelines, checklists, and procedure manuals informed by experiences in technical problem-solving. Third, to improve the familiarity of Indian engineers with Tempcomp's products and value chain, the firm established short-term assignments of Indians to Germany and visiting programmes to suppliers and production plants. Fourth, further organizational rules were implemented in India to overcome internal hierarchical communication barriers. Lastly, the firm implemented a gatekeeper model, transferring three Indian engineers to the German headquarters and having three Germans/Americans at the Indian location to capture the tasks, inform their colleagues (in India), and check the quality of the deliverable.

7. Conclusion

The case studies described above show that the offshoring of knowledge-intensive activities is beginning to appear in an industry that is known more than others for centralizing most such activity close to headquarter locations and always in developed economies. It is also evident that this phenomenon is not just based on Northern MNEs taking advantage of advanced capabilities in developing countries. Firms from the South, too, *in*shore the relevant knowledge through acquisitions of strategic assets in the North. As a result, GINs may evolve (see Figure 1).

The experience of the firms makes it clear that strategic intent and a stock of local capabilities are not sufficient conditions for the emergence of GINs. The tacit character of relevant knowledge in the industry, combined with different work practices that, in turn, are influenced by the respective cultural environment, necessitates dedicated knowledge management in the context of cross-cultural communication. The difficulties of such communication are related to the distance, cultural and otherwise, of firms from different backgrounds.

The management of knowledge transfer is key because owning a knowledge asset is not equivalent to know-why, much like joint ventures do not guarantee knowledge transfer from

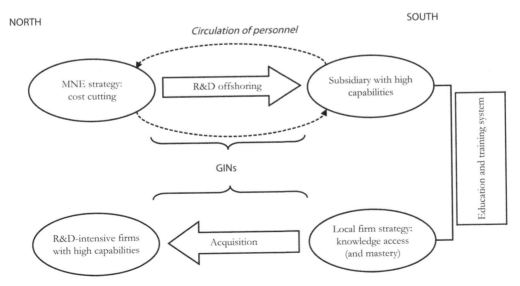

Figure 1. GINs in the automotive sector.

the senior to the junior partner, as hoped for in policies incentivizing equity partnerships between foreign and local firms (Sadoi, 2008). For example, although Elecsys1 now owns advanced engineering capabilities, it has not yet internalized these competencies. Doing so takes time, and in this industry it is likely to require more time than in others where knowledge is more codified. The same applies to the Chinese and Indian OEMs that have acquired European or US carmakers.

The education and skill system obviously influences average capabilities and is thus an important indicator of the attractiveness of a region or a country for knowledge-intensive investments. But the more relevant finding is that firms in economies with severe human capital constraints can find solutions to overcome these constraints. Most commonly these are aimed at increasing the supply of skills or at increasing access to knowledge sources – examples include recruiting graduates from universities, collaborating with universities, internal training programmes, internal staff circulation within the group, online internalized knowledge networks, and collaboration with suppliers and customers. Sometimes, the solution is at the engineering level: skill shortages at the lower and medium levels can be overcome by exploiting high-level capabilities while adjusting to lower-level skill constraints through dedicated process engineering.

Acknowledgements

This research was partially funded by the European Community's Seventh Framework Programme (Project INGINEUS, Grant Agreement No. 225368, www.ingineus.eu). The authors are responsible for its contents, which do not necessarily reflect the views or opinions of the European Commission; nor is the European Commission responsible for any use that might be made of the information appearing herein. The authors are grateful to Luke Muller for research assistance, Fabian Arends and Joan Roodt for background inputs on South Africa's education and skill system as well as on FDI in the country, Eike Schamp and Andreas Stamm for undertaking the German case studies, and Glenda Kruss for mentorship, encouragement, and commenting on the final draft.

References

Archibugi, D., and Iammarino, S. (2002) The globalization of technological innovation: Definition and evidence. *Review of International Political Economy*, 9, pp. 98–122.

Barnes, J., and Kaplinsky, R. (2000) Globalisation and the death of the local firm? The automobile components sector in South Africa. *Regional Studies*, 34, pp. 797–812.

Barnes, J., and Morris, M. (2008) Staying alive in the global automotive industry: What can developing economies learn from South Africa about linking into global automotive value chains? *The European Journal of Development Research*, 20, pp. 31–55.

Becker, H. (2006) *High Noon in the Automotive Industry* (Berlin: Springer).

Birchall, D.W., Tovstiga, G., and Chanaron, J.J. (2001) Capabilities in strategic knowledge sourcing and assimilation: A new look at innovation in the automotive industry. *International Journal of Automotive Technology and Management*, 1, pp. 78–91.

Black, A. (2009) Location, automotive policy, and multinational strategy: The position of South Africa in the global industry since 1995. *Growth and Change*, 40, pp. 483–512.

Borensztein, E., De Gregorio, J., and Lee, J.W. (1998) How does foreign direct investment affect economic growth? *Journal of International Economics*, 45, pp. 115–135.

Brandt, L., and Van Biesebroeck, J. (2008) *Working Report for Industry Canada: Capability building in China's auto supply chains* (Ottowa: Industry Canada).

Carrillo, J. (2004) Transnational strategies and regional development: The case of GM and Delphi in Mexico. *Industry and Innovation*, 11, pp. 127–153.

Chanaron, J.J., and Rennard, J.P. (2007) The automotive industry: A challenge to Schumpeter's innovation theory, in: E. Carayannis and C. Ziemnowicz (eds) *Re-discovering Schumpeter: Creative destruction Evolving into 'mode 3'*, pp. 320–343 (New York: Sage).

Chang, S.J. (2008) *Sony vs. Samsung* (Hoboken: John Wiley and Sons).

Chuang, Y. (2000) Human capital, exports, and economic growth: A causality analysis for Taiwan, 1952–1995. *Review of International Economics*, 8, pp. 712–720.

Cohen, W.M., and Levinthal, D.A. (1989) Innovation and learning: The two faces of R&D. *Economic Journal*, 99, pp. 569–596.

Cohen, W.M., and Levinthal, D.A. (1990) Absorptive capacity: A new perspective on learning and innovation. *Administrative Science Quarterly*, 35, pp. 128–152.

Dehoff, K., and Jaruzelski, B. (2009) Beyond borders: The global innovation 1000, report for Booz and Company. *Strategy+Business Magazine*, 53, pp. 53–67.

Dilk, C., Gleich, R., and Wald, A. (2006) State and development of innovation networks: Evidence from the European vehicle sector. *Management Decision*, 46, pp. 691–701.

Dunning, J. (1993) *Multinational Enterprises and the Global Economy* (New York: Addison-Wesley).

Dutrénit, G. (2004) Building technological capabilities in latecomer firms: A review essay. *Science Technology & Society*, 9, pp. 209–41.

Gastrow, M. (2008) An overview of research and development activities in the South African automotive industry. *Journal of New Generation Sciences*, 6, pp. 1–15.

Gastrow, M. and Gordon, A. (2010) Technological evolution in the South African and Argentine automotive manufacturing sectors: policy responses and results. Presentation at the 8th conference of the Global Network for Economics of Learning, Innovation, and Competence Building Systems, Kuala Lumpur, 1–3 November 2010.

Gereffi, G. (2005) The global economy: Organisation, governance and development, in: S. Smelser and R. Swedberg (eds) *Handbook of Economic Sociology*, pp. 160–182 (Princeton, NJ: Princeton University Press and Russel Sage Foundation).

Goldstein, A.E. (2003) Regional integration, FDI, and the competitiveness of SADC. Paper prepared for the OECD African Investment Roundtable (downloaded on 15 May 2011 from http://www.oecd.org/dataoecd/11/48/18595394.pdf)

Grossman, G.M., and Helpman, E. (1991) *Innovation and Growth in the Global Economy* (Cambidge, Massachusetts: MIT Press).

Hobday, M., Rush, H., and Bessant, J. (2004) Approaching the innovation frontier in Korea: The transition phase to leadership. *Research Policy*, 33, pp. 1433–1457.

Humphrey, J., and Memedovic, O. (2003) , The global automotive industry value chain: What prospects for upgrading by developing countries? UNIDO Sectoral Studies Series paper, Vienna.

Humphrey, J., Mukherjee, A., Zilbovicius, M., and Arbix, G. (1998) Globalization, foreign direct investment and the restructuring of supplier neworks: The motor industry in Brazil and India, in: M. Kagami (ed.) *Learning, Liberalization and Economic Adjustment*, pp. 117--189 (Tokyo: Institute of Developing Economies).

Ivarsson, I., and Alvstam, C.G. (2005) Technology transfer from TNCs to local suppliers in developing countries: A study of AB Volvo's truck and bus plants in Brazil, China, India, and Mexico. *World Development*, 33, pp. 1325–1344.

Jung, M., and Lee, K. (2010) Sectoral systems of innovation and productivity catch-up: Determinants of the productivity gap between Korean and Japanese firms. *Industrial and Corporate Change*, 19, pp. 1037–1069.

Kim, L. (1997) *Immitation to Innovation: The dynamics of Korea's technological learning* (Cambridge, Massachusetts: Harvard Business School Press).

Lall, S., 2001. *Competitiveness, Technology and Skills*. (Cheltenham: Edward Elgar).

Lall, S., and Narula, R. (2004) Foreign direct investment and its role in economic development: Do we need a new agenda? *The European Journal of Development Research*, 16, pp. 447–464.

Lorentzen, J. (2007) MNCs in the periphery: DaimlerChrysler South Africa (DCSA), human capital upgrading and regional economic development, in: G.R.G. Benito and R. Narula (eds) *Multinationals on the Periphery*, pp. 158–187 (New York: Palgrave Macmillan).

Lorentzen, J. (2009) Learning and innovation: What's different in the (sub)tropics and how do we explain it? A review essay. *Science, Technology & Society*, 14, pp. 177–205.

Lorentzen, J., and Barnes, J. (2004) Learning, upgrading, and innovation in the South African automotive industry. *European Journal of Development Research*, 16, pp. 465–498.

Lorentzen, J., Møellgaard, P., and Rojec, M. (2003) Host-country absorption of technology: Evidence from automotive supply networks in Eastern Europe. *Industry and Innovation*, 10, pp. 415–432.

Maxton, G.P., and Womald, J. (2004) *Time for a Model Change. Re-engineering the global automotive industry* (Cambridge: Cambridge University Press).

Moran, T.H. (1998) *Foreign Direct Investment and Development* (Washington, DC: Institute for International Economics).

Nam, K. (2010) Learning through the international joint venture: Lessons from the experience of china's automotive sector. Presentation at the 8th conference of the Global Network for Economics of Learning, Innovation, and Competence Building Systems, Kuala Lumpur, 1–3 November 2010.

Noorbakhsh, F., Paloni, A., and Youssef, A. (2001) Human capital and FDI inflows to developing countries: New empirical evidence. *World Development*, 29, pp. 1593–1610.

OECD (2007) *The Internationalisation of Business R&D: Evidence, impacts and implications* (Paris: OECD).

Osterman, D. and Neal, B. (2009) The global automotive industry crisis: A way ahead. *An IMVP position paper*. IMVP, MIT, Cambridge, Massachusetts.

Rutherford, T., and Holmes, J. (2008) The flea on the tail of the dog': Power in global production networks and the restructuring of Canadian automotive clusters. *Journal of Economic Geography*, 8, pp. 519–544.

Sadoi, Y. (2008) Technology transfer in automotive parts firms in China. *Asia Pacific Business Review*, 14, pp. 147–163.

Sturgeon, T. and Van Biesebroeck, J. (2010) Effects of the crisis on the automotive industry in developing countries: A global value chain perspective. *Policy Research Working Paper 5330*. World Bank, Washington, DC.

Sturgeon, T.J., Memedovic, O., Van Biesebroeck, J., and Gereffi, G. (2009) Globalisation of the automotive industry: Main features and trends. *International Journal of Technological Learning, Innovation and Development*, 2, pp. 7–24.

Tan, H.W., and Batra, G. (1995) *Enterprise Training in Developing Countries: Incidence, productivity effects and policy implications* (Washington, DC: World Bank).

UNCTAD. (2005) World Investment Report, UNCTAD, Geneva.

UNESCO. (2010a) United Nations Educational, Scientific, and Cultural Organization Institute for Statistics Data Centre [online], available at: http://stats.uis.unesco.org/unesco/TableViewer/document.aspx? ReportId=143andIF_Language=eng (5 December 2010).

UNESCO. (2010b) United Nations Educational, Scientific, and Cultural Organization Science Report 2010 [online], available at: http://www.unesco.org/new/en/natural-sciences/science-technology/prospective-studies/unesco-science-report/ (5 January 2010).

Van Tunzelmann, N. (2009) Competencies verses capabilities: A reassesssment. *Economia Politicia*, 26, pp. 435–464.

te Velde, D.W. (2005) Globalisation and education: What do the trade, investment and migration literatures tell us? *Working Paper 254*. Overseas Development Institute, London.

te Velde, D.W., and Xenogiani, T. (2007) Foreign direct investment and international skill inequality. *Oxford Development Studies*, 35, pp. 83–104.

Wad, P. (2010) Impact of the global economic and financial crisis over the automotive industry in developing countries, *United Nations Industrial Development Organisation (UNIDO) Working Paper 16/2009*. Vienna.

Wooldridge, A. (2010) The world turned upside down – special report on innovation in emerging markets, The Economist, *Special report*, 17 April 2010.

World Bank. (2010) Data [online], available at: http://data.worldbank.org/ (4 December 2010).

Appendix 1. Response rates and total sample distribution by sector, country, and firm size.

Sector/ county	Data set	Responses	Response rate (%)	Percentage of over total sector observations	R&D-active firms	Percentage of R&D-active firms over national sample
China[a]	9119	243	2.7	26	181	74.5
Estonia	121	17	14	1.8	2	11.8
Norway	519	179	34.5	19.1	53	29.6
India[b]	1287	324	25.2	34.7	195	60.2
Sweden	1662	171	10.3	18.3	76	44.4
Total EU	2302	367	15.9	39.3	131	35.7
Total emerging	10,407	567	5.4	60.7	376	66.3
Total ICT	**12,709**	**935**	**7.3**	**100**	**507**	54.2
Denmark	210	49	23.3	37.1	5	10.2
Norway	2	2	–	1.5	0	–
South Africa	325	81	24.9	61.4	27	33.3
Total EU	212	**51**	24	38.6	5	9.8
Total emerging	325	81	24.9	61.4	**81**	24.9
Total Agro	**535**	**132**	19.6	100	32	24.2
Brazil[c]	241	69	28.6	46.6	17	24.6
Germany	963	53	5.5	35.8	31	58.5
South Africa	2	2	–	1.4	0	–
Sweden	168	24	14.3	16.2	13	54.2
Total EU	1131	77	6.8	52	44	57.1
Total emerging	243	71	29.2	48	17	23.9
Total Auto	**1374**	**148**	10.8	100	61	41.2
TOTAL EU	3645	495	13.6		180	36.4
TOTAL	10,975	719	6.6		420	58.4
TOTAL	14,620	**1214**	8.3		600	

[a]The Chinese sample was extracted from two regional databases: (i) the *Beijing database* and (ii) the *Schenzhen database*. The questionnaire was distributed in the five most developed provinces in China: 146 questionnaires came from Beijing, which account for 60% of the total questionnaires; 51 came from the Guangdong province, which account for 21%; 35 from Shanghai, 14%; 10 from the Zhejiang province, representing the 4%; and only 1 from the Shandong province.

[b]The Indian sample was extracted from the *NASSCOM Directory of IT firms 2009–2010*, distributed across the main cities and regions as follows: 281 in Bangalore, which account for 21.8% of NASSCOM Directory; 256 in Delhi/Noida/Gurgaon representing the 19.9%; 185 in Mumbai(14.4%); 72 in Pune (5.6%); 147 in Chennai (11.4%); 184 in Trivandrum (14.3%); 107 in Hyderabad (8.3%); and 55 in Kochi (4.3%).

[c]The Brazilian sample was extracted from the *Annual Registry of Social Information (RAIS)*, a registry of social and balance sheet information collected by the Brazilian Labour and Employment Ministry. The total number of firms classified in the automotive sector in Brazil is 2625. Of these, 233 companies are located in the state of Minas Gerais and, of these, 107 (46%) have employed, in 2008, 30 workers or more. From the data set, all automotive firms from the state of Minas Gerais were selected, provided the firms declared over 30 employees.

Appendix 2

Indicator	SA	Brazil	India	China	Germany	Source
Public sector education expenditure as percentage of GDP (1999)	6.03	3.88	4.47	1.91	n/a	(a)
Public sector education expenditure as percentage of GDP (2007)	5.34	5.21	3.18[a]	3.22[b]	n/a	(a)
Public sector education expenditure per capita (2007) USD	316.86	374.27	27.21[a]	231.35[b]	n/a	(a)
Gross tertiary enrolment as a percentage of the total 18–24 age cohort (2000)	12.9[c]	16	10	7.8	n/a	(b)
Gross tertiary enrolment as a percentage of the total 18–24 age cohort (2007)	16.2[c]	30.01	13	22.05	n/a	(b)
Brain drain ranking[d]A19	62	39	34	37	31	(c)
Quality of educational system[e]	130	103	39	53	18	(c)
Quality of math and science education[e]	137	126	38	33	39	(c)
Availability of scientists and engineers[e]	116	68	15	35	27	(c)
Quality of management schools[e]	21	73	23	63	31	(c)
Quality of scientific research institutions[e]	29	42	30	17	6	(c)
Internet access in schools[e]	100	72	70	22	39	(c)
Extent of staff training[e]	26	53	59	57	8	(c)
University–industry linkages[e]	24	34	58	25	9	(c)
Local availability of R&D services[e]	49	36	51	50	2	(c)
Top 200 ranked universities	1	0	1	9	10	(d)
Percentage of tertiary graduates in science fields (2008)	4	6.77	n/a	n/a	13	(e)
Percentage of labour force with a tertiary education	13	8.6[c]	n/a	7[f]	24	(e)
Thompson Reuters' Science Citation Index publications percentage change (2002–2008)	48.3	110.6	91.7	174.7	24.1[g]	(f)
Patent output 2007 per million of population	1.86	0.65	0.64	118.02	9713	(g)

Sources: a = World Bank (2010); UNESCO (2010a), b = World Bank (2010); # Department of Education, 2007, c = WEF Global Competitiveness Report 2010–2011, d = QS World University Rankings 2010, e = UNESCO 2010a, f = UNESCO 2010b, g = UNESCO Science Report 2010.

[a] 2006.
[b] Source: People's Daily 2009.
[c] 2006.
[d] A lower ranking indicates greater brain drain.
[e] WEF rankings out of 139 countries.
[f] http://english.peopledaily.com.cn/
[g] EU total.

New trends in an old sector: exploring global knowledge and HR management in MNCs and the North–South divide in human capital formation

Eike W. Schamp[a,b] and Andreas Stamm[b]

[a]*Institute for Human Geography, Goethe University, Frankfurt, Germany;* [b]*German Development Institute, Bonn, Germany*

Multinational Companies (MNCs) from the global North still are major players in globalization. In response to increased competition based on knowledge and innovation, MNCs are currently trying to implement new forms in 'transnational' knowledge and human resource (HR) management which are appropriate to the company's knowledge base. The paper focuses on the specifics of a synthetic knowledge base in the automobile sector, and presents an explorative analysis of new tools in global knowledge and HR management, using the example of three German companies. These tools refer both to skill enhancing on the shop floor and improvements in global knowledge sharing among engineers in R&D. The paper concludes by discussing the interplay of MNC management and national education and training policies in the shaping of globalization.

1. Introduction

It is now widely acknowledged that globalization as we knew it has changed. MNCs from the global North, in particular in the manufacturing sector, have long since learnt how to organize globally divided production, although they still struggle with the diversity of human resources available. Increasing global competition and the turn to the 'knowledge society' have recently brought knowledge and skills, i.e. 'human capital', to the fore as major resources for MNCs in the global game. New challenges for human resource (HR) management in MNCs arise from two directions. Firstly, the quality of the labour force at many subsidiaries in emerging economies has to be improved substantially when MNCs wish to relocate more or less sophisticated production abroad; with the dual aims of gaining access to lower production costs and regional markets. In terms of skills and knowledge available, it seems that the world is full of 'blind spots' where the labour force has to be repeatedly trained and qualified. Secondly, MNCs can increasingly tap into newly emerging 'hot spots' where knowledge and highly educated 'talent' seem to be available at lower costs for knowledge-based activities such as R&D. Here, MNCs face even more diversity in the 'cultural' dimensions of human resources which may render efficient communication between talent at different locations difficult, thus impeding an efficient globally divided labour force. As a result, MNCs are driven to develop new approaches at the interfaces of global HR management and global knowledge management in order to overcome these barriers. This paper wishes to shed some exploratory light on recently established tools in global HR management in a manufacturing sector which is characterized both by skill and R&D intensity, i.e. mechanical engineering, and more precisely, sections of the automotive industry. We argue that the particular context of origin of the MNC and its sector-specific knowledge base have to be considered when companies introduce new tools in global HR management.

The paper is structured as follows. We first discuss the conceptual framework of our study which we see at the borders of different strands in scientific debate. We then introduce the particular context of the country of origin of our case companies, i.e. the German automotive production system, discuss in brief the specifics of the synthetic knowledge base in the sector and present the case study companies. The main part of the paper is devoted to new practices which have been introduced recently in global knowledge management in the companies studied. These relate to two functional levels of the company which are essential to the MNC's competitiveness. The first level involves improving the subsidiary's capability for producing innovative products which are new to the host country; this is a crucial task to ensure the MNC's flexibility in production and (regional) market access, particularly with a view to markets in emerging economies, where the MNC is attempting to establish a level playing field for quality production 'worldwide'. The second level is where MNCs expand their capabilities and reduce labour costs in R&D by offshoring some of their R&D to so-called hot spots (Manning et al., 2010) where they can find qualified engineers in sufficient numbers. A major challenge in the organization of divided labour in knowledge-intensive activities such as engineering is the governance of knowledge sharing and of communication in communities of practice. This improves the MNCs' capabilities to innovate 'new to the world'. We conclude with a broader discussion of how these processes relate to the current state of globalization and to past and present education and training policies in emerging economies. This includes a look at policy requirements for reducing the 'blindness' of places in terms of the knowledge base for global production.

2. Conceptual framework

This paper focuses on organizational shifts and changing routines within the multi-locational system of the MNC. We claim that organizational shifts become effective only if innovation occurs in management practices, i.e. in routines governing shared activities internal to the MNC. As such, it is embedded in the abundant literature on the theory of the firm, recent issues in the resource-based perspective of the firm, and more specifically on the internationalization strategies of the MNC aiming at strengthening the capabilities to manage an increasing diversity of tasks that have been offshored to developing countries and emerging economies. While much attention has recently been paid to the offshoring of R&D in the MNC, mostly in terms of 'who has relocated what, where and why' (Demirbag and Glaister, 2010; Ambos and Ambos, 2011; Moncada-Paternò-Castello et al., 2011), developing skills at the production sites have not yet been discussed much. The internationalization of R&D is, of course, an important fact that changes the organizational and locational structure of the MNC. However, we do not wish to discuss the establishment of new kinds of sites in different functions of the company here. We concentrate instead on changes of routines within the MNC. In particular, we examine new practices internal to the MNC designed to improve skills and knowledge at subsidiaries which are not located in highly developed 'industrial' nations. Obviously, there is a certain overlap of knowledge management and HR management, as knowledge is embedded in human beings. In our analysis, we draw on different strands in organizational theory, knowledge and innovation theory, and HR theory.

Most recent issues in *organizational research* have revealed the difficulty of managing an increasing global division of labour in knowledge-intensive activities, caused by the accelerated relocation of quality production to emerging economies and the offshoring of some R&D activities. For example, Lema et al. (2012, p. 11) recently observed that 'over the last decade a fundamental change has occurred in the way innovation is organised', and they investigated the 'organizational decomposition of the innovation process' (ODIP) in two sectors – automotive and software – and two countries – Brazil and India. Based on a global value chain perspective, the authors develop four types of ODIP, two of which are important for our purpose as they consider organizational decomposition internal to the MNC. The authors highlight the strong connection between production and innovation activities, which is our motivation to look at both functions in our paper. The production of sophisticated products which have emerged from a synthetic mode of knowledge creation often requires a highly skilled and experienced labour force. The new forms of organizational decomposition in knowledge-based activities call for new practices in 'interface management', e.g. in global engineering networks (Manning et al., 2009).

In their recent literature review on 'governing knowledge sharing in organizations', Foss et al. (2010, p. 456) state that '"knowledge governance" has recently become a distinct issue in management and organization [but the] concept [..] has not yet been well explored and understood'. They claim that 'the relationship between governance issues and knowledge processes remains under-researched'. While the authors draw on different perspectives at the macro-level (the organization) and the micro-level (the individual and his/her behaviour), we wish to emphasize the importance of introducing management practices, or in the words of Nelson and Winter (1982) new routines, in global knowledge management.

In the realm of *knowledge and innovation theory*, several recent strands are relevant. Economic geographers have observed the changing spatial patterns of innovation on a global scale for more than a decade. More recently, a new concept for the typology of knowledge bases has been suggested. These have a different spatiality at the global scale and are characterized by different forms of governance internal and external to the company. Asheim et al. (2007) suggested three types of knowledge base, i.e. the science-based 'analytical' knowledge base, the experience-based 'synthetic' knowledge base, and the creativity-based 'symbolic' knowledge base. Although this has elements of an ideal typology, knowledge bases are generally assigned to a particular sector (see also Malerba and Nelson, 2011, p. 1651), e.g. the analytical knowledge base to biotechnology (Moodysson et al., 2008), the synthetic knowledge base to engineering, or the symbolic knowledge base to the media, advertising, architecture, etc. Only a few empirical studies have been published, mostly on the analytical knowledge base. We wish to use the concept of the synthetic knowledge base for our empirical study of the automotive sector. The skills of a qualified labour force and the experience of qualified engineers play a crucial role in knowledge management in the automotive industry, as most knowledge creation in the automotive sector is experiential (Dankbaar, 2007). Recent management literature has identified the automotive sector as 'pioneers in relocating [..] engineering and design work across globally distributed locations' (Manning et al., 2009, p. 9). However, there is a strong component of 'tacit' knowledge in the sector, which is not easy to transmit and is therefore often assessed as 'local'. This type of tacit knowledge is found in both skilled production and creative engineering. The knowledge of engineers in product development in the automotive sector is based on specific, professionally shared visions and experience. It is mainly oriented towards combining existing knowledge in a new way, it is cross-disciplinary, and is based on interactive learning, often with customers (Asheim et al., 2010). A crucial point in shared understanding among engineers applies to the interface between different modules which are assembled in the final stage of production. Unlike other sectors such as electronics, interfaces in the automotive industry are not precisely defined and are certainly not standardized. As a result, personal communication between engineers is very important.

Transfer of tacit knowledge refers to both 'the moment of innovation' and the 'distribution of innovation' (Gertler, 2003, p. 83), meaning that in engineers' communities of practice, the transfer and exchange of tacit knowledge matters in product development as well as in the execution of skilled activities on the shop floor. Tallmann and Chacar (2010) emphasize informal networking as a major management tool for the transfer of tacit knowledge in communities of practice of the MNC. Their focus is mostly on proximity in co-location in the transfer of tacit knowledge and they propose 'managerial intervention [..] to develop such activities across isolated units of the MNC' (p. 295). In this paper, however, we wish to explore explicitly new formal practices in enabling the transfer of tacit knowledge to subsidiaries in emerging economies.

Knowledge at both levels of activities resists easy internationalization, as tacit knowledge is embodied in individuals and, according to the early research of Nonaka (1994) and others on knowledge transfer mechanisms, often can only be transmitted by personal face-to-face communication, i. e. through 'socialization'. How can this be managed by the company when internationalization crosses huge cultural boundaries? Although similar questions have been of interest for a long time, at least on the shop floor – since MNCs relocated production to developing countries – they have recently become a new and more pronounced issue in *HR theory* with the growing internationalization of knowledge-based activities. However, it seems, as in the case global knowledge management, that the global perspective in HR management is new to academics and companies (Brewster and Suutari, 2005; Festing and Eidems, 2011). Brewster and Suutari (2005, p. 5) see 'three major challenges concerning global human resource management (HRM): getting the right skills to where they are needed easily, spreading up-to-date knowledge and practices throughout the organisation [and] identifying and developing talent on a global basis'.

In our exploratory study, 'upgrading' of production abroad refers to the first two of these challenges while the offshoring of engineering services to R&D encompasses all three of them. In focusing on new practices which facilitate knowledge transfer in the global MNC, we wish to explore what Minbaeva (2005, p. 126) called a novelty (to HR literature), i.e. 'bringing together two fields, which have not met very often: knowledge and HRM'. In this author's view, (HR) literature has for a long time overlooked the fact that MNCs have the capability to innovate in global knowledge transfer practices. In this way, they augment the absorptive capacity of subsidiaries and, as a result, upgrade subsidiaries abroad for quality production and the adoption of new functions such as R&D services. While Minbaeva discusses a diversity of dimensions of the HR system within the company, we wish to concentrate on what has been recently called 'competence management' on the part of the companies studied.

It goes without saying that knowledge and its governance and management are highly context-specific. The paper has a broader *geographical perspective*, finally, where the interplay of places (such as cluster regions, nations) and spaces (of MNCs) provides further explanation of current globalization. According to the literature on internationalization, the nation state – whether it is configured as nationally variegated capitalism (Hall and Soskice, 2001), a national business system (Whitley, 2000), or a national innovation system (Lundvall, 2007) – has a considerable impact on the firm's organization and practice of internationalization. We chose the context of a specific home country of MNCs, Germany, and a specific sector, the automotive industry or, more precisely, the first-tier component suppliers to automobile producers. With the recently increasing competition for innovative products in emerging economies such as Brazil, China, or India, companies are squeezed to improve the capabilities of their local production sites and to use some 'lower edge' R&D activities abroad. Recent attempts to improve skills through standardization in training and to integrate local 'talent' in engineering, particularly in newly established engineering service centres, caused a major challenge to global knowledge management in this sector where a synthetic knowledge base and the transfer of tacit knowledge dominate.

MNCs nowadays realize that a rapidly changing environment, particularly in skills and knowledge, is available in the global South. While skilled and educated human capital has long been considered a major factor for the economic development of nations, it has become paramount for MNCs with the emergence of the global knowledge society. Malerba and Nelson (2011) recently pointed out that skilled human capital needs to be sector-specific to contribute to development. Some countries have invested heavily in tertiary education, giving rise to a huge amount of well-educated 'talent'. This is particularly true for large emerging economies such as Brazil, China, and India. Moreover, re-migration of 'experts' from the USA to these economies has tremendously increased the availability of talent, as highlighted by Saxenian's term 'New Argonauts' (2006). Some countries have also invested in primary education and vocational training, increasing the skills of their labour force. As a result, MNCs are pushed to introduce new management practices to make use of these new opportunities and to develop human capital abroad. Their strategies prove to be geographically generic with regard to the improvement of 'blind spots' but are highly selective in choosing talent and 'hot spots'.

3.   The German automotive production system as a hub for internationalization

Germany is well known as the leader in European automobile production and one of the largest exporters in the world, mainly in premium cars. It is currently also the fourth largest producer of commercial vehicles (as of 9 March 2011, see VDA, 2011). Powerful original equipment manufacturers (OEMs) lead in the segments of premium cars (three), volume production (three), and commercial vehicles (two). These OEMs are the very demanding customers of the automotive supplier industries, pushing them towards learning and innovation and follow-the-client investments in internationalization. The German automotive companies have become powerful multi-nationals in recent decades, in particular during the 1990s (e.g. Ambos, 2005). In the short period from 1995 to 1998, the automotive sector's share in German FDI in manufacturing rose from 18% of total investment to nearly 30%. Since then, this figure has been fairly constant (Legler et al., 2009, p. 86f.). Between 2005 and 2008, foreign direct and indirect investment by the German automotive industry fluctuated around €100 billion, with the bulk concentrated in Europe and the USA, and increasing investment only in Brazil, China, and India.

The industry has become the most important driver of innovation in Germany, in terms of sectoral R&D expenditures. Most R&D in the automotive industry is intramural but extramural R&D grew from 15.3% in 1995 to 25.8% in 2001 (Legler et al., 2009, p. 90; VDA, 2010, p. 23). Most of this is still domestic, as the automotive sector seems to be slower in internationalizing than other segments of the manufacturing industry R&D (Belitz, 2010, p. 7). There is ample theoretical and empirical evidence for the specific hierarchical governance of the automotive value chain both in Germany and worldwide (Sturgeon et al., 2008). The sector is often seen as a 'pyramid' of powerful car assemblers (OEMs), a limited number of first-tier systems and second-tier components suppliers, and a host of third-tier suppliers. Governance of the pyramid differs, however, according to the type of capitalism practised. Thus, German OEMs, particularly those in the premium segment, most often maintain long-term relationships as 'partners' to their principal system and components suppliers in model development and purchasing, based on trust and long-term collaboration. This is rather different from the governance patterns in Japanese or US-American automotive value chains (Sturgeon et al., 2008, p. 308f.).

Recent research on the organization of R&D and innovation in the industry has revealed a similar hierarchical situation in innovation activities (Schamp et al., 2004). OEMs and first-tier suppliers still carry out most of their R&D at home. Here, the companies are embedded in a specific domestic social organization of production and innovation. In the German system of coordinated market capitalism (Hall and Soskice, 2001), companies benefit from an institutional environment with a highly qualified domestic labour force based on the combination of the dual system of vocational education and training (VET) and a host of technical universities and universities of applied sciences, co-management strategies of the powerful trade unions, and a sophisticated R&D landscape. Based on an in-depth analysis of companies' strategic behaviour, Kinkel and Zanker (2007) have characterized the majority of German MNCs in the automotive sector as 'home-based players'. These companies form part of a fairly hierarchically governed automotive value chain and they also prefer quite hierarchical forms of internal governance.

4. Methodology and data

As far as we are aware, only a small number of publications deal with the interweaving of global knowledge management and global HR management both theoretically and empirically. Companies in the German automotive sector only fairy recently started to organize knowledge management formally and, as will be shown later, introduced new practices in *global* knowledge and HR management. Both trends are not only new to the sector but also highly complex. Thus, in order to grasp the main characteristics of these phenomena, we decided to follow an exploratory approach using selected case studies. We are attempting to pin down a new phenomenon, new at least in the perception of important actors in the sector. We are explicitly interested in identifying tendencies and emerging traits and not so much in making generalizations.

The selection of case studies explored has been prepared by data gathering at a broader scale. As automotive components suppliers stem from a variety of sectors, we first established our own data bank on relevant companies in Germany based on a special call for data from Hoppenstedt, our own corrections, and supplements. Sixty-two per cent of the 583 companies with more than 50 employees belonged to NACE Rev. 2 sector 2932 (manufacturing of other parts and accessories for motor vehicles). We took the case studies from this subsector. We expected large companies to have a multi-locational and international production system. Further selection was guided by the idea that the largest MNCs were most probably eligible for new practices in global knowledge and HR management. However, comprehensive statistics on the internationalization of these companies are not available. Using an earlier list from VDA (2004) of subsidiaries in the automotive sector abroad, we selected those companies which were present on at least at two of the three continents Asia, Africa, and Latin America and which had several thousands of employees globally. We finally approached three companies of global reach which we believed to be fairly similar in terms of the type of knowledge used and in their requirements with regard to a skilled labour force and R&D organization. They have a common field of technology in different components of the combustion engine system where they have accumulated technological experience and knowledge in sophisticated problem solving over quite a long time, resulting in the development of increasingly complex products. Among the major drivers for technological change are increasing requirements for environmental protection. Companies in this product range are therefore obliged to search continuously for innovations and to combine knowledge inputs from various other technologies. As a consequence, the following case studies represent one of the most R&D-intensive subsectors in the automotive industry, which can hardly be compared with other supplier industries such as assembly in seats or wiring harnesses.

Approaching German companies for case studies is difficult and time-consuming. In this study, up to 10 months were required to gain access to the companies studied. As we looked for new practices in both quality production and innovation activities, we conducted in-depth interviews with in total 10 managers from a variety of departments such as Development and Knowledge Management, Personnel Development and Change Management, International HR Management, International Production Coordination, Competence Management, and, in one company, the sales manager for new products and product managers. This diversity simply reflects different forms of organization within the companies and may be an expression of still unsettled routines in the organization. In each company, we conducted 3–4 h interviews with three or four persons between September 2010 and February 2011, augmented by follow-up telephone interviews. We considered the information generated from the relatively small number of interviews sufficient to explore a new phenomenon, inspired by the grounded theory approach (Glaser and Strauss, 1968). The interviews were transcribed and supplemented by various documents, both public (website) and private (company).

The companies are located in the area around Stuttgart in Southern Germany where a unique cluster of OEMs and automotive suppliers has emerged, including many international suppliers and world market leaders in their specific market niches. They are quite mature companies, going back at least 100 years. They internationalized in Europe a long time ago and went global more recently, mainly to BRICS countries. They are family-based companies of considerable size nowadays (5000–23,000 employees), and belong to the so-called German 'Mittelstand'. As such, they are typical of the dominating 'home-based (global) players' in the German automotive components industry (Kinkel and Zanker, 2007) following a long-term strategy. The companies are highly specialized in respect of technology, so that they play the role of forerunners in innovation. Another important observation is that they learn from producing different product lines, both for domestic and foreign OEMs and the passenger car and commercial vehicle markets. Different product lines and segments present different challenges. Systems and components for passenger cars are almost standardized, but often require certain adaptations for the different models, and are price-sensitive. Systems for commercial vehicles are highly complex technical solutions and require significant investment in R&D. Technical solutions for commercial vehicles cannot easily be transferred to passenger cars. However, the companies studied saw an internal learning relationship between both markets.

The selected companies have sufficient similarities, on the one hand, but differ according to size and experience in internationalization, on the other. We would expect diverse forms of new practices in global knowledge and HR management on the basis of the latter observation and a degree of comparability on the basis of the former observation.

Comp1 started as a small workshop for car radiators in 1905 and is now a leading producer of air conditioning and engine cooling systems, for both passenger cars and trucks. While the company has been strongly oriented towards the premium model sector in passenger cars and sophisticated truck markets, it has recently started to enter low-cost markets, such as modules for the Indian Tata Nano model (Wells, 2010). It still is a family-owned company in the third generation, owned by three families.

The company is still largely operating on European markets, with half of its trade based in Germany. Nevertheless, it has 22 production locations worldwide, and 11 development centres. However, there are only two fully equipped R&D centres, at the company headquarters and in Michigan, USA. Comp1 used a typical 'follow-the-client' strategy in its early internationalization and went first to the Americas (USA, Mexico, Brazil). Only recently, the company identified other emerging countries such as China, India, and Turkey as the growth markets of the future. However, it followed a cautious strategy by starting with joint ventures and only later investing in fully owned subsidiaries. In 1997, the company opened a JV in India, supplemented by an engineering service company in 2000. Later, Comp1 became involved in China and Turkey.

Comp2 was founded in 1865, but only entered the automobile production system in 1932, when it started to produce heating systems and sound absorbers. After the Second World War, it grew with the increasing demand of a German volume producer at that time. The company started to internationalize during the 1980s, but only recently (in 2000) established a R&D centre abroad, in the USA. It currently produces in eight European countries, in the Americas (USA, Canada, Brazil), in South Africa, East Asia (Korea, China), and India, and has some other licensed foreign production. Again, most of the production sites abroad carry out pre-assembly work in proximity to OEM assembly plants. The company has R&D centres in India and Brazil, mostly for adaptation, and currently is extending its capacities for development by establishing close contact with an Indian engineering service provider.

Comp3 is in fact part of a very large German system supplier with a rather complex organization. Comp3 is concerned with one of 10 activity fields in the automotive sector, i.e. gasoline systems. The company was founded in 1886 and soon grew into an international company, selling 88% of its production abroad by 1913. Thus, the company has a very long experience in going global. Furthermore, it has been well-known for its innovative activities for a long time, with an average R&D intensity of 8% in recent years. More than 32,600 employees are involved in R&D and innovation processes worldwide, in the very different segments of the company. Thousand three hundred are employed in the corporate research centre (basic research and pre-development) in Germany. The company has a global innovation policy that involves approaching basic R&D labs abroad. For example, it opened its own software centre in India in 1998 and established close R&D collaboration with Stanford University in 2008.

5. Skills development at subsidiaries abroad

Over the decades, automotive companies in Germany have become embedded into the sophisticated and specifically German education and training system. In this system of education and *dual* vocational training in Germany, supervisors, foremen, and skilled workers can acquire a broad and competent knowledge base (Uhly et al., 2006; Leszczensky et al., 2010).[1]

Thus, one of the major reasons for the strong core competence automotive companies claim at home is their human capital. This refers to competences in regular manufacturing activities. In the context of the new challenges in globalization due to the shift to emerging economies, new human resources requirements emerge abroad. An increasing need for 'upskilling' the labour force comes to the fore when MNCs plan to increase the capabilities of subsidiaries abroad in order to shift qualified production (at lower costs) across the world and thus to become more flexible in locational terms. They hereby attempt to make the world 'flatter' in accordance with their strategic goals. However, such formalized VET systems do not exist in most developing or emerging economies, or exist only in specific geographical and/or sectoral pockets.

Managing human capital locally at different locations abroad was apparently not a major challenge when (automotive) MNCs orientated most of their foreign direct investment towards the Triad countries and occasionally established small plants in emerging economies and developing countries. This was partly due to similarities in social systems, culture, and work practices between European countries and North America, for example. Human knowledge management was implemented traditionally through the expatriate manager, the mobile expert responsible for training, and mobile global support teams for solving technological problems or for introducing new production lines abroad. However, these schemes increasingly involved high costs, e.g. for travelling, and tended to provide idiosyncratic ad hoc training.

With growing investments in emerging economies, MNCs from the European North faced an increasing diversity in the formal qualifications, culture, and habits of their global workforce, both in repetitive work on the shop floor and in creative work carried out by engineers in development. One response to these new challenges was to establish new roles in the company. As Festing and Eidems (2011, p. 163) put it, 'a lot of MNCs need to develop an appropriate *transnational* HRMS' (Human Resource Management System, authors' italics). Festing and Eidems identify a tendency whereby MNCs 'align the geographically fragmented workforce around common principles and a set of common objectives' (p. 165), which is confirmed by recently introduced practices of standardizing training and task allocation at a global scale in our case studies.

It is evident from our case studies that the new practices do not replace but supplement traditional practices. The traditional patterns of knowledge management are still valid, especially in cases where a new plant is established abroad to which the company sends experts even at the shop floor level for quite a while and/or invites much of the new technical staff to the German lead plant to be trained there. However, they no longer respond in a satisfactory way to the requirements of an increasingly 'flat' flexible world of production based on standardized procedures. Sometimes, traditional practices may be new to the subsidiaries abroad – and therefore new to the global company – but not new to the sector. This is exemplified by Comp2 that recently introduced the so-called 'four-phases-method' in training abroad. For local instructors, this means (1) preparing the person to be trained, (2) demonstrating the process to the learning person, (3) supervising the person who copies the process, and (4) monitoring the person's tasks until he or she has a complete grasp of the process. This method has been used in Germany for decades to teach the simplest practices to young people who had no prior contact with the crafts or industrial sector. There is a large amount of anecdotal evidence that these forms of training from the scratch are now becoming increasingly important globally.

Changes in global knowledge and HR management become explicit in connection with a new issue in management and organization. This is global 'competence management' as a new tool for 'up-skilling' the workforce at locations abroad. Competence management can be seen as part of a new transnational HR management particularly oriented towards middle and senior managers (Festing and Eidems, 2011, p. 163), and lower management, whose more recent tasks include improving productivity and efficiency to global standards on the shop floor abroad. As an interviewee in one of our case studies puts it, 'the aim of competence management is to provide, *through a structured and systematic process*, at the right time and at the right place for those competences which are necessary today and in future and support the company's business targets' (Comp3, our italics). However, two of our three case study companies that had recently implemented competence management at a global level claim that full implementation requires a tremendous amount of time (and costs). Comp3, for example, had started 'competence management' in the early 2000s at home and begun to implement it globally late in 2005. But at the time of the interview, in late 2010, competence management had not yet been established at all locations abroad.

Comp3 seems to be at the top of these new practices as it has introduced a sophisticated and 'scientifically' based competence management system. Target competences for each workplace have to be defined globally, deviations from the actual competences measured, and new instruments for building up competences developed. Ultimately, this type of competence management is a new device for managers to define requirements for training current employees and hiring new staff in a globally standardized way. For a global company, this means developing standards for workplace competences across all plants wherever they may be. Competence management is seen as the task of a team organized vertically (across production planning and production) and horizontally (across all business fields of the company).

In implementing competence management, companies also make use of a more traditional tool which is the definition of 'lead' plants which are responsible for any change in technology and production within the multi-locational organization. These lead plants act as best practice locations and models for subsidiaries abroad. They are responsible for the implementation of competence management in other countries. It comes as no surprise that lead plants are generally located in Germany and close to the headquarters. As the case study companies have often established subsidiaries in emerging economies in the course of capacity extension and a follow-the-client strategy, they have mostly built on quasi-similar technology. However, even where new products are first introduced at a subsidiary abroad, support is given from a European lead plant (in the relevant technology) given that European – and sometimes US-American – plants get new tools first, even if they are not formally a lead plant.

Box 1. Phasing in the 'competence management' of Comp3.

Phase 1: Clear-cut definition of workplace requirements (in production and in other functions) in order to explore the state of performance and define the nature and dimensions of deficiencies as a basis for the development of curricula in training. The standard basis for the definition of workplace requirements are workplaces in 'lead plants' in Germany or Europe.
Phase 2: Adaption of the nature and scope of training requirements to the variety of local situations abroad, generally pursued by a joint team from the headquarters and large subsidiaries abroad.
Phase 3: Co-development of curricula for training by HR managers from the headquarters and subsidiaries abroad.
Phase 4: Implementing training courses, mostly by 'local' trainers (internal and external to the subsidiary).

Both companies (1 and 3) developed curricula for basic courses to be used by instructors at the plants abroad in the training of the shop floor labour force. They also established 'training centres' in different world regions which are, however, virtual. Local trainers, either from the subsidiary's HR management or external to the subsidiary, are trained by HR managers from the headquarters in short-term courses. Intercultural barriers to the transfer of skills across the global company should also be overcome with the help of these organizational forms of teaching, but the main target is the acquisition of technical competences.

Fostering global HR management in these ways leads to an increasing standardization of work processes. Most current literature examines the opportunities for local learning in subsidiaries abroad (e.g. Fuchs, 2005) and discusses the intricate balance between standardization and localization in transnational HR management (Festing and Eidems, 2011). In contrast, this paper focuses on the ongoing difficulties in standardizing experience-based activities across countries which are very diverse in terms of education, culture, and institutions. Competence management is a broad tool to standardize tacit know-how on managing staff assessment, workflow improvement, and know-how in teaching and training. As such, it is an indirect instrument to improve the efficiency and quality of work at the shop floor level. As already noted, companies increasingly need a level playing field among their subsidiaries in terms of efficiency and productivity in a globalized market. In the governance of this level playing field, companies enforce a geographical core–periphery relationship, where German or European lead plants form the knowledge core and are the governing instrument for developing skills at plants on other continents.

6.   Where to acquire and how to insert 'talent' into the global R&D organization of the company

It has been argued recently that MNCs striving for lead positions in global markets increasingly face 'a lack of talent' at home, and are consequently obliged to look for talent abroad in the global South (e.g. Lewin et al., 2009). 'Talent' at comparatively low costs is mostly required in R&D functions. Companies are increasingly becoming aware that such talent is often 'sticky' and therefore unevenly distributed across the world. 'Hot spots' in specialized talent have emerged at a very limited number of locations, partly due to long-term national investment in higher education and partly due to the cumulative effects of attracting foreign firms to such places – which has fostered further migration of talent to these places (Manning et al., 2010). MNCs try to 'tap into' hot spots, meaning that their subsidiaries have to become embedded in local networks. However, they have to master a precarious balance between local networking with other institutions at the hot spot and global networking within the MNC. While recent literature increasingly examines the local embeddedness of MNCs (e.g. Andersen and Christensen, 2005), it appears that the emerging challenges in organizing and controlling global internal R&D networks are still under-researched.

The automotive industry is considered to be a leading sector in this respect (Lewin et al., 2009). The internationalization of companies' R&D systems has become an important topic in recent literature (see Moncada-Paternò-Castello et al., 2011, for a recent literature review, and Ambos, 2005, for a study of the German automobile industry). In most cases, MNCs look for product adaptation in R&D for local markets, however, and therefore need talent for local development, not research. However, in some cases, MNCs realize – and simultaneously contribute to – the emergence of hot spots of a particular kind of (sticky) knowledge and try to integrate a hot spot into their global system of R&D by investing in a local R&D lab.

As we already mentioned, German automotive MNCs mostly behave as home-based players maintaining strong control over global activities. They spend considerable resources on R&D in order to maintain their position as first-tier suppliers and market leaders. The case study companies have a long experience in the hierarchical organization of the international division of labour in R&D processes. During the 1990s, they invested in full R&D centres in the USA. Later they established R&D labs in emerging economies such as Brazil, China, and India. These are functionally quite different from the branch in the USA as they either are limited to product adjustments for the local market and mostly located at production sites, or were established as listening posts to observe trends in the global automotive market. This was mainly initiated by the dominant follow-the-client (large OEMs) strategy in the sector. Since the early 2000s, changes in the global markets have encouraged the case companies to invest in engineering service units abroad, either in the form of subsidiaries or joint ventures. Compared with an ordinary R&D lab abroad which is responsible for product adjustment, these units are considerably larger in size. Their function is to deliver ordinary and sophisticated engineering services to the central R&D labs at home or the USA. Thus, a new form of global division of labour in creative engineering processes seems to be emerging.

As a matter of fact, engineering services in the automotive sector are generally based on software but also require experience in automotive technologies. There are not that many regions in the world where MNCs can find favourable conditions for locating an engineering service unit. Moreover, locational decisions are path-dependent and often rely on earlier investments in production abroad, even if service units are ultimately not allocated to production sites. The literature currently discusses locations in Latin America, but for other sectors (Manning et al., 2010), but the case study companies have decided to locate their engineering service units in India. It seems that India has a first mover advantage for this type of engineering services which are mostly based on knowledge in IT. The case study companies established their only engineering service centre in Bangalore (Comp3), which is well known as an IT hub, and in Pune (Comp1+2), one of the Indian hubs in automotive production. Both locations have recently been described as hot spots with large pools of highly qualified young experts and well equipped with educational and public R&D institutions (Basant and Chandra, 2007; Plechero and Chaminade, 2010).

The main motivation for relocating engineering services is not a perceived lack of talent but part of the companies' growth strategies and driven by lower costs in R&D. Comp1 recently relocated – in the proper sense of the word – some engineering tasks from the USA to India, as a consequence of the crisis. There were at least two reasons for relocating engineering tasks from the USA, not Germany. First, labour market regulation in the USA makes lay-offs much easier compared with

Germany. Second, the US R&D centre is not involved in the company's strategic research, which is still carried out solely in Germany. Thus, a new type of global innovation network is emerging within the MNC which is oriented towards the collaborative creation of innovation which is new to the MNC and the world. Mastering cross-border creative processes in the design of new products therefore becomes crucial to the companies. Collaboration between professionals in the context of the divided labour organization depends essentially on communication among experts, where communication is based both on formal and informal networks within the company but across various types of borders. These may be organizational – from headquarters to a foreign subsidiary, a joint venture or an 'independent' subsidiary organization; cultural – according to work practices, professional understanding, etc.; institutional – in educational systems, labour regulation, and the like; and not least language, as recent literature underlines the difficulties that non-native speakers have in professional debates and bargaining (Will-Zocholl, 2011, p. 209).

While in many instances these barriers are not new to an MNC, and MNCs again have long since developed instruments to overcome these, communication between engineers on 'tacit' knowledge in a sector with a synthetic knowledge base implies challenges with a new quality (see also Manning et al., 2009). As a recent study of cross-cultural management in engineering in Comp1 has claimed, Indian engineers 'lack internal company know-how and product-specific experience' (Lehner and Warth, 2010a, p. 592), while they are quite familiar with IT tools such as different CAD systems. Clear-cut solutions to the problem have not yet been developed but the companies are working to achieve learning ('by doing') in a considered way.

It may sound quite easy to implement new procedures in knowledge transfer at an R&D centre abroad. However, this is a time-consuming and costly process involving many individuals and it may even ultimately prove unsuccessful. Lehner and Warth (2010b) have recently presented a detailed case study from the automotive sector of a knowledge transfer process to an engineering service centre in India which took more than 18 months, i.e. from February 2009 to September 2010. Our interview partners emphasized that establishing and learning cross-cultural communication in knowledge-intensive activities is a challenge. To summarize a number of interviews, there appear to be various methods first to reduce the extent of a barrier and then to bridge it.

Companies developed a set of different measures in order to establish efficient collaboration among engineers at the headquarter's (HQ) location and the Indian engineering service centres. These encompass four instruments: (1) fragmentation and standardization in engineering tasks; (2) a concise policy to foster inpatriate development; (3) the careful selection and appointment of boundary spanners; and (4) the elaboration of global IT-based support tools. These will be discussed in greater depth in the following.

(1) *Fragmentation and standardization in engineering tasks*: Tacit knowledge in creative engineering tasks which requires a sophisticated experience in different disciplines has to be disaggregated from more repetitive tasks which can more easily be standardized and digitalized. Standardization here means creating a well-defined interface with other tasks and a well-defined project, and using a well-known methodology. Thus, fragmentation of hitherto combined creative processes into a tacit, still locally sticky knowledge segment and another 'codified' knowledge segment is of paramount importance for the ability to offshore at least some knowledge-based tasks in engineering (Cohendet and Steinmueller, 2000). This seems to be more complicated for Comp2 which offshores parts of engineering tasks in co-development with the central R&D lab than for Comp3 which has definitively offshored all of its software development to its subsidiary in India. Accordingly, Comp1 and Comp2 still do the creative engineering work in 3D design at home while they have relocated, for instance, 2D drawings for production purposes,

simple design, and calculations to the Indian service lab. Offshoring in this sense can be used for enlarging the MNC's R&D capacities and increasing 'speed to market' on the one hand, and cost reduction in design, on the other.

(2) *Fostering inpatriate development*: Companies increasingly draw upon inpatriates to improve communication across large distances, national borders, and different departments. Inpatriates are 'third country nationals transferred or hired locally into the parent organization on a semi-permanent or permanent basis' (Harvey et al., 2000, p. 386) or 'employees who are transferred from a MNC's subsidiary to the headquarters for a limited period' (Reiche, 2011, p. 366). Reiche also states that less is known about the role of inpatriates in MNCs compared with the role of expatriates. It seems from the interviews with the case companies that engineer inpatriates have to perform quite difficult tasks. Firstly, they must be trained in understanding the visions of the engineers at the central R&D lab, then in translating precise tasks to their counterparts at the subsidiary, and thus transferring vision and practices to them, and finally, in controlling the outcome. In Nonaka's (1994) terms, the role of the inpatriate is to act as a 'tool' for learning how to span boundaries in tacit knowledge. Inpatriate development has not yet been established formally in the case study companies but still occurs in an ad hoc manner. Companies are always afraid of high fluctuation rates in emerging economies. Training inpatriates is not yet based on a standard programme but is carried out on short-term assignments to Germany and through visiting programmes to suppliers and production plants. Only recently, one of the companies granted fellowships to some foreign students in Germany, who were later to be employed in their home country. It seems that the 'diaspora' and the growing number of international student migration are not yet really explored for HR management in these MNCs.

(3) *Appointment of (formal) boundary spanners*: When Comp1 established its own engineering service subsidiary in India, the company experienced increasing problems in communication between engineers across distances and cultures. Basic misunderstandings occurred between the older and experienced German engineers at the headquarter location and the young and inexperienced engineers in India. Based on public co-finance and cooperation with a university chair (PhD project) in Germany, the company developed a new policy on intercultural communication management. In organizational terms, the company established boundary spanners[2] both at home and at the Indian location (Lehner and Warth, 2010a). It was, however, extremely difficult to find a person with both knowledge of the company's routines and the specific knowledge of the community of practice of engineers (in different fields of technology). Ultimately, this was an Indian engineer from within the company who, together with the MNC's HR department, co-developed curricula for courses in intercultural management. He then became the chief boundary spanner for his Indian compatriots in India. Boundary spanners complement earlier and traditional patterns of sending expatriates to the R&D service centres abroad and inviting some employees from the host country to long-term training at the headquarters, which had proved to be no longer adequate. These boundary spanners not only 'translate' between engineers in Germany and their counterparts in India but also train engineers on both sides of the relationship in intercultural practices, using newly developed curricula.

(4) *Implementation of IT-based information tools*: The case study companies have elaborated various standardized IT-based tools for the improved cross-boundary implementation of tasks, such as manuals, check-lists for quality standards in task execution, and various guidelines.

7.   What lessons can be learned and for whom?

This paper has looked at new practices in the global knowledge and HR management of some large innovative and R&D-intensive German automotive MNCs. We believe that these case studies illustrate new tendencies in management practices and increased learning on how to improve the capabilities of subsidiaries in emerging economies and, finally, their absorptive capacities. The paper stressed the importance of context to the behaviour of MNCs, focusing on the particular knowledge base of the automotive sector that makes particular efforts in the transfer of tacit knowledge necessary, and on the special case of German MNCs which are strongly embedded in their home base. As the sector's production and innovation are mostly based on experience (synthetic knowledge), global knowledge transfer encompasses tacit knowledge in both skills on the shop floor and engineers' communication in divided work in R&D. It should be borne in mind that other companies in other sectors, using different knowledge bases, have been forerunners in global knowledge and HR management. In the German automotive sector, however, evidence from interviews and documents points to the fact that the large R&D-intensive case study companies develop the most sophisticated practices in this realm. Given that the automotive production system is organized in quite a hierarchical manner between companies, we expect a trickle-down process in the near future, both vertically to the second-tier component suppliers and horizontally to the smaller first-tier suppliers (as exemplified with Indian suppliers, Okada, 2004).

The case studies have revealed that global knowledge management in MNCs has at least two general outcomes: Firstly, knowledge management adapts to and simultaneously contributes to a geographically uneven world of many blind spots and a few hot spots. Secondly, we find that MNCs are heterogeneous in their global knowledge management. However, for the sector of automotive suppliers in general and home-based players and family-based companies in particular, the case study companies are forerunners in these forms of global knowledge management.

These findings correspond to statements by some scholars concerning a presumed 'next wave of globalization' (Dossani and Kenney, 2007; Manning et al., 2008). As our explorative study shows, new challenges for global knowledge and HR management are emerging. However, mastering knowledge-intensive activities in production and innovation and governing knowledge management globally are complex tasks where MNCs need time for learning and which may result in failures and unexpected outcomes. The paper also pointed to an increasing diversity of available skilled and educated labour force for MNCs, making a difference between many blind spots and a few hot spots (of knowledge available) in emerging economies. MNCs invested in improving skills abroad, standardizing training schemes, with the aim of creating a level playing field (among blind spots) for the relocation of sophisticated production (at lower costs), and they invested in new communication practices to use opportunities from knowledge available at hot spots. In both fields, the case study companies took the geographical distribution of available skills and knowledge for granted.

However, we believe that the MNCs utilize and even promote the efforts national governments have made in their education policies. Therefore, we would like to add a brief outlook concerning policy issues in developing countries and emerging economies. For development policy, two different relationships between the outward-oriented activities of technology-oriented MNCs (such as OEMs and first-tier automotive suppliers) and the skills base of developing and emerging countries are of importance and have been discussed extensively in the literature. Firstly, the availability of skilled human resources at relatively low cost can be an important locational factor for multi-national companies in their search for improved conditions for both exploitative and explorative learning. Recent literature explores the difficulties of pursuing both learning modes, considered essential to ensure a firm's long-term success and even its survival (Lackner et al., 2010, p. 3). This means that the larger the local basis of skilled human resources, the more likely it is that an internationally oriented company will relocate advanced production and innovation-oriented activities to a third country. State investment in vocational training appears to play an important role, creating opportunities for exploitation strategies of MNCs. The presence of global players has an impact on the demand for vocational training in many countries. In order to manage high-end knowledge and to incorporate technologies into existing production, companies' demand for technically trained staff rises. This can give incentives to young people to seek VET opportunities. Unfortunately, vocational training has to struggle with considerable image problems, as ambitious young people in most countries are still focused on white-collar jobs, and prefer general education courses that offer a path to these (e. g. Hoogerwaard, 2006, p. 8).

On the supply side, many countries have embarked on ambitious programmes to boost VET. By 2010, China was estimated to have a national network of 2000 VET centres, and in 2007, India announced plans to open some 50,000 new skill development centres and 10,000 new vocational schools (CEDEFOP, 2009). Since its early stages, development cooperation has carried out a large number of programmes and projects in the field of VET, mainly driven by donors like Germany or the Netherlands,[3] which have advanced and internationally renowned vocational training systems at home. VET is seen as an important tool for poverty reduction through the creation of employ-ment in the formal business sector.[4] However, VET programmes run by national governments and development cooperation often had obvious shortcomings involving the simplistic copying of systems from industrialized countries. They are usually embedded in broader employment pro-grammes, often beginning with measures to improve the employability of young people, addres-sing gaps in basic skills and work attitudes. A recent evaluation of policy transfer in VET from Germany to China clearly identified a number of obstacles relating to the broader societal system of the host country (Barabasch et al., 2009). The ambiguous significance of skill improvement through vocational training becomes obvious when two recent messages are considered. Firstly, Barabasch et al. (2009, p. 15) claim that there are 'increasing difficulties for vocational graduates to find gainful employment' while, a recent report states that China faces an increasing excess in the higher educated labour force but a striking lack in technically skilled workers (Demos, 2012).

If the broad-based and modern VET system can convert blind spots of the international div-ision of labour into 'eligible spots' for skill-intensive international investments, it will not convert them into potential 'hot spots' in international innovation networks. This will require systems to train and educate young people able to manage complex and constantly updated technical and managerial knowledge, including forming the basis for boundary spanning functions (advanced language and inter-cultural skills). Only a few countries beyond the BRICs have taken decisive steps in this direction and started to modernize their higher education systems.

Hot spots for the relocation of knowledge-intensive services – internal and external to the MNC – have emerged where governments have invested in higher education for a long time, in particular in technical disciplines such as IT or engineering, and sciences. An abundant litera-ture has recently evolved on the evolution of university systems as part of national innovation systems in developing countries (e.g. Göransson and Brundenius, 2011). The automotive MNCs have been very selective in taking advantage of talent in engineering in India. From their point of view, educated employees still lack 'experience' in many technical fields – as revealed by new practices in knowledge and HR management discussed here. From the host coun-try's point of view, the MNC subsidiaries, especially those delivering knowledge-based services, should become increasingly embedded in local and national knowledge systems. From various academic points of view, the 'local' needs to be combined with the 'global' in global knowledge and HR management (e.g. Manning et al., 2009, 2010; Malerba and Nelson, 2011).

Acknowledgements

Research for this paper was funded by the European Commission's Seventh Framework Programme (Project INGINEUS, Grant Agreement No. 225368, www.ingineus.eu). The authors alone are responsible for its contents which do not necessarily reflect the views or opinions of the European Commission, nor is the European Commission responsible for any use that might be made of the information appearing herein. Parts of the paper have been presented at the Globelics Conference 2011 in Buenos Aires and the eurolio conference 2012 on the Geography of Innovation in St. Etienne/France.

Notes

1. The unique character of dual vocational training lies in the combination of training conducted in private business companies under the supervision of a 'master', and more theoretical education in a vocational school.
2. A boundary spanner is a person who is able to connect two different communities of practice within and between organizations, according to the literature on social networks. Reiche (2011, p. 366) says: 'Specifically, I define inpatriates' boundary spanning as their brokerage between the social ties they have established at the HQ and the social ties they maintain at their home unit'. Generally, organizational literature focuses on informal boundary spanners. However, the formal establishment of the role of a boundary spanner is discussed here as a tool for global communication among engineers.
3. In 2007, the BMZ made some 77 million euros available to projects in the field of vocational training; available at: www.bmz.de (accessed 27 February 2012).
4. A 2005 VET sector strategy of the German Federal Ministry of Economic Cooperation and Development, for instance, explicitly mentions the role of VET as a key location factor and therefore for businesses' international competitiveness (BMZ, 2005, p. 10).

References

Ambos, B. (2005) Foreign direct investment in industrial research and development: A study of German MNCs. *Research Policy*, 34(4), pp. 395–410.

Ambos, B., and Ambos, T.C. (2011) Meeting the challenge of offshoring R&D: An examination of firm- and location-specific factors. *R&D Management*, 41(2), pp. 107–119.

Andersen, P.H., and Christensen, P.R. (2005) From localized to corporate excellence: How do MNCs extract, combine and disseminate sticky knowledge from regional innovation systems? *Druid Working Paper no. 05–16*. Available at: www2.druid.dk/conferences/working_papers.php (accessed 26 June 2007).

Asheim, B., Coenen, L., and Vang, J. (2007) Face-to-face, buzz, and knowledge bases: Sociospatial implications for learning, innovation, and innovation policy. *Environment and Planning C: Government and Policy*, 25(5), pp. 655–670.

Asheim, B.T., Ebersberger, B., and Herstad, S.J. (2010) MNCs between the local and the global: Knowledge bases, proximity and distributed knowledge networks Druid, Paper submitted to the Summer Conference 2010 at Imperial College London Business School, 16–18 June, 2010.

Barabasch, A., Huang, S., and Lawson, R. (2009) Planned policy transfer: The impact of the German model on Chinese vocational education. *Compare*, 39(1), pp. 5–20.

Basant, R., and Chandra, P. (2007) Role of educational and R&D institutions on city clusters: An exploratory study of Bangalore and Pune regions in India. *World Development*, 35(6), pp. 1037–1055.

Belitz, H. (2010) Internationalisierung von Forschung und Entwicklung in multinationalen Unternehmen. Studien zum deutschen Innovationssystem 6-2010, Berlin.

BMZ (German Federal Ministry of Economic Cooperation and Development). (2005) Technical and vocational education and training and the labour market in development cooperation. BMZ Strategies 140, Bonn.

Brewster, C., and Suutari, V. (2005) Global HRM: Aspects of a research agenda. *Personnel Review*, 34(1), pp. 5–21.

CEDEFOP (European Centre for the Development of Vocational Training). (2009) World class competition in training: Emerging economies. CEDEFOP Briefing Note July 2009, Thessaloniki. Available at: http://www.cedefop.europa.eu/EN/Files/9013_en.pdf (accessed 26 February 2012).

Cohendet, P., and Steinmueller, W.E. (2000) The codification of knowledge: A conceptual and empirical exploration. *Industrial and Corporate Change*, 9(2), pp. 195–209.

Dankbaar, B. (2007) Global sourcing and innovation: The consequences of losing both organizational and geographical proximity. *European Planning Studies*, 15(2), pp. 271–288.

Demirbag, M., and Glaister, K.W. (2010) Factors determining offshore location choice for R&D projects: A comparative study of developed and emerging regions. *Journal of Management Studies*, 47(8), pp. 1534–1560.

Demos. (2012) Zu viele Hochqualifizierte, zu wenig gering Qualifizierte. *Demos Newsletter* 137, June 8, 2012. Institut fuer Bevoelkerung und Entwicklung, Berlin.

Dossani, R., and Kenney, M. (2007) The next wave of globalization: Relocating service provision to India. *World Development*, 35(5), pp. 772–791.

Festing, M., and Eidems, J. (2011) A process perspective on transnational HRM systems – a dynamic capability-based analysis. *Human Resource Management Review*, 21(3), pp. 162–173.

Foss, N.J., Husted, K., and Michailova, S. (2010) Governing knowledge sharing in organizations: Levels of analysis, governance mechanisms, and research directions. *Journal of Management Studies*, 47(3), pp. 455–482.

Fuchs, M. (2005) Internal networking in the globalising firm: The case of R&D allocation in German automobile component supply companies, in: C.G. Alvstam and E.W. Schamp (eds) *Linking Industries Across the World. Processes of Global Networking*, pp. 127–146 (Aldershot: Ashgate).

Gertler, M. (2003) Tacit knowledge and the economic geography of context, or the undefinable tacitness of being (there). *Journal of Economic Geography*, 3(1), pp. 75–99.

Glaser, B.G., and Strauss, A.L. (1968) *The Discovery of Grounded Theory. Strategies for Qualitative Research* (London: Weidenfeld and Nicholson).

Göransson, B., and Brundenius, C. (eds) (2011) *Universities in Transition. The Changing Role and Challenges for Academic Institutions* (New York: Springer).

Hall, P.A., and Soskice, D. (2001) An introduction to varieties of capitalism, in: P.A. Hall and D. Soskice (eds) *Varieties of Capitalism: The Institutional Foundations of Comparative Advantage*, pp. 1–68 (Oxford: Oxford University Press).

Harvey, M.G., Novicevic, M.N., and Speier, C. (2000) An innovative global management staffing system: A competence–based perspective. *Human Resource Management*, 39(4), pp. 381–394.

Hoogerwaard, W. (2006) Vocational education and training in developing countries. An exploration of the quality and a design of guidelines. University of Twente, Enschede. Available at: http://essay.utwente.nl/56929 (accessed 26 February 2012).

Kinkel, S., and Zanker, C. (2007) *Globale Produktionsstrategien in der Automobilzulieferindustrie. Erfolgsmuster und zukunftsorientierte Methoden zur Standortbewertung* (Berlin: Springer).

Lackner, H., Güttel, W. H., Garaus, Ch., Konlechner, St., and Müller, B. (2010) Different ambidextrous learning architectures and the role of hrm systems, *DRUID Working Paper no. 11–10*. Available at: www.druid.dk/wp/20110010.pdf (accessed 25 February 2012).

Legler, H., Gehrke, B., Krawczyk, O., Schasse, U., Rammer, Ch., Leheyda, N., and Sofka, W. (2009) Die Bedeutung der Automobilindustrie für die deutsche Volkswirtschaft im europäischen Kontext. *Endbericht an das Bundesministerium für Wirtschaft und Technologie* (Karlsruhe: ZEW).

Lehner, F., and Warth, C. (2010a) Structured knowledge transfer for the implementation of a new engineering service centre in India. Results from a captive offshoring project in the automotive supplier industry, in: R.J. Howlett (ed.) *Proceedings of the 2nd International Conference on Knowledge Transfer*, 7–8 December 2010, Coventry.

Lehner, F., and Warth, C. (2010b) Knowledge transfer processes in the automotive supplier industry – designing an integrated knowledge transfer model, Proceedings of the 11th European Conference on Knowledge Management, Universidade Lusiada de Vila Nova de Famalicao, Portugal, 2 September, 2010, vol. 2, pp. 591–601.

Lema, R., Quadros, R. and Schmitz, H. (2012) Shifts in innovation power to Brazil and India: Insights from the auto and software industries. *IDS Research Report 73*. Institute of Development Studies, Brighton, Sussex.

Leszczensky, M., Frietsch, R., Gehrke, B., and Helmrich, R. (2010) *Bildung und Qualifikation als Grundlage der technologischen Leistungsfähigkeit Deutschlands* (Berlin: Studien zum deutschen Innovationssystem), 1–2010.

Lewin, A., Massini, S., and Peeters, C. (2009) Why are companies offshoring innovation? The emerging global race for talent. *Journal of International Business Studies*, 49(6), pp. 901–925.

Lundvall, B.-A. (2007) National innovation systems – analytical concept and development tool. *Industry and Innovation*, 14(1), pp. 95–119.

Malerba, F., and Nelson, R. (2011) Learning and catching up in different sectoral systems: Evidence from six industries. *Industrial and Corporate Change*, 20(4), pp. 1645–1675.

Manning, S., Massini, S., and Lewin, A.Y. (2008) A dynamic perspective on next-generation offshoring: The global sourcing of science and engineering talent. *Academy of Management Perspectives*, 22(3), pp. 35–54.

Manning, S., Hutzschenreuter, T. and Strathmann, A. (2009) Emerging capabilities or continuous challenge? Managing interfaces in shifting global engineering networks. *Duke CIBER Short Working Paper*, January 2009. Available at: http://faculty.fuqua.duke.edu/oswc/2009/submissions/Manning.pdf (accessed 2 November 2011).

Manning, S., Ricart, J.E., Rosatti Roque, M.S., and Lewin, A.Y. (2010) From blind spots to hotspots: How knowledge services clusters develop and attract foreign investment. *Journal of International Management*, 16(4), pp. 369–382.

Minbaeva, D.B. (2005) HRM practices and MNC knowledge transfer. *Personnel Review*, 34(1), pp. 125–144.

Moncada-Paternò-Castello, P., Vivarelli, M., and Voigt, P. (2011) Drivers and impacts in the globalization of corporate R&D: An introduction based on the European experience. *Industrial and Corporate Change*, 20(2), pp. 585–603.

Moodysson, J., Coenen, L., and Asheim, B. (2008) Explaining spatial patterns of innovation: Analytical and synthetic modes of knowledge creation in the Medicon Valley life-science cluster. *Environment and Planning A*, 40(5), pp. 1040–1056.

Nelson, R.R., and Winter, S.G. (1982) *An Evolutionary Theory of Economic Change* (Cambridge, MA: Belknap Press).

Nonaka, I. (1994) A dynamic theory of organizational knowledge creation. *Organization Science*, 5(1), pp. 14–37.

Okada, A. (2004) Skills development and interfirm learning linkages under globalization: Lessons from the Indian automobile industry. *World Development*, 32(7), pp. 1265–1288.

Plechero, M. and Chaminade, C. (2010) Different competences, different modes in the globalization of innovation? A comparative study of the Pune and Beijing regions. *Lund University, Circle Paper 2010/03*. Available at: www.circle.lu.se/publications (accessed 29 November 2011).

Reiche, S. (2011) Knowledge transfer in multinationals: The role of inpatriate's boundary spanning. *Human Resource Management*, 50(3), pp. 365–389.

Saxenian, A. (2006) *The New Argonauts: Regional advantage in a global economy* (Cambridge, MA: Harvard University Press).

Schamp, E.W., Rentmeister, B., and Lo, V. (2004) Dimensions of proximity in knowledge-based networks: The cases of investment banking and automobile design. *European Planning Studies*, 12(5), pp. 607–624.

Sturgeon, T., van Biesenbroeck, J., and Gereffi, G. (2008) Value chains, networks and clusters: Reframing the global automotive industry. *Journal of Economic Geography*, 8(3), pp. 297–321.

Tallmann, S., and Chacar, A.S. (2010) Knowledge accumulation and dissemination in MNEs: A practice-based framework. *Journal of Management Studies*, 48(2), pp. 278–304.

Uhly, A., Troltsch, K., and Walde, G. (2006) Challenges to the German dual system, in: U. Schmoch, C. Rammer and H. Legler (eds) *National Systems of Innovation in Comparison*, pp. 205–225 (Berlin: Springer).

VDA. (Verband der Automobilindustrie). (2004) Auslandsaktivitäten der Deutschen Automobilindustrie (Berlin: VDA).

VDA. (2010, 2011) *Jahresbericht* (Berlin: VDA).

Wells, P. (2010) The Tata Nano, the global 'value' segment and the implications for the traditional automotive industry regions. *Cambridge Journal of Regions, Economy and Society*, 3(3), pp. 443–457.

Whitley, R. (2000) *Divergent Capitalisms: The social structuring and change of business systems* (Oxford: Oxford University Press).

Will-Zocholl, M. (2011) *Wissensarbeit in der Automobilindustrie* (Berlin: Edition Sigma).

Skills and the formation of global innovation networks: a balancing act

Michael Gastrow and Glenda Kruss

Human Sciences Research Council, South Africa

In seeking to understand the linkages between skill development and the formation of global innovation networks (GINs), we develop an analytical framework that incorporates concepts of dynamic upgrading with the distinction between centripetal and centrifugal forces that act to expand or contract these networks. Using a multiple case-study analysis methodology, we find that on the whole innovation follows skills, which act as a centrifugal force distributing innovation around the globe. Our cases also reveal that this general pattern overlays many other influential factors at the macro, meso, and micro levels, including factors related to skill availability, market characteristics, sectoral characteristics, policy contexts, and micro-level determinants. While these factors are influential, in principle, in shaping GINs, within each individual network, there is a unique and complex interaction between particular sets of forces.

The impact of skill availability on the formation of global innovation networks

Global innovation networks (GINs) are networks of innovation activity in which some knowledge-intensive activities are based in both developed and developing countries. Variability in the level of globalization, proximity to the innovation frontier, and network strength provides a matrix of possible GIN structures. A 'strong-form' GIN is part of a highly globalized network that includes developed and developing countries, conducts new-to-the-world innovation, and participates in an extensive network that includes actors beyond its value chain. Conversely, a 'weak-form' GIN participates in a weakly internationalized network, for example, one restricted to Europe, conducts incremental or adaptive innovation, and participates in a weak network restricted to an internalized structure or within a single value chain. The range of combinations in between these two extremes renders a number of distinct GIN formations.

There is a considerable history of scholarship examining the globalization of innovation, seeking to clarify conceptual models and interpret empirical evidence (e.g. Grossman and Helpman, 1991; Archibugi and Iammarino, 2002; Carlsson, 2006; Dilk et al., 2006; Cummings, 2007). A closer examination of the links between skill development and the formation of innovation networks forms an important component of this literature (e.g. Cohen and Levinthal, 1989, 1990; Brown and Duguid, 1991; Granstrand et al., 1992; Dutrénit, 2004; te Velde, 2005; Disher and Lewin, 2007; Lewin and Couto, 2007; Massini et al., 2008). At the same time, there is a focus on the rise of innovation in developing countries (Ernst, 2002, 2005; Woodridge, 2010) and the impact of learning and dynamic upgrading on local economies (e.g. Reddy, 1997; Lorentzen, 2007). A concern is that, despite the potential for growth (Quinn, 2000), developed countries may be threatened by the growing capabilities of developing countries and the accompanying internationalization of innovation (Lieberman, 2004; Freeman, 2006).

These analyses include several conceptual distinctions that may be usefully applied towards understanding GINs better, including the notions of absorptive capacity (Cohen and Levinthal, 1989), the transfer of knowledge from the 'centre' to the 'periphery' (Albuquerque et al., 2011), and the outsourcing of innovation activity from the 'North' to the 'South' (Ernst and Lundvall, 2000). One way of conceptualizing the structures and dynamics of GINs is as a result of the interplay between 'centripetal forces' which favour concentration and which induce firms to centralize their innovation activities in their headquarters or home countries and opposing 'centrifugal forces' that work towards the dispersion of R&D activities across different locations beyond the home country. This approach has been widely applied in the literature examining the internationalization of firms (e.g. Benito et al., 2002) but has also been applied to the analysis of innovation networks (Paoli and Guercini, 1997; Pearce, 1990, 1999; Patel and Vega, 1999; Narula and Zanfei, 2003; Maftei, 2007). Centripetal forces postulated in this literature include

- the need to protect firm-specific technology from unwanted leakage;
- the significance of scale economies and critical mass that can be achieved by a high degree of concentration of R&D and innovation activities;
- the high cost of globalized co-ordination and control; and
- the availability of competences embedded in the home organization and the domestic innovation system surrounding it.

Centrifugal forces include

- access to new markets;
- lower costs – particularly access to lower cost scientific and technological skills and infrastructures;
- proximity to customers in other markets in order to be sensitive to the specific needs and characteristics of foreign demand;
- the need for product adaptation to local market conditions;
- the need for closer communication with marketing and production activities in other countries; and
- political factors such as policy incentives or access to research-funding programmes.

Other factors can act as either centripetal or centrifugal forces, depending on their context. For example, value chain dynamics, sectoral drivers, market characteristics, and input characteristics can all in some cases enable GIN formation and in others hinder it.

The existing research on GINs (UNCTAD, 1995; Manning et al., 2008, 2011; Toner, 2011) suggests that they are forming at an increasing rate, which means that certain factors are changing the balance of centripetal and centrifugal forces in favour of centrifugal forces (Albuquerque et al., 2011), thereby compelling firms to locate their R&D activities outside their home countries. In the context of the broad range of centripetal and centrifugal forces that shape evolving GINs, the changing distribution of skills across the world influences these GIN formations. One of the main reasons is the availability at a lower cost of skills in emerging economies such as China and India (Stembridge, 2007).

This paper seeks to understand more clearly the centripetal and centrifugal forces that act upon GINs – with a focus on the role of skills in these processes. A useful framework for understanding how changing patterns of skill development and distribution might affect innovation activity is that of dynamic upgrading developed by Lall (2001). We extend the range of Lall's analysis to include capabilities for innovation and R&D. We highlight processes of dynamic upgrading, for example, in-house training, knowledge networks, capital equipment flows, and staff exchange. Whether these factors enable or constrain GINs allows us to understand them as centripetal or centrifugal forces. We use the broad term 'skills' to include a variety of aspects related to human capital, including knowledge assets embedded in firms at the capability level and at the technological level.

At the macro level, a country's education and training institutions and pool of talent are key considerations in the global distribution of knowledge-intensive activity. At the micro level, firm-level capabilities are key. Lall's framework seeks to understand how the distribution of skills changes over time, with a focus on the determinants of firm-level capability-building. First, since different technologies make different demands on learning requirements, the learning process is technology-specific. Each sector has a distinct profile of skills required for innovation, including differing utilizations of codified and tacit knowledge. Second, different technologies depend to differing degrees on external sources of information – some sectors may operate in isolation, while others require a broad range of knowledge partners. Third, the entire range of skills within a firm is relevant to its upgrading process. Although the design of a new product may primarily be undertaken by scientists and engineers, the successful application of this design requires workers, supervisors, technicians, and management. Fourth, advancing technological trajectories cannot rely entirely on the mastery of operational 'know-how'. Firms must also master 'know-why', which requires an understanding of the principles of the technology they are acquiring or developing. Fifth, learning occurs in the context of externalities and linkages which are influenced by institutional characteristics. Education and training institutions and policy environments thus shape processes of learning and upgrading. Finally, when examining linkages between multinational corporations (MNCs) and the availability of skills in host countries, it is important to differentiate between internalized and externalized technology transfers. When an MNC chooses to keep strategically valuable technology to itself, the transfer of 'know-how' may take place, but the transfer of 'know-why' may be impaired.

By applying Lall's conceptual framework to the distinction between centripetal and centrifugal forces acting on GINs, we place the network itself at the centre of our analytical approach. The GIN is the unit of analysis and is subject to forces that motivate for the extension or deepening of the network and opposing forces that motivate for the network to contract or weaken. We therefore apply an understanding that innovation, and the networks within which it takes places, is dynamic and is subject to simultaneous forces of integration and disintegration. Such an approach differs from a 'North–South' framework, in which most innovation is seen to be centred in the 'North' and firms (and other actors) seek to extend their innovation networks to acquire desirable knowledge and institutional assets in the 'South'. Our approach centres on the innovation network itself as the unit of analysis in the context of a globalized world. This avoids a 'North–South' dichotomy, since the location of the network is seen as a contingent rather than as a fundamental property. We seek to understand the determinants that cause innovation networks to expand or contract in the global context, whether they originate or are centred in developed or developing countries. In a globalized world, economic and institutional drivers are global in nature, and only the contingencies of local conditions (whether in Beijing, Lisbon, Cape Town, or Sao Paolo) are different. In other words, we seek to understand global rules that interact with local contexts, wherever these happen to be.

Our analysis is based on a set of case studies conducted for the INGINEUS project.[1] We examine the centripetal and centrifugal forces acting on the case-study GINs, with a focus on the role of skills, and the articulation between skills and other influential factors. We find patterns among these forces which allow us to postulate an abstracted model of the key variables influencing the expansion or the contraction of GINs. Critically, however, we also find that each case study represents a unique balance of multiple forces that form a 'fingerprint' that determines the final shape of each GIN.

Methodology

Our international set of 19 case studies (see Table 1) includes firms in the automotive, agro-food, and Information and Communication Technology (ICT) sector, making it possible to examine the influence of sectoral factors. The cases include large multinational firms as well as medium and smaller firms with an international footprint. Five were 'matched' cases of large globalized firms, in which interviews were conducted in both the home country of the firms and at subsidiaries in host countries. While most of the firms are headquartered in Europe, the cases include two firms from developing countries that invested in subsidiaries in Europe. One firm is headquartered in a transition economy (Estonia) and developed a GIN that spread into nearby Nordic countries.

The first step of the firm selection process was to identify European MNCs (from Germany, Denmark, and Sweden) with subsidiaries in the BICS (Brazil, India, China, South Africa) countries, in each of the sectors. The firms were assured confidentiality. Research teams in each country arranged interviews with managers in charge of R&D, technology, or innovation as well as of human capital. This choice of key informants was based on accessing managers with the most relevant knowledge of the articulation between the firm's skill requirements and innovation strategies.

The interviews took place in 2010 and lasted up to 2 h. The researchers produced a synthesis of the conversation which was submitted to the interviewees for vetting of accuracy. The interviews were semi-structured and explored the factors that enable or constrain the development of innovation linkages between the home country and the host country. A focal point was the identification of a particular instance of technological change with a potential impact on GIN formation. Each focal point represents a set of strategic decisions taken by firms seeking to articulate

Table 1. Case-study sample.

Firm	Sector	Interview locations
ICT1	ICT (software)	Sweden, India, and China
ICT2	ICT (hardware)	Sweden and South Africa
Agro1	Agro-processing	Denmark and South Africa
Auto1	Automotive	Germany and South Africa
Auto2	Automotive	Germany and South Africa
Auto3	Automotive	Brazil
Auto4	Automotive	Brazil
Auto5	Automotive	Brazil
Auto6	Automotive	Brazil
Auto7	Automotive	Brazil
Agro2	Agro-processing	Denmark
Agro3	Agro-processing	Denmark
Agro4	Agro-processing	Denmark
ICT3	ICT	Estonia
ICT4	ICT	Estonia
Auto8	Automotive	Germany
Auto9	Automotive	South Africa
Auto10	Automotive	South Africa
Auto11	Automotive	South Africa

their innovation requirements with the global distribution of human capital. These decisions often represent the dynamics present in the firm's broader context, such as sectoral drivers, or the availability of competencies at the national level.

The first step of the analysis was to apply our conceptual and analytical framework to review all the case-study material, including drawing inductively from the empirical material. Since each case study involved a home country and a host country, our methodology focused on centripetal forces that motivate for and centrifugal forces that motivate against the strengthening of connections. The set of cases used for this analysis excluded those that presented insufficient detail to

Table 2. Determinants of GIN formation.

Firm	Countries	Centrifugal forces	Centripetal forces
Agro1	Denmark/South Africa	Regional gateway, local demand for adaptation, regional commonalities (with Brazil), tacit knowledge acquisition, specialized knowledge acquisition, and local network acquisition	Small size of domestic market
Auto1	Germany/South Africa	Regional gateway, long logistical pipeline, and demand for local product development and adaptation	Management constraints on innovation activity at the subsidiary
Auto1	Germany/India	Large domestic market and growth potential and large available human capital pool at lower cost	Tacit knowledge barriers and cultural barriers
Auto2	Germany/India	Large domestic market and growth potential and large available human capital pool at lower cost	Tacit knowledge barriers and cultural barriers
Auto3	Italy/Brazil	Regional gateway, demand for local product development and adaptation, and policy incentives	Shortage of high-level skills
Auto4	Italy/Brazil	Regional gateway and demand for local product development and adaptation	Shortage of high-level skills
Auto9	Germany/India	Large domestic market and growth potential and large available human capital pool at lower cost	Tacit knowledge barriers and cultural barriers
Auto9	Germany/South Africa	Regional gateway, demand for local product adaptation, and regional commonalities with Brazil	Shortage of high-level skills and small domestic market
Auto10	South Africa/UK/USA	Local skill shortages and proximity to customers	
Auto11	South Africa/Australia/New Zealand	Proximity to customers	
ICT1	Sweden/China/India	Large domestic market and growth potential, large available human capital pool at lower cost, and innovation management structures	
ICT2	Sweden/China/India	Large domestic market and growth potential and large available human capital pool at lower cost	
ICT2	Sweden/South Africa	Regional gateway and demand for local product development and adaptation	Small domestic market
ICT3	Sweden/Estonia	Availability of specialized human capital, geographical proximity, and low cultural barriers	

assess the balance between centripetal and centrifugal forces (rendering 14 case studies covering 11 multinational firms – see Table 2).

Through this analytical process, a set of key determinants was developed. A quantitative coding methodology was then applied to identify the centrifugal and centripetal forces exerted upon each case. The resulting data illuminate patterns of determinants across the case studies, allowing us to develop an abstracted model of the key forces enabling or constraining the development of GINs.

The second step of the analysis was to use this set of determinants to examine four cases that illustrate distinct types of GINs. These show that each network is subject to a unique balance of centripetal and centrifugal forces as they play out at the firm level, at the sectoral level, and at the national level. The balance can lead to the formation of a strong GIN or a weak GIN or prevent a GIN from appearing at all. While the literature suggests a positive relationship between market size and GIN formation and the availability of a pool of talent and GIN formation, our case studies illustrate that these generalized relationships exist in the context of micro-, meso-, and macro-level factors that together form a 'fingerprint' for each particular case. We show that the relationship between skill availability and GIN formation is complex and nonlinear, subject to a broad array of variables that determine the final effect.

Determinants of GIN formation

In each case, actors balance a number of dynamic and interacting factors when developing their unique strategies, including multiple strategies playing out within different parts of the same corporate group. The cases therefore reveal differing strategic patterns as firms allocate their resources towards technological upgrading and innovation activities around the world. The high-level findings, illustrating the main centripetal and centrifugal forces in each case, are presented in Table 2.

Skills at the macro level

The cost of skills has been highlighted as a key factor driving innovation activity away from high-cost locations and towards low-cost locations (Manning et al., 2011). This generalized relationship is reflected in the case studies: India is regarded by Auto1, Auto2, Auto8, Auto9, ICT2, Agro2, and Auto11 to offer cheap qualified labour for R&D. ICT1, ICT2, and Agro1 consider China's qualified labour to be cheap. Auto2 chooses to offshore R&D to India rather than retain it in Germany because of the competitive price of hiring engineers. However, as suggested by Maskell et al. (2006), cost considerations are taken in the broader context of a multitude of factors, with the most important ones being the availability of a critical mass of skills and the availability of the specific skills required.

Strong national education and training systems in the home country act as centripetal forces, enabling local innovation and disincentivizing the offshoring of knowledge-intensive activity. All the firms interviewed in Europe reported that they could find the skills they needed in their home market, with the exception of certain rare high-level skills, for which they scan globally. The German automotive firms emphasized that Germany's dual vocational education and training system provides a strong home base in qualifications at the shop-floor and supervisory level. A national decline in manufacturing employment has increased the pool of experienced labour. Smaller countries such as Denmark and Sweden might have local shortages of specific skills encouraging them to look elsewhere in Europe and more recently in Asia. However, these skill shortages were described as minor and of low significance in shaping firms' strategies for the global fragmentation of innovation.

The more dynamic strategic arena for the expansion of Europe-based GINs appears to be the developing countries: in all the European MNC case studies, firms reported that the key factors influencing the fragmentation of GINs related to conditions in host countries. The availability of a wide scope and large scale of skills in a host country acts as a centrifugal force. The case-study firms perceived both of these factors to be available in China and India, making them attractive locations for knowledge-intensive activity. ICT1, ICT2, Agro1, and Agro2 noted that India and China have large-scale pools of talent. Auto1, Auto2, and Auto8, all with subsidiaries in India that conduct some innovation, highlighted that the local pool of skills has a wide scope and there are no problems finding staff. ICT1 pointed out that in Shanghai, the addition of 183,000 new graduates per year is a major incentive to locate a large R&D centre there. The US multinational has now opened a second corporate headquarters in Bangalore (India), with a major reason being to access talent.

For GINs based in developing countries, skill availability in the host (developed) country is equally a critical centrifugal force. Weaker national education and training systems incentivize these firms to expand their GINs to locations with more abundant skills. The well-functioning education and training systems and plentiful skill supplies (especially at the higher levels) in developed economies attract knowledge-intensive activities from the developing world. This pattern characterized Auto10 and Auto11 and has parallels in the recent purchases of knowledge assets in Europe by firms from Asian economies, such as the purchase of Jaguar/Landrover by Tata and the Chinese purchase of the MG automotive brand.

The growth in skill availability – including processes of dynamic upgrading – in emerging economies is thus key (Figures 1 and 2). The massification of higher education in India, Brazil, China, and South Africa since the 1990s has increased the global pool of talent and greatly increased the proportion of competencies that reside in developing countries. This is reflected in an increase in tertiary enrolment figures between 2000 and 2007, particularly in Brazil, which may reflect their policy of free public higher education (World Bank, 2010). The near tripling of China's enrolment rate, given its large population, represents a massive new cohort of skilled people that has a significant impact on the global distribution of innovation. However, the BICS countries still have a long way to go before catching up with Europe: in Germany, the proportion of the labour force that has a tertiary education is 24%, in Sweden 29.8%, in Denmark 30.6%, and in Estonia 33.7% – this figure is only 7% in China, 8.6% in Brazil, and 13% in South Africa (World Bank, 2010).

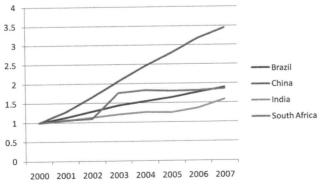

Figure 1.   Growth of public and private tertiary enrolment for developing countries (normalized to unity in 2000).
Source: UNESCO (2010a).

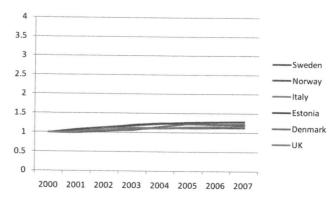

Figure 2. Growth of public and private tertiary enrolment for developed countries (normalized to unity in 2000).
Source: UNESCO (2010a).

Rapid expansion has put strain on education quality. Firm-level case studies repeatedly reported problems with the quality of graduates in developing countries. The high levels of inequality in these countries affect their educational outputs. Nevertheless, in an environment of great inequality, it is possible for pockets of excellence to exist within a generally weak system. In all four developing countries, the ranking for the quality of scientific research institutions, and local availability of R&D services, was far higher than the rankings for the overall quality of their education system (see Table 3).

It thus appears that in the search for skills, firms are seeking pockets of excellence that emerge from the challenging environment of rapidly expanding education systems in developing countries.

At the national level, policy incentives can also play a role in attracting innovation-intensive activities to a country (Kumar, 1996). Industrial policies supporting the automotive sector in South Africa were seen by Auto1, Auto9, Auto10, and Auto11 as essential to the maintenance of innovation linkages with European firms, as they supported the production activities which created demand for that innovation. In the ICT sector, Intellectual Property Rights (IPR) protection is seen as critical. Weak IPR protection in China was cited as a challenge in terms of

Table 3. WEF rankings out of 139 countries.

Country	Quality of educational system	Quality of math and science education	Availability of scientists and engineers	Quality of management schools	Quality of scientific research institutions	Internet access in schools
Denmark	10	19	19	14	12	10
Germany	18	39	27	31	6	39
India	39	38	15	23	30	70
Estonia	42	21	58	41	26	2
China	53	33	35	63	17	22
Brazil	103	126	68	73	42	72
South Africa	130	137	116	21	29	100

Source: WEF (2010).

increasing the level of R&D in that country for ICT1. On the other hand, stronger IPR protection in South Africa was seen as an enabler of innovation in the agro-food sector by Agro1.

In extending their GINs, the case-study firms thus seek 'pockets' of skills that respond to their demand for innovation. For all the cases (with the exception of Auto firms 3, 4, 10, and 11), the great depth and scope of skill availability in China and India, together with the larger market size, have facilitated the establishment of R&D centres that serve both the local market and the needs of the global group. By contrast, the relatively limited size of the skill pool in Brazil and South Africa has acted as a constraint, with local innovation activities largely confined to adaptation to local markets. This distinction holds at the lower scale: Brazil has a larger market and a larger skill pool than South Africa, and consequently the case-study firms in Brazil host more R&D and more evolved GINs than the South African operations, which host very little R&D and often participate in low-intensity or incipient GINs.

Skills and markets

Thus, the case studies suggest that the articulation between market characteristics and skill availability is a key factor in GIN formation. Emerging countries with large populations and growing markets are more likely to have the market pull and human capital base to retain the R&D functions of domestic firms and to attract European MNCs to invest in large R&D centres. Four firms (ICT1, ICT2, Auto9, and Agro2) found the Chinese market size to be attractive. Four firms (Auto1, Auto2, ICT1, and ICT2) found the Indian market size to be attractive. Medium-sized emerging countries have smaller market potential and more restricted human capital. They attract fewer and smaller R&D centres, and innovation demand is more focused on adaptation and product development for local markets. At the same time, large markets in Europe and the USA incentivize the extension of GINs from firms in developing countries – for example, the purchase of R&D centres in the UK and USA by Auto10, and by product adaptation and sales centres in Australia and New Zealand by Auto11 – both South African firms.

For GIN linkages from a home country in Europe to a host country in a developing economy, two key centrifugal forces are local demand for product adaptation (the adaptation of products with specifications aimed at developed countries in order to suit the market conditions of developing countries) and local demand for new product development. Local demand for adaptation is a strong factor attracting R&D into China, India, Brazil, and South Africa. Nine of the 19 firms noted demand for adaptation in emerging countries. For example, subsidiary firms in the Brazilian and South African automotive sectors required innovation activity to redesign transmission systems that could deal with low adherence road conditions. In both cases, the host country subsidiary collaborated with a supplier to develop a low-cost system. Local demand for new products in emerging markets is a less significant factor than demand for product adaptation. Only two firms (Auto3 and Auto7) reported demand for new products in Brazil.

Skills and sectoral drivers

The sectoral context of each firm influences the drivers and characteristics of innovation, which in turn affects the manner in which firms seek the skills they require in support of their innovation activities. Sectors (and sub-sectors) operate at different levels of technological intensity, have different levels of dependence on tacit and codified knowledge, and have differing distributions of global demand for innovation. Sectors also have differing levels of demand for incremental development, adaptive development, new product development, and basic research.

In the agro-food sector, customers continuously demand new products, and ingredient companies must anticipate future needs and identify technological opportunities relevant to the customers ahead of time (Haakonssen, 2012). Our agro-food case-study firms are headquartered in Denmark. Their R&D collaboration is mostly within the supply chain, with firms reporting collaboration mostly with customers, suppliers, and consultancies, all predominantly located in Denmark and Western Europe (Ministry of Science and Technology, 2010). This concentration is related to the localization of the sector: first, Denmark is home to agglomeration in the sector. Second, the nature of the agro-food industry favours local incremental innovation that can quickly respond to local customer needs and variations in local inputs.

Sector-specific skills are generally available in Denmark. The Danish food cluster is export-oriented and among the most innovative in the EU. Denmark ranks 3rd in the Organisation for Economic Co-operation and Development for food patenting *per capita* and has the highest number of scientific publications related to food *per capita* (Ministry of Science and Technology, 2010). The sector is also prominent in South Africa, home to several large agro-food companies, of which some have become global players exporting knowledge services. South Africa has the most developed food-processing and -manufacturing sector in Southern Africa (DTI, 2006). Consequently, the sector has attracted a number of international and local companies that use South Africa as a base to reach domestic and regional markets. Existing sectoral knowledge and physical infrastructure, together with the country's strategic position, thus act as centripetal forces.

The automotive sector case-study firms are located in Germany, South Africa, and India. The value chain structure of the automotive sector is more hierarchical and concentrated than the ICT or agro-food sectors, and this has a major influence on innovation and GIN formation. Innovation is concentrated within large firms at the top of the value chain (Humphrey and Memedovic, 2003). Basic research is concentrated at the main R&D facilities of assemblers and major suppliers, while applied research can be cascaded down the value chain. Assemblers create unique standards and specifications, necessitated by the high level of inter-relationships in the performance characteristics of components that differ for every model. This creates a consistent demand for R&D among the large firms in the sector, but it also acts as a centripetal force that concentrates R&D within the highest tiers and largest firms. Since barriers to entry are raised by investment requirements and by the top-down direction of design specifications, the scope for innovation among smaller firms is further reduced. Close collaboration between suppliers and assemblers also leads to agglomerations of firms near the headquarters of assemblers and large tier 1 suppliers, further concentrating innovation in these clusters.

At the same time, contrasting dynamics are influencing the conduct of innovation in the industry. Very large and growing markets such as Brazil, China, and India make it profitable for assemblers to adapt existing or even to produce specific models for these markets (Brandt and Van Biesebroeck, 2008). Original Equipment Manufacturers (OEMs) thus establish regional headquarters as well as regional design and innovation centres. In turn, this creates pressure for lead suppliers to follow suit and to source inputs from local second-tier suppliers which might end up supplying assemblers directly. Similarly, OEMs use advanced developing countries, whose markets do not justify specific models but are large enough to warrant local assembly (e.g. South Africa), as regional production hubs. Opportunities for technological upgrading can take place when a European supplier transfers technology to an assembly plant in a developing country (e.g. Ivarsson and Alvstam, 2005; Nam, 2010) or when an assembler from a developing country acquires competencies by purchasing a European firm (Lorentzen and Gastrow, 2012).

The ICT sector is distinguished by the greater role of codified technology, both in the hardware sub-sectors and in the software sub-sectors. This lowers cultural and geographical barriers and facilitates the globalization of innovation. The rewards for radical innovation in the sector are great: the rapid spread of the internet and the development of more advanced underlying communication technologies has brought about major technological disruptions and opportunities in the telecommunication software industry (Ernst and Lundvall, 2000), including possibilities of catch-up (Chang, 2008; Ernst, 2009). Firms seek to take the advantage of these opportunities through innovation – the rapid growth and success of the ICT case-study firms were predicated on radical software innovations. There is also a continuous demand at the local level for customized ICT solutions. Emerging markets are changing rapidly, and a critical strategy for ICT firms is to keep track of changing demands and develop appropriate solutions – a factor which was one of the incentives for R&D investments in India and China by all the ICT sector case-study firms.

Micro factors

Skill factors also articulate with firm-level determinants affecting GIN formations. Management styles and choices can affect innovation outcomes. German automotive firms reported that innovation management was concentrated at their headquarters in the home country, leaving little space for innovation at the subsidiary level and exercising tight control over all innovation activity. On the other hand, Agro1, ICT1, and ICT2 encouraged local innovations to respond to domestic market requirements.

Geographical proximity can act as a centripetal or a centrifugal force. Firms and subsidiaries in developing countries (Auto1, Auto2, Auto9, Auto10, Auto11, Agro1, Agro2, Agro3, Agro4, and ICT3) highlighted that geographical proximity to developed country value chains and customers facilitated innovation linkages. On the other hand, for Auto1, the large geographical distance between the South African subsidiary and European customers created a demand for quality-enhancing process innovation to mitigate the cost risks and capital commitments of long transportation lead times. Geopolitical roles can also influence GINs, as we have noted: Brazil and South Africa were perceived to be gateway countries to their respective regions, which strengthened innovation linkages for Auto1, Auto3, Auto4, Auto9, and Agro1.

Cultural and linguistic proximity act as centripetal or centrifugal forces. German automotive firms with innovation-performing subsidiaries in India (Auto1, Auto4, Auto8, and Auto9) reported that linguistic and cultural differences were significant barriers to the strengthening of innovation network linkages. Agro1 and Agro2 reported that cultural and linguistic differences in China discouraged the establishment of R&D centres. To overcome this obstacle, firms establish specialized 'boundary-spanning' functions. For example, Auto1, Auto4, and Auto9 bring engineers from India and China to work with German engineers for a period to help ease communication problems. Where countries share a common language, innovation linkages are facilitated. Auto10 and Auto11 (based in South Africa) invested in R&D centres in the UK, the USA, Australia, and New Zealand, where English is the shared language. Automotive subsidiaries in Brazil (Auto firms 3, 4, 5, 6, and 7) all reported some innovation linkages with parent companies and suppliers in Latin-language-speaking countries (Italy and Spain).

Whether innovation relies on tacit or codified knowledge also influences the role of skills in GIN formation. Tacit knowledge is more difficult to transfer across linguistic boundaries, cultural gaps, and geographical space (Subramaniam and Venkatraman, 2001). Sectors rely on different levels of tacit knowledge. The ICT sector is characterized by a greater proportion of codified knowledge, while the automotive sector is more heavily reliant on tacit knowledge built up over time by experience in solving engineering problems (Jung and Lee, 2010). German automotive firms with R&D centres and subsidiaries in India reported significant barriers to the transfer of certain forms of tacit knowledge and had to initiate programmes of cultural bridging to mitigate communication gaps. By contrast, the ICT firms with innovation-performing subsidiaries in India and China did not report substantial obstacles in terms of the transfer of tacit knowledge.

Macro-, meso-, and micro-level forces

The overall analysis of these cases reveals that GIN formations are influenced by skill availability factors at the macro, meso, and micro levels. Macro-level factors include

- the strength of the national education and training system;
- the scale of the local pool of skills;
- the scope of the local pool of skills (especially high-end and specialized skills);
- the availability of technology-specific skills;
- the strength of the National System of Innovation; and
- the availability of local network assets.

Other macro-level factors include

- market characteristics: market size, market growth potential, local demand for adaptation, and local demand for new product development; and
- the policy context: the strength of national IPR regimes and policy incentives.

At the meso level, sectoral drivers play a role in articulating market demands and global sectoral trends with local skill availability. Aspects here include

- differing levels of tacit and codified knowledge in innovation processes;
- sector-specific skill demands;
- the influence of value chain dynamics on the organizational structure of innovation; and
- differing sectoral innovation drivers shaped by differing characteristics of market demand for adaptation and new production development.

At the micro level, considerations include

- cultural and linguistic commonality;
- the ease of tacit and codified knowledge transfer;
- management styles and decisions within firms: the nature of innovation management structures, the strength of internalized knowledge networks, and the strength of value chain knowledge networks; and
- geographical proximity, the role of regional gateways, logistical challenges, and regional commonalities.

Illustrative case studies

While an overview of our case studies allows us to postulate general patterns of factors that cause GINs to expand or contract, no individual GIN can be understood without reference to a host of particularities, since each case is a unique balancing act of multiple and sometimes opposing forces. Our illustrative case studies demonstrate this. These selected cases range from the most basic (incipient GINs) to intermediate (GINs focused on product adaptation) to the most complex (large GINs with a global distribution of new-to-the-world innovation). The selected cases illustrate well-defined strategic stances and general trends. The balance of centripetal and centrifugal forces at play in each case is mapped in a matrix that distinguishes between factors originating in the home and the host country (Figures 3–6).

Our first illustrative case study is Auto10, a South African electronic components supplier to OEMs, with a focus on customized engine management systems. After market liberalization and

	Centrifugal forces		Centripetal forces	
	Home country (SA)	Host country (UK)	Home country (SA)	Host country (UK)
Skills	Skills shortages	Specialised skills availability	Lower cost of skills	Expensive skills
Markets	Small market	Large market		
Sectoral factors	Follow-source and follow design lock domestic firms out of the automotive value chain	Specialised knowledge assets provide access to the value chain		
Geography	No proximity to customers (who are based in Europe)	Proximity to customers		
Culture and tacit knowledge		No linguistic barriers (English-speaking); cultural barriers are minor		
Policy				
Management	Management strategy of seeking knowledge assets and access to customers on a global front			

Figure 3. Auto10.

value chain changes in the 1990s, the firm was in danger of being substituted by global suppliers. In order to retain access to its customers, the firm needed a development facility that was recognized by the OEMs. The firm could not find the requisite high-level skills locally; in addition, since global value chain re-alignment favoured suppliers based near the headquarters of OEMs, it was imperative that the firm establish a foothold near its customers. Thus, the firm acquired an engineering services consultancy based in Europe, previously owned by an OEM. The acquisition gave it access to one R&D centre each in the European and North American markets. This purchase established the basis of an emerging GIN, in which knowledge began to flow between the South African headquarters and the newly purchased US and UK subsidiaries. This does not imply immediate technological upgrading; the division of labour remains similar, in that the developed country operations undertake R&D, while the South African operation focuses on manufacturing, using the designs originating in the subsidiaries. The locus of control remains in South Africa, and the developed country operations have become a tool for access to customers and product development to meet their needs.

For this firm, sectoral dynamics created centrifugal forces, driving an expansion of a low-intensity GIN from South Africa into the UK and the USA. At the same time, increasing knowledge intensity in the sector meant that some skills were not available locally. Hence, the management adopted a strategy of searching globally for knowledge assets and a better position from which to access customers. In this case, language and cultural barriers were minimal, since the firms shared a common language (English). Skills in the UK were more expensive, but on balance these forces favoured the emergence of a South Africa-based GIN, where some innovation activity remained in South Africa, and innovation activities commensurate with the skills available in the UK and US centres were carried out there.

Overall, the centrifugal forces of skill availability, market access, sectoral drivers, low cultural barriers, and management decisions outweighed the centripetal force of higher skills costs in the

	Centrifugal forces			Centripetal forces	
	Home country (Dk)	Host country (SA)		Home country (Dk)	Host country (SA)
Skills	Some skills gaps; High cost	Acquisition of specialised knowledge; Acquisition of valuable network assets		Large and competent skills pool	Limited availability of specialised skills
Markets	Limited market size; stagnant growth.	High local demand for product adaptation and new product development. Growth market.			Limited market size
Sectoral factors		Agro-food sector is characterised by the need to adapt to local input and market conditions			
Geography		Regional gateway to Africa; Commonalities with other emerging markets (e.g. Brazil)			No geographical proximity
Culture and tacit knowledge		Acquisition of valuable tacit knowledge. Only minor cultural and linguistic barriers.			
Policy		Strong IPR protection			
Management	Partially decentralised global internalised knowledge network. SA grouped with Brazil. Group strategy of knowledge acquisition through purchases.				

Figure 4.   Agro1.

host countries, resulting in the formation and strengthening of ties between these nodes in an incipient (weak-form) GIN.

Our second illustrative case study is a large Danish multinational firm that develops and manufactures flavourants and ingredients. The focal point was the purchase, in 2010, of a specialist South African firm and its incorporation into the Agro1 Group as a subsidiary. The South African firm was a local player with a small laboratory supporting bread-producing customers. In particular, the company was working on adaptation for local markets, including solutions to get low-quality wheat rising with yeast, in order to supply international customers moving into South Africa. The key motives for this purchase were the acquisition of skills, strategic knowledge assets, insight into local market conditions, and a plug-in to an existing local innovation system. The key strategic knowledge asset was the capability to achieve rapid turnaround times when developing mixtures for customers in the baking sector. This required, in addition to codified knowledge, unique tacit knowledge of local conditions, particularly the characteristic of local inputs such as flour and yeast. The South African firm had well-developed links with local universities, research institutes, and other firms active in the value chain.

After the purchase, the subsidiary continued to draw on previously existing local knowledge networks, but supplemented by collaboration and knowledge exchange with Agro1 headquarters and with the regional headquarters in Brazil. Its primary engagement in the firm's internalized knowledge network was interaction with Brazil for product development. There have been numerous cases where intellectual property from South Africa is used in Brazil. If Brazil does

| | Centrifugal forces | | Centripetal forces | |
	Home country (US/Swd)	Host country (China)	Home country (US/Swd)	Host country (China)
Skills	Limited size of skills pool; Gaps in specific skills sets; High cost.	Large pool of human capital with the required competences and capabilities - at lower cost		Occasional problems with skills quality. Skills cost is escalating due to increased demand - approaching EU levels in major cities.
Markets	Stagnant growth	Very large market with massive growth potential; Demand for local product adaptation and development of products for local market.		
Sectoral factors				In ICT software sector the importance of geographical proximity and tacit knowledge are reduced.
Geography				
Culture and tacit knowledge				Some difficulties with cultural and linguistic gaps
Policy		Policy requires R&D investment as a prerequisite to market entry		Poor IPR regime
Management		Globalised and decentralised innovation management structures		

Figure 5. ICT1.

not have the required knowledge, a broader global base can be accessed. Access to other regions is horizontal and need not be channelled through Brazil. This example illustrates how market commonalities between South Africa and Brazil create centrifugal forces by facilitating the strengthening knowledge and technology networks between the two countries.

Agro1's national context in Denmark shifts emphasis to the availability of human capital elsewhere. The skills required for innovation are generally available in Denmark, although due to the small size, firms occasionally seek supplementary skills. Firms face barriers when it comes to importing skilled foreigners: it is difficult to integrate them into the Danish system, so firms sometimes need to open in other locations that are attractive places for specialized labour. Hence, firms' internationalization has predominantly taken place within Europe or the USA, but destinations in Asia increasingly attract innovation related to foreign direct investments from Danish companies.

From the Danish perspective, centrifugal forces for the internationalization of innovation are, first, market-specific knowledge for the region and, second, complementary and specialized knowledge for global operations. Importantly, incentives for internationalizing research are not related to the need for cost reductions. According to the interviewees, qualified people abroad earn as much as those in Scandinavia. In the case of Agro1, the South African national context offers a range of centrifugal forces. The agro-food industry is an important trading partner because of its counter-seasonality to Europe and its well-developed infrastructure. One of the more recent important developments is the establishment of a cold chain in the transport sector. It also acts as a gateway economy to sub-Saharan Africa. However, in the case of the purchase of the South African subsidiary, it was specialized local knowledge, including knowledge networks, that was the key consideration.

A key reason for the Danish investment was related to the tacit knowledge component of agro-food research: the capability to develop bread mixtures in a very short lead time using tacit knowledge

	Centrifugal forces			Centripetal forces	
	Home country (Ger)	Host country (Ind)		Home country (Ger)	Host country (Ind)
Skills	High cost	Sufficient scale of skills - at a lower cost		General availability of the required skills, both in terms of scope and scale	Skills quality not always sufficient. Lack of trust in domestic educational institutions
Markets	Stagnation in domestic market; Risk in EU market	Large market with significant growth potential; High demand for local adaptation		Domestic and EU still account for largest markets	
Sectoral factors				Strategic incentive to retain core R&D in home country to minise risk and retain control	Automotive sector places emphasis on tacit knowledge, which increases the challenge
Geography		Long logistical pipeline creates demand for some process innovation to improve quality levels			
Culture and tacit knowledge	Management programme for crossing cultural barriers			Difficulty in crossing deep cultural barriers. Necessary to expend considerable resources to do so	
Policy					Erratic policy and political environment
Management				Strategic incentive to retain core R&D at home	

Figure 6.   Auto1.

rather than codified methods which require much more time – a major advantage in a time-sensitive sector. Since the tacit knowledge could not be simply purchased and shipped to Denmark, Agro1 was incentivized to purchase the South African subsidiary. This was part of Agro1 group's broader strategy of knowledge acquisition through purchases: the company has generally grown through takeovers and uses venture capital to buy equity in promising start-ups. It therefore represents a strategy of GIN development through the purchase of an existing innovation network, effectively bolstering the group's existing GIN. The transaction allows the South African subsidiary to exploit Intellectual Property (IP) from all over the world when introducing new products into sub-Saharan Africa, while also augmenting the group's innovation network through linkages into the region's sectoral innovation network. This example shows that MNC strategies for GIN formation need not have lower cost as a main consideration and can instead focus on knowledge access, the search skills, and the search for existing networks, in this case leading to the inclusion of the South African subsidiary into a highly globalized, highly networked, and moderately innovative GIN.

The case of ICT1 illustrates how the global distribution of human capital influences the global distribution of innovation in the relative absence of tacit knowledge-related impediments. ICT1 is a large multinational, with 550 offices and 30 manufacturing sites across 165 countries. This Global Production Network (GPN) houses an extensive GIN, including a global network of R&D centres, with major centres in both India and China. Innovation activity relies on a strong internalized network and also incorporates an externalized network in an open innovation model. ICT1 is therefore a large strong-form GIN – highly globalized, highly innovative, and highly networked.

The interviews highlighted three main motivations for R&D offshoring to India and China: first, access to large and growing markets; second, the capacity to react quickly to changes in those markets; and third, access to their large pool of human capital. ICT1 interviews in China and India did not highlight any significant cultural or tacit knowledge barriers to these processes. Within the ICT1 group, the process of GIN formation is noticeably different in Asia and Europe. In Asia, the firm established new R&D centres, sometimes in partnership with local actors. By contrast, when ICT1 opens an R&D centre in Europe, it is primarily through the acquisition of local firms with R&D centres that are then maintained within the group. Thus, while in Asia the expansion of innovation capabilities in important growing markets is the primary purpose and motivation, in Europe the presence of specialized knowledge held locally is the primary motivation for inclusion into the firm's GIN.

Auto1's South African subsidiary provides an example of participation in an incipient GIN where the centripetal and centrifugal forces are finely balanced, resulting in a limited or incipient GIN. The Auto1 Group has a global innovation network, with large R&D facilities in Germany and India. The South African subsidiary has no formal R&D unit and participates only in very limited product and process innovation. A large geographical distance acts as a centrifugal force: because of the large finished goods stock held in the logistical pipeline to its international customers, the subsidiary suffers far higher costs from production rejects than the German production plants. It thus undertook production process innovation to lower reject rates to below that of the German plant. The firm had the capabilities to undertake this independently.

Other centrifugal forces include demand for local product adaptation. Auto1 South Africa has developed parts for local vehicle assemblers that design vehicles specifically for the local market and has therefore had permission from its headquarters to collaborate directly with local customers and suppliers in the design process. However, these new technologies did not feed back into the group. Auto1 South Africa's involvement in a GIN is thus weakly globalized (it collaborated mostly with local actors), weakly innovative (mostly minor product and process changes), and weakly networked (its collaboration was restricted to inside the value chain).

At the micro level, management practices within the global group act as a centripetal force. In the interpretation of the South African management, the existing division of innovation labour is due to group internal hierarchies rather than a reflection of lack of capabilities on their part: management at the headquarters in Germany does not accept any innovation originating from South Africa. Thus, while the requisite human capital for increased innovation is generally available at the subsidiary, innovation management at group level acts as a constraint. This incipient GIN may evolve further if management constraints are lifted and if market demand for new products creates enough incentive.

A balancing act

The literature examining the links between skills and innovation suggests that on the whole innovation follows skills, which act as a centrifugal force distributing innovation around the globe. Our case-study analysis reaches the same conclusion, but also reveals that this general pattern overlays many other influential factors at the macro, meso, and micro levels. An abstract overview of the centrifugal and centripetal forces emerging from the case studies is presented in Figure 7. Here the boundary of the GIN (where new actors and links may be added, removed, strengthened, or weakened) is represented by the boundary of a circle, within which key centripetal forces (reducing the size and scope of the GIN) and outside which key centrifugal forces (expanding the size and scope of the GIN) are illustrated. While these factors are influential, in principle, in shaping GINs, within each individual network, there is a unique and complex interaction between particular sets of forces.

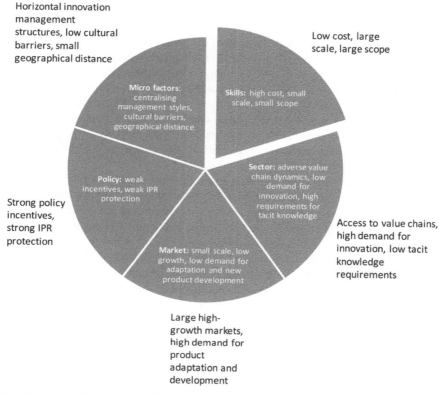

Figure 7.   Overview of centripetal and centrifugal forces.

Our analytical framework thus provides a useful approach to understanding the forces which shape GINs. The flexibility to both identify general patterns and interpret individual cases makes this approach particularly suitable for the interpretation of multiple case-study data, but could also be applied to a larger quantitative study.

Acknowledgements

This research was partially funded by the European Community's Seventh Framework Programme (Project INGINEUS, Grant Agreement No. 225368, www.ingineus.eu). The authors are responsible for its contents, which do not necessarily reflect the views or opinions of the European Commission; nor is the European Commission responsible for any use that might be made of the information appearing herein. The authors are grateful to the research team of Work Package 6 of the INGINEUS project for their work in undertaking the case studies. The authors also thank Cristina Chaminade, Stine Haakonsson, Eike Schamp, Marek Tiits, Tarmo Kalvet, Ana Valéria Carneiro Dias, Maria Pereira, Gustavo Britto, and KJ Joseph. This paper is dedicated to the memory of Jo Lorentzen.

Note

1.   Conducted for the European Community's Seventh Framework Programme (Project INGINEUS, Grant Agreement No. 225368, www.ingineus.eu).

References

Albuquerque, E.M., Britto, G., Camargo, O.S. and Kruss, G. (2011) Global interactions between firms and universities: Global innovation networks as first steps towards a global innovation system. *Discussion Paper No. 419* (Belo Horizonte: CEDEPLAR/FACE/UFMG).

Archibugi, D., and Iammarino, S. (2002) The globalization of technological innovation: Definition and evidence. *Review of International Political Economy*, 9(1), pp. 98–122.

Benito, G.R.G., Larimo, J., Narula, R., and Pedersen, T. (2002) Multinational enterprises from small economies: Internationalization patterns of large companies from Denmark, Finland and Norway. *International Studies of Management and Organization*, 32(1), pp. 57–78.

Brandt, L., and Van Biesebroeck, J. (2008) *Working Report for Industry Canada: Capability Building in China's Auto Supply Chains* (Ottawa: Industry Canada).

Brown, J.S., and Duguid, P. (1991) Organizational learning and communities-of-practice: Toward a unified view of working, learning, and innovation. *Organization Science*, 2(1), pp. 40–57.

Carlsson, B. (2006) Internationalization of innovation systems: A survey of the literature. *Research Policy*, 35(1), pp. 56–67.

Chang, S. (2008) *Samsung vs. Sony: The Inside Story of the Electronics Giants* (Singapore Hoboken, NJ: John Wiley & Sons).

Cohen, W.M., and Levinthal, D.A. (1989) Innovation and learning: The two faces of R&D. *Economic Journal*, 99(397), pp. 569–596.

Cohen, W.M., and Levinthal, D.A. (1990) Absorptive capacity: A new perspective on learning and innovation. *Administrative Science Quarterly*, 35(1), pp. 128–152.

Cummings, J. (2007) Fostering innovation in organizations through geographically dispersed teams and networks. Paper presented at the Duke CIBER Research Conference and Workshop on Offshoring, Cary, NC.

Dilk, C., Gleich, R., and Wald, A. (2006) State and development of innovation networks: Evidence from the European vehicle sector. *Management Decision*, 46(5), pp. 691–701.

Disher, C., and Lewin, A.Y. (2007) The power link between innovation and the globalization of talent. Paper presented at the 2007 IAOP World Outsourcing Summit, Las Vegas, NV.

DTI (2006) Department of Trade and Industry: The South African agro processing sector overview. Paper presented at the Kwazulu-Natal Trade and Investment Faire and Conference. Available at: http://www.kznded.gov.za (accessed 31 March 2010)

Dutrénit, G. (2004) Building technological capabilities in latecomer firms: A review essay. *Science Technology & Society*, 9(2), pp. 209–241.

Ernst, D. (2002) Global production networks and the changing geography of innovation systems. Implications for developing countries. *Economics of Innovation and New Technology*, 11(6), pp. 497–523.

Ernst, D. (2005) Complexity and internationalization of innovation: Why is chip design moving to Asia? *International Journal of Innovation Management*, 9(1), pp. 47–73.

Ernst, D. (2009) A new geography of knowledge in the electronics industry? Asia's role in global innovation networks. *Policy Studies #54*, August, East-West Center, Honolulu, HI.

Ernst, D. and Lundvall, B.A. (2000) Information technology in the learning economy: Challenges for developing countries. *Working Paper No. 8*, East-West Center, Honolulu, HI.

Freeman, R. (2006) Does globalization of the scientific/engineering workforce threaten U.S. economic leadership? *NBER Innovation Policy & the Economy Working Paper* (Cambridge, MA: National Bureau of Economic Research).

Granstrand, O., Håkanson, L., and Sjölander, S. (1992) *Technology Management and International Business: Internationalization of R&D and Technology* (Chichester: John Wiley and Sons).

Grossman, G.M., and Helpman, E. (1991) *Innovation and Growth in the Global Economy* (Cambridge, MA: MIT Press).

Haakonssen, S. (2012) Globalisation of innovation in the Danish food industry: The exploitation and exploration of emerging markets. *Innovation and Development*, in press.

Humphrey, J., and Memedovic, O. (2003) The global automotive industry value chain: What prospects for upgrading by developing countries? *UNIDO Sectoral Studies Series Paper* (Vienna: UNIDO).

Ivarsson, I., and Alvstam, C.G. (2005) Technology transfer from TNCs to local suppliers in developing countries: A study of AB Volvo's truck and bus plants in Brazil, China, India, and Mexico. *World Development*, 33(8), pp. 1325–1344.

Jung, M., and Lee, K. (2010) Sectoral systems of innovation and productivity catch-up: Determinants of the productivity gap between Korean and Japanese firms. *Industrial and Corporate Change*, 19(4), pp. 1037–1069.

Kumar, N. (1996) Intellectual property protection, market orientation and location of overseas R&D activities by multinational enterprises. *World Development*, 24(4), pp. 673–688.

Lall, S. (2001) *Competitiveness, Technology and Skills* (Cheltenham: Edward Elgar).

Lewin, A.Y. and Couto, V. (2007) Next generation offshoring: The globalization of innovation. *Duke University CIBER/Booz Allen Hamilton Report* (Durham, NC: Duke CIBER).

Lieberman, J.I. (2004) Offshore outsourcing and America's competitive edge: Losing out in the high technology R&D and services sectors. *U.S. Senate Report* (Washington, DC: U.S. Senate).

Lorentzen, J. (2007) MNCs in the periphery: DaimlerChrysler South Africa (DCSA), human capital upgrading and regional economic development, in: G.R.G. Benito and R. Narula (eds) *Multinationals on the Periphery*, pp. 158–187 (New York: Palgrave Macmillan).

Lorentzen, J. and Gastrow, M. (2012) Multinational strategies, local human capital, and global innovation networks in the automotive industry: Case studies from Germany and South Africa. *Innovation and Development*, in press.

Maftei, V. (2007) R&D internationalization. An overview of the driving forces. *Analele Stiintifice ale Universitatii 'Alexandru Ioan Cuza' din Iasi – Stiinte Economice*, 54, pp. 138–143.

Manning, S., Massini, S., and Lewin, A. (2008) A dynamic perspective on next-generation offshoring: The global sourcing of science and engineering talent. *Academy of Management Perspectives*, 22(3), pp. 35–54, SSRN. Available at: http://ssrn.com/abstract=1287369 [last accessed 7 September 2012].

Manning, S., Sydow, J., and Windeler, A. (2011) Securing access to lower-cost talent globally: The dynamics of active embedding and field structuration. *UMB College of Management Working Paper* (UMB), Boston, Mass.

Maskell, P., Pedersen, T., Petersen, B., and Dick-Nielsen, J., (2006) Learning paths to offshore outsourcing: From cost reduction to knowledge seeking. *CBS Center for Strategic Management and Globalization Working Paper 13/2006* (Copenhagen: Copenhagen Business School).

Massini, S., Lewin, A.Y., and Manning, S. (2008) Offshoring innovation and the emergence of new organizational capabilities: A co-evolutionary research perspective. *Duke CIBER Working Paper* (Durham, NC: Duke CIBER).

Ministry of Science and Technology (2010) Survey of Danish food. Research: Analysis and evaluation, April. Danish Agency for Science Technology and Innovation. Copenhagen.

Nam, K. (2010) Learning through the international joint venture: Lessons from the experience of China's automotive sector. Presentation at the 8th Conference of the Global Network for Economics of Learning, Innovation, and Competence Building Systems, Kuala Lumpur, 1–3 November 2010.

Narula, R., and Zanfei, A. (2003) Globalisation of innovation: The role of multinational enterprises. *DRUID Working Paper No 03–15* (DRUID), Copenhagen.

Paoli, M. and Guercini, S. (1997) R&D internationalisation in the strategic behaviour of the firm. *STEEP Discussion Paper No. 39*, University of Sussex, January 1997. Available at: http://www.sussex.ac.uk/Units/spru/publications/imprint/steepdps/39/steep39.doc (accessed 14 April 2007).

Patel, P., and Vega, M. (1999) Patterns of internationalisation of corporate technology: Location vs. home country advantages. *Research Policy*, 28(2/3), pp. 145–155.

Pearce, R. (1990) *The Internationalisation of Research and Development* (London: Macmillan).

Pearce, R. (1999) Decentralized R&D and strategic competitiveness: Globalized approaches to generation and use of technology in MNEs. *Research Policy*, 28(2–3), pp. 157–178.

Quinn, J.B. (2000) Outsourcing innovation: The new engine of growth. *Sloan Management Review*, 1(4), pp. 13–28.

Reddy, P. (1997) New trends in globalization of corporate R&D and implications for innovation capability in host countries: A survey from India. *World Development*, 25(11), pp. 1821–1837.

Stembridge, B. (2007) *Eastward ho! – The Geographic Drift of Global R&D* (Philadelphia, PA: Knowledge Link newsletter from Thomson Scientific).

Subramaniam, M., and Venkatraman, N. (2001) Determinants of transnational new product development capability: Testing the influence of transferring and deploying tacit overseas knowledge. *Strategic Management Journal*, 22(4), pp. 359–378.

Toner, P. (2011) Workforce skills and innovation: An overview of major themes in the literature. *OECD Education Working Papers, No. 55*, OECD Publishing. http://dx.doi.org/10.1787/5kgk6hpnhxzq-en [last accessed 7 September 2012].

UNCTAD (1995) Incentives and foreign direct investment. Background report of UNCTAD Secretariat, 6 April (Geneva: United Nations).

UNESCO (2010a) United Nations Educational, Scientific, and Cultural Organization Institute for Statistics Data Centre. Available at: http://stats.uis.unesco.org/unesco/TableViewer/document.aspx?ReportId=143andIF_Language=eng (accessed 5 December 2010).

te Velde, D.W. (2005) Globalisation and education: What do the trade, investment and migration literatures tell us? *Working Paper 254* (London: Overseas Development Institute).

WEF (2010) World Economic Forum: The Global Competitiveness Report 2010–2011. Available at: http://www3.weforum.org/docs/WEF_GlobalCompetitivenessReport_2010-11.pdf (accessed 6 January 2011).

Wooldridge, A. (2010) The World Turned Upside Down. Special Report on Innovation in Emerging Markets. *The Economist*, April 17.

World Bank (2010) *Data*. Available at: http://data.worldbank.org/ (accessed 4 December 2010).

Index

Note: Page numbers in *italics* represent tables
Page numbers in **bold** represent figures
Page numbers followed by 'n' refer to notes

For Product Safety Concerns and Information please contact our EU
representative GPSR@taylorandfrancis.com Taylor & Francis Verlag GmbH,
Kaufingerstraße 24, 80331 München, Germany

Printed and bound by CPI Group (UK) Ltd, Croydon, CR0 4YY
08/05/2025
01864331-0004